BEYOND BELIEF

KATIE BASKERVILLE

BEYOND BELIEF

ONE PLACE. MANY STORIES

HQ
An imprint of HarperCollins*Publishers* Ltd
1 London Bridge Street
London SE1 9GF

www.harpercollins.co.uk

HarperCollins*Publishers*
Macken House, 39/40 Mayor Street Upper,
Dublin 1, D01 C9W8, Ireland

This edition 2026

1

First published in Great Britain by HQ,
an imprint of HarperCollins*Publishers* Ltd 2026

Copyright © Katie Baskerville 2026

Katie Baskerville asserts the moral right to be identified as the author of this work. A catalogue record for this book is available from the British Library.

HB ISBN: 978-0-00-873060-4
TPB ISBN: 978-0-00-873061-1

This book is set in 10.7/15.5 pt. Sabon by Type-it AS, Norway

All rights reserved. No part of this publication may be reproduced, stored in a retrieval system, or transmitted, in any form or by any means, electronic, mechanical, photocopying, recording or otherwise, without the prior permission of the publishers.

Without limiting the exclusive rights of any author, contributor or the publisher of this publication, any unauthorised use of this publication to train generative artificial intelligence (AI) technologies is expressly prohibited. HarperCollins also exercise their rights under Article 4(3) of the Digital Single Market Directive 2019/790 and expressly reserve this publication from the text and data mining exception.

Printed and bound in the UK using 100% Renewable
Electricity by CPI Group (UK) Ltd

This book is dedicated to my grandmothers, Doris and Menai, who chose to live fiercely.

'... women, confined within the generality of their destiny as women, are united by a kind of immanent complicity. And what they seek first of all from each other is the affirmation of their common universe.'
— SIMONE DE BEAUVOIR, *The Second Sex*

Contents

Introduction................................... 1
Chapter One: A History of Gossip................. 12
Chapter Two: Friend or Foe?..................... 45
Chapter Three: Locker-Room Talk................. 67
Chapter Four: Social Media...................... 101
Chapter Five: Whisper Networks.................. 140
Chapter Six: Defamation........................ 191
Chapter Seven: Rags to Reality TV............... 218
Chapter Eight: Biddies, Codswallop and Witches..... 242
Chapter Nine: Tea.............................. 268
Chapter Ten: Unbelievable...................... 292

Acknowledgements............................. 310
Endnotes..................................... 315

Introduction

Have you ever found out something so devilishly delicious, something so juicy, so private, so utterly fascinating, that you've had to run and tell your best friend and confidant immediately?

Gossip is entwined with our daily life, though we might not realise it. Whether you're chiming into the WhatsApp group chat to dissect a dating profile, or screenshotting conversations of an argument in preparation to vent, it's thrilling, titillating and scandalous.

Gossip has a bad reputation, though – one, I think, it doesn't wholeheartedly deserve. Gossip is commonly associated with bitchiness, or criticised as a discredited mode of speech based on nothing more than rumour and speculation. I disagree with these positions. Gossip is so much more than that. Its duality as a great connecter and weapon of social destruction is perhaps why I – or rather, we – treasure moments shared with people who partake in a bit of gossip, and why we relish *Schadenfreude* behind closed doors.

Gossip demands privacy. When that privacy is broken, you might feel ashamed. Getting called out for gossiping, or being called a gossip, can feel like such an insult. But why is that, if we're all at it?

The truth is that gossip in all its forms is a deeply complex subject, interwoven with so many other things that impact women's credibility.

If I'm being honest, there is nothing I find more delightful than gossip. I'll shamelessly ask my girlfriends what's going on in their village life – a village I've never actually lived in, but where I spent a lot of time growing up – wanting to know all the gory details of who's sleeping with who; whose husband has had an affair; how so-and-so's doing now that they're in rehab, and so on, and so forth. They'll tell me about recent deaths, community dramas and houses up for sale, just in case I finally make good on that promise to move home to North Wales for good.

Gossip is a tool for protection too. I've watched friends turn stiff and pale-faced watching a man walk into the room, only to find it's common knowledge that he was a perpetrator of sexual assault. No legal intervention. No court case. No police. Just a whisper network and knowing looks that say: *Cover your drink. Don't let him walk you home alone.*

This sort of gossip is necessary; lifesaving, even. And while gossip can be light-hearted, or even silly, it's worth questioning how else we might discuss the goings-on in our world. I suppose that's the point: if we didn't gossip, we *wouldn't* discuss the goings-on in our world. We wouldn't laugh about the silly drama of old school acquaintances and celebrities. We wouldn't share intimate knowledge about our communities and the relationships within them. We wouldn't warn one another of the dangers living down the road.

Nevertheless, there is a juncture where gossip and morality meet. It may sound contradictory, but gossip is first and foremost dutiful, tied to a code of conduct and complex rules and ethics that demand compliance for the safety of the group. It is conditional, relationship-based speech. And the most entertaining pastime. The reality is, if you have ever uttered the words, *If I tell you this, you have to swear to keep it a secret*, or, *Not to be a bitch, but* ... then you'll know just how potent – and deliciously fun – gossip can be.

That said, it is also a powerful force majeure. Gossip has the potency to destroy reputations, careers and livelihoods. It can propel people into extremism; be a radical force that can wield manipulative misinformation and reinforce gender and racialised stereotypes. There are sides to gossip that are ugly. It can sever relationships, ostracise individuals and be the ultimate act of betrayal.[1] Ultimately, gossip is a tool for social control,[2] both within the group and outside of it, and one that positions women as 'unbelievable'.

When considering the title for this book, I knew it had to embody this impossible dynamic. 'Unbelievable' as a word has many meanings, depending on its context. It means untrustworthy, suspicious, lacking in credibility. But the word is subversive too, because to be a woman is to live a truly unbelievable existence. Woman are filled with so much joy, friendship and love, yet we live under a suffocating systematic oppression in every aspect of our lives that can at times feel unrelentingly dangerous and exhausting. Being a woman is to know that, no matter how well you play by the rules laid before you, no matter how thin you stay, how pretty you are, how well you tread the line between sexually available and 'pure', when something happens to you, or when you have something important to say – or anything to say at all – it is highly likely that you won't be listened to; that you'll be disregarded, discredited or ostracised for speaking out.

As far as our experiences of sex and gender go, our words and our accounts are regarded as *beyond belief*, and so too is our life experience. What other term is best placed to describe it? Imagine if you were an alien and someone told you the nonsensical rules women had to live by; the statistics of gender-based violence and the rampant inequality within societies around the world. The story in itself feels perversely fantastical: the idea that a woman can be attacked, but the first question she might be asked is what she was wearing to tempt the attacker, not what can be done to prevent attacks on women by men. Or, why, when a ten-year-old American child is raped, and a female doctor in a neighbouring state performs an abortion, that doctor might be reprimanded by their medical board instead of revered.[3]

The year is 2025, the world has become very ugly, and I fear it's only going to get uglier still. As I write this, the daily news deluge is a mire of genocide, rollbacks on reproductive rights, fascism and staunchly anti-LGBTQ+ rhetoric. The truth is that we are living through wildly unequal times, and inequality is the lifeblood of fascism and the far right-isms (of which there are plenty, notwithstanding misinformation and disinformation – or propaganda). This book is my urgent appeal to take on that inequality and unlearn some of the biases we can't help but absorb as part of our socialisation as women. It isn't our fault we live under a patriarchy, but we can – and must! – do something about it, even if all we do is equip ourselves with the knowledge to free ourselves from that patriarchy's expectations – a self-determined emancipation from misogyny and sexism; freedom of the mind. In this way, we're travelling beyond our own beliefs.

Whether we are born female, or become women, our socialisation under the girlhood and womanhood umbrella means we can't help but metabolise the patriarchal world, leading to internalised misogyny, misogynoir and all forms of self-hatred that come with not being able to fit into the impossibly contradictory identity. To be a woman, or to be associated in some way with the identity, either due to your assigned sex at birth or your expression of gender, is to experience a Sisyphean struggle. As soon as we've marched that boulder towards the top of the hill, patriarchy kicks us back down again. But no man or woman or person is an island. Lone wolves seldom survive. And so, I thought about the great connection between women and their world – our world. How do we suck out the poison? Is it through finding community? Ridding ourselves of ideologies that harm us and others around us? How can we recognise the value of our shared experiences? As with most big questions, I turned to the people who had some, if not all, of the answers. Silvia Federici, bell hooks, Angela Davis, Simone de Beauvoir – and then I stumbled upon a quote that stuck into the pith of me, a shard of truth that tied my questions to one fundamental answer: '... women, confined within the generality of their destiny as women, are united by a kind of immanent complicity. And what they seek first of all from each other is the affirmation of their common universe.'

There is a reason why de Beauvoir's *The Second Sex* is a seminal piece of feminist philosophy, even today. What, then, does it mean to share a 'destiny' as women? How are we united by that immanent complicity – does it have a name? Can it divide us? How do women seek to affirm their common universe from each other? Is it in the way we talk? Is gossip our common ground? I'm sorry to say, there aren't any simple answers to be found, at least not in the introduction. There are perhaps even more questions. But it is *good* to have questions. It is good to seek knowledge, especially when anti-intellectualism seeks to destroy what is truth to champion the lie. And when gossip is both the lens and the answer, in part, to the question I've posed above, having a critical eye and mind is par for the course. We must continuously ask questions.

De Beauvoir famously wrote that 'One is not born, but rather becomes, a woman.' As marginalised members of society, whether you were assigned female at birth, have experienced gendered socialisation, present effeminately, gender bend, have transitioned into womanhood, or out of it, by having either an adjacency or a sense of belonging to the umbrella term of 'woman' in some way, shape or form, you'll know that being a woman – whether this term fits you, or is attributed to you by gender stereotyping and socialisation – *is really fucking difficult.*

And so, there is no one coherent answer. The answer isn't simple, nor is it needed. To prove this, feminism asks the question 'What is a woman?' rhetorically.[4] Nevertheless, we are united by the commonality of our experiences. Patriarchy, misogyny, sexism and chauvinism are symptoms of a sick, unequal society. How could those experiences *not* galvanise our sense of camaraderie?

Here is the beginning of the answer to our first question: what does it mean to be 'destined' to become a woman? It means to live in a society with rigid parameters for what is an acceptable presentation of the identity of womanhood, which is broadly defined and imposed by those who are not themselves women.

As for the question of how are we united by that immanent complicity – does it have a name? – I believe we are bound in our experiences imperfectly. I believe that, unlike the very narrow definition of 'woman', these bonds that unite us in our immanent complicity have *many* names: minority stress; sisterhood; sorority; some kind of 'girl code'. An unspeakable, untouchable – yet universally understood – set of ground rules we hold one another to and do our best to abide by, because en masse, women are unbelievable, which creates a code of ethics that binds us so that we may survive against the odds.

Whether it's something as seemingly innocuous as *sugar, spice and all things nice*, or the fact that women have a far higher likelihood of being the victims of domestic abuse and sexual violence, perceptions and consequences of gender stereotyping are intrinsically interwoven with our need to seek out one another, congregate, affirm and care for one another.

It is important to note, though, that the belief that we are all experiencing oppression in the same way feeds into white feminism, a term that describes the refusal to consider the racial privilege of whiteness and one that places emphasis on and pulls focus towards the concerns, agendas and beliefs of white women as being universally representative of the collective struggle towards equality.[5] Often, it's related to other sects of feminism, like 'girl boss' feminism or liberal feminism, which can be flattened into phraseologies like SHE-E-O and commodifies and infantilises feminism in a bid to be palatable and profitable.[6]

The exclusionary nature of white feminism makes it problematic and dangerous. It's entrenched with biases rooted in racism and misogynoir, homophobia, transphobia and transmisogyny, Islamophobia and antisemitism. So, an expectation for marginalised people to share their energy, time, resources and activism to fight solely for white feminism is an act of violent entitlement. That's not to say that white, middle- to upper-class, cisgendered women aren't oppressed under patriarchy – they most certainly are, but their experiences of oppression are not compounded by other intersectional factors like class, sex, identity, race, religion, education, disability, wealth and life-course[7] in the same way. They are still able to, and do, act oppressively towards marginalised people, including marginalised men.

This means that solidarity and girl code require empathy and a true and equal understanding of oppressive circumstances. 'Sisterhood is a mutual relationship between equals. And as anyone with sisters can tell you, it's not uncommon to fight or hurt each other's feelings,'[8] writes Mikki Kendall in *Hood Feminism*. This is why girl code is more complex than the idea of us all being equal-standing members of a 'sisterhood', because we are not all treated equally in society, even though degrees of oppression are experienced by all women. So, while solidarity might feel like something we should all participate in, solidarity isn't something we can all share – the playing field is not level.

This moral obligation attached to girl code is important for us to know before we embark on the journey through gossip in the rest of the book, because this sense of community and union is how we are motivated to affirm our 'common universe', as de Beauvoir puts it. 'Girl code' is imperfect and hard to define, but it is an anchor-point that shows us we have evolved to react to our minority stress by trying to stick together through our empathy and collective understanding of the struggle it has taken to get to where we are and how much work there is still left to do, from suffrage to protesting the implementation of the Equality and Human Rights Commission guidance on single-sex spaces. That's not to say that we cannot transcend the intersectional factors that create space between us; it just means that we need to keep working to close the gaps, because the moment we become complacent, those bridges we form are easily dismantled by powers greater than our own, as we've seen in recent times.

Now, then, the penultimate question: *how do women seek to affirm their common universe from each other?* In addition to girl code's politically charged nature and caregiving service, it is also motivated by a desire for safety, which can be heavily influenced by fear. This means that, while we might experience something like a kinship, the codes of conduct we adopt under girl code are different depending on how we are experiencing oppression. It changes the game considerably, whether through solidarity or competition, decolonisation and liberation, or oppression and exclusion. Often, we don't know which game those around us are playing. Sometimes, we don't even realise which game *we're* playing. This means that girl code can be consciously and unconsciously weaponised because of our internalised biases, to detrimental effect.

Through researching this book, I realised that while girl code, solidarity, feminism – whichever name *you* feel comfortable using for our shared empathy – is a part of the answer that explains how women's credibility is determined, ultimately, as being beyond belief. If we share in our common identity, or at least share empathy for the enforced socialisation we are destined to experience as women, and the rules of solidarity are based on the ethics we hold towards one another are based on this shared suffrage, then why is our existence and our experience as women discredited? To answer the final Beauvoirian question, *is it in the way we talk? Is gossip our common ground?* I would argue that it is, absolutely.

This book is the culmination of years of reflection, experience, research, and hours and hours of interviews. It led me to examine women's speech and the role that gossip plays within it. I saw the threatening hypocrisy of locker-room talk, the digital Wild West that is social media and the burgeoning threat of weaponised defamation. I reflected on the impact it has on our identities and our existence when we aren't believed, and why the bonds of female connection are cherished by every woman I spoke with. I realised that our world is woven through the oral histories and coping strategies of our friends, sisters, mothers, grandmothers and great-grandmothers – and if not them, then those of our chosen families. We navigate the world hand in hand with other women and marginalised folks. We share stories. We talk.

CHAPTER ONE

A History of Gossip

I heard it in the night
Words that thoughtless speak.
Like vultures swooping down below
On the devil's radio.
I hear it through the day
Airwaves getting filled
With gossip broadcast to and fro
On the devil's radio.
— GEORGE HARRISON, 'DEVIL'S RADIO', 1987

Tittle-tattle, prattle, whispers, hearsay, rumour, talk – gossip goes by many names, each one with its own meaning and essence.

Gossip can fill a room with electricity, spill dread into the depths of one's stomach and create a narrative so fanciful that the line between truth and fiction becomes blurred. It can create a web of distrust and confusion or be a great connector of experience. This is why I believe that there is no one singular definition of what gossip is – how could there be?

However, the historical roots of the word 'gossip' tell us a lot. While pinpointing the origins of the word might not be the beginning of gossip's story, it still provides us with a good place to start in its history. The etymology tells us that the earliest known use of the word 'gossip' comes from Old English, which puts us somewhere in the Early Middle Ages of England (500–1000 CE).

During this time, 'gossip' – derived from the Old English word, *Godsibb* – meant something entirely different to what it means today. Rather than also functioning as a verb, 'gossip' was solely a noun, denoting a person related to God. In our modern English, we would translate it directly as 'godparent', or someone who stands in relation to God,[1] like a baptismal sibling, or God-sibling. Historically, the usage of the word wasn't gendered in the way that it is today, but over the years, its meaning became broader and more feminised.[2] It grew to refer to a midwife or a birthing chamber; a group of girlfriends found nattering in a tavern, or the chitter-chatter shared between women serfs working in noble households. Your 'gossip' was your most trusted confidante, privy to your most precious and salacious information.[3] Being a gossip, or someone else's gossip, was a privilege.

For women in this period, speaking plainly wasn't always wholly permissible, making gossip a vital part of their lives. Rules surrounding what women could and couldn't do in the medieval era were strict and enforced. They couldn't preach or teach, nor could they partake in business or marry without special permissions from familial patriarchs, with their husbands taking over any formal decision making on their behalf after marriage. Essentially, women had very little autonomy. This was broadly because women were believed to be inferior in every sense, it was felt that giving them access and the rights to these things would only end in disaster.[4] Women were perceived as being inherently deceitful and weak-minded, and therefore, the very idea that a woman would dare to act with agency would have been unthinkable. Everything they did was through the permission of the men in their lives. As Eleanor Janega writes in her brilliant book *The Once and Future Sex: Going Medieval on Women's Roles in Society*: 'It was men who knew what women should be, and men who were best able to understand and tame the nature of women to be exactly that.'[5]

In many respects, it's easy to see how feelings towards gossip began to shift during the Early Middle Ages. Author and academic Ned Schantz states in his book *Gossip, Letters, Phones: The Scandal of Female Networks in Film and Literature* that gossip is an example of early feminist consciousness and a method for women to create networks that resist patriarchy.[6] Whether this was intentional or not, it shows women choosing to disobey patriarchal structures in favour of building the foundations of camaraderie through privileged information exchanges. Even in oppressive times, women have long been drawing on the power of words to build community. Gossiping and connecting with trusted friends in a way that excluded men was not without consequence, and ultimately, there was a growing sense of unease around how much freedom women had when it came to sharing information. It was this gender-based discomfort that caused gossip to fall from grace.

Women have long been stained by the devil's mark. It is an inescapable attribution given to us since the dawning of Mesopotamia – and therefore, the historical beginnings of us all – as the cradle of civilisation. Female anatomy, or, more specifically, the reproductive organs, have an immense propensity for pleasure. Additionally, women's ability to give life, as well as suffer the tragedies of infant death, pregnancy loss, miscarriage and maternal death, all mean that women have symbolically sat in close proximity to a primordial 'evil'.

The female body has always represented the capacity to give life, and so women's purpose has always been entwined with servitude to the continuation of family, and therefore the burden of responsibility to ensure the passing on of possessions and wealth. Women's fertility has been instrumental in these generational exchanges of status and security, though its necessity and value have, throughout history, largely been waved off as simply being a woman's duty, and therefore of no great sacrifice to the individual. When our functionality as a vessel is perceived as being at risk, or – perhaps worse – is found to be faulty in some way, the worth and value of our lives immediately hang in the balance. This isn't hyperbole, either – just ask Anne Boleyn. Without the comprehensive view modern science gives us on female reproductive health (though admittedly, even today, knowledge remains woefully inadequate),[7] demons, gods and goddesses provided explanations for the inexplicable unfairness of infertility and pregnancy loss.

In the Middle East, which included Mesopotamia, Egypt and the Levant, if a person was unlucky enough to find themselves infertile, it was perceived by those in the community as being a sickness of the soul caused by the touch of demons and evil spirits.[8] During this period, and for many centuries later, women's bodies have, by default, represented temptation, and a gateway for demonic interference. As such, patriarchal society has created a belief that women must be protected from their propensity to summon the wrath of demonic forces, just as much as from the demons wreaking havoc in their lives. For these women of the past, who couldn't do right for doing wrong when it came to protecting themselves against the very real, earthly threats they were facing, gossip, or a *type* of gossip, would come to their rescue, and act as a comfort in dark times.

It all began with the demon goddess Lamashtu,[9] of the Mesopotamian era, who is described by Dr Sarah Clegg in her book *Woman's Lore* as 'the grand matriarch' of all monstrous women. From Lamia (subject of a narrative poem by John Keats), to Lilith (the disgraced first wife of Adam – and subsequent feminist icon), sirens, mermaids, serpents and succubi: if there is a demon out there who beguiles, ensnares and murders babies, it's likely that Lamashtu is her ancient relative. Lamashtu had a predilection for plucking babies from their mother's wombs with her long, sharp fingers, killing women during childbirth and murdering young children, and it is through stories of Lamashtu that women were first recorded as using oral traditions to teach one another how to protect themselves against maternal death – a likely fate.

Women of the past faced disempowerment and a dismantling of rights that parallel those taking place today. Their incantations, salves, prayers, rituals and familial knowledge were chipped away at by a strengthening patriarchal society, governed by the burgeoning power of the Roman Catholic Church. Women would come to rely on bonds of trust, and a willingness to share the knowledge of those who had come before them, to survive. Due to high rates of illiteracy, oral traditions were paramount. Women would teach one another about midwifery, caregiving, sex, pregnancy and childbirth. Through ancestral networks of tenderly gathered knowledge, these were the forerunners of women's healthcare, and these networks of care became a powerful tool in helping to protect women from illness and death.[10]

Women would be given talismans from midwives to ward off any spirits or demons responsible for infant death; they would bury bowls inscribed with incantations to protect their husbands from seductresses and infidelity and more, all in the hopes of saving themselves, and one another, from the hands of Lamashtu and her terrifying offspring.[11]

As women continued to try to safeguard their mortality with incantations, men blamed the virgin ghost-demon Lilitu for wet dreams. It was believed that male chastity was being stolen by countless sex-mad women-creatures and demons who were driven by jealousy and voracious sexual appetites. It is within these folktales and mythologies that we can see how gender-based social mistrust and blame for women's sexual desires, appetites and autonomy fomented over the centuries.[12]

The notion that women's speech is idle and non-productive – in direct contrast to the words of men – can be found in texts that date back to the Graeco-Roman period, in Aristotle's infamous works on philosophy and politics.

Aristotle's belief that women 'lacked authority' to deliberate is blamed for the confinement of women to the home in his *Politics*,[13] and it set the theoretical groundwork for the omission and elimination of female voices from arenas that would essentially dictate how they could lead their lives. Essentially, Aristotle's masculinist view bound women to domesticity,[14] and his sexist characterisation of women as shameless and false; more readily deceived than men; more watchful, idle, excitable; more compassionate and ready to weep; more jealous, contentious and querulous[15] enshrined a blueprint that would be bastardised by religions, governments and political institutions, and used to oppress women into subordination and shackle them to notions of purity and rituals of purification.[16]

Mistrust in women was compounded by the strengthening of Roman Catholicism in Europe, which denounced the belief in mythological, feminised monsters, therefore undermining the wisdom of women. Yet, despite this, belief in them persisted, usually in those who still needed protection from the baby-stealing demons, poverty-induced sickness and husband-ensnaring creatures – more often than not, women and peasantry folk.

Although the Roman Catholic Church in early-thirteenth-century Europe banned all ritualistic practices apart from their own,[17] no alternative care system was put in place, leaving people reliant on superstitions and women's knowledge within their social networks to survive – superstitions that still exist today in a range of cultures and societies across the globe. In America, superstitious beliefs eke into medical care, with more than 40 per cent of the general public believing in superstitious treatments over Western medicine. In India, 62 per cent of schizophrenic patients are known to turn to witches for treatment in a country still rich in superstitions.[18] Both India and the United States have healthcare systems that are notorious for failing the working classes and those living on the poverty line, leading to a necessary return to alternative forms of care.

The intervention of the Roman Catholic Church in women's bodily autonomy, notably through its restriction of abortion access and its teachings surrounding sex, sexuality and general reproductive freedoms,[19] created something of a melting pot of contradictions and cultural misalignments surrounding oral traditions, rituals and spell casting, not least because it led to superstitious, health-related beliefs becoming interwoven with concepts of chastity, purity and obedience – notions that continue to haunt us thousands of years later.

During the Middle Ages, specifically, a vast number of texts were written to remind women of their place in the world, predominantly centring around Eve and original sin. An example that illustrates the extent to which women's credibility and 'goodness' was under constant scrutiny comes from the popular early Christian author Tertullian. His books, which were hugely influential during this time, addressed women directly. In one, he writes:

> Do you not realise that Eve is you? That the curse that God pronounced on your sex weighs still on the World. Guilty, you must bear its hardships. You are the devil's

gateway, you desecrated the fatal tree, you first betrayed the law of God, you softened up with your cajoling words the man against whom the devil could not prevail by force.

By all accounts, a stark reminder for women, both of their inescapable destiny as biblical harbingers of doom, and of the tremendous and terrible influence their words held.

From the Roman Catholic Church to governments the world over, institutions have set a dangerous precedent for silencing women. Despite this, women continued to use the oral tradition, folk tales and what we would now call gossip to share histories, happenings and, of course, healthcare. Washerwomen in particular enjoyed unusual freedom of movement, congregating by rivers to gossip and work.[20] While this was, for the most part, ignored by the Roman Catholic Church, who dismissed it as unimportant and the women as powerless, this passive attitude wouldn't last forever.

In thirteenth-century England, legislators had begun to police speech in earnest, making it illegal to defame the king under the Statutes of Westminster Act 1275. This was compounded in the fourteenth century, when it became illegal to slander powerful men of the kingdom. Then came the criminalisation of the 'babbler', 'rabble-rouser' and 'court time waster', variations of titles given to people disrupting the peace, more commonly known as a 'barrator', or someone who frequently stirs up trouble for personal or financial gain. These laws disproportionately impacted peasant people, but also affected some noble litigators, who could be found guilty of barratry by inciting disputes and causing quarrels under common law.

The criminalisation of those seen to be speaking up and speaking out would have sent a clear message to both common people and the nobility alike about who was in charge, as well as making clear what was at stake when challenging the powers that be – whether through mass organisation, word of mouth, rumour or slander. However, it also shows us something else: as we have seen so often throughout history, and around the world, the need to suppress voices of dissent and opposition makes clear that the authorities recognise the danger of the people coming together, and the potential for dissent and uprising.

Following this attempt at mass censorship in the fourteenth century, brewing civil dissent culminated in 'the Great Rumour', which took place in 1377. The Great Rumour itself was a conspiracy theory and acted as a precursor to the Peasants' Revolt in 1381, subsequently leading to the charge of treason for those who used speech to disturb the status quo. The Great Rumour was circulated in England after King Edward III's death and centred on the belief that the ten-year-old Richard II's regency government would bring England under French rule. This was a falsehood, but nevertheless, the rumour spread like wildfire among the common folk and noble circles alike. The result of this was a peasantry on strike, refusing to work for their lords, and growing dissent among the public as faith in the king dwindled.

This 'fake news', if you will, took place at a time in England's history when the Black Death had ripped through much of the population, meaning that by the 1400s, the country's population was around half what it had been one hundred years prior.[21] There was also a great deal of economic instability during this period, and the peasantry were depleted by the extortionate taxation to fund the Hundred Years' War in France. People were discontented and ready for change, and after the death of the much-beloved King Edward III, the inflamed class tensions and the continued exploitation of the peasantry, revolt and a rejection of the bourgeoisie were, perhaps, predictable responses.

The Great Rumour shows us how destructive disinformation and misinformation can be at times of great hardship and civil unrest. However, the laws that followed the Peasants' Revolt didn't necessarily prevent falsehoods from spreading, although they did prevent, or at the very least, make it much harder for the peasantry to challenge their oppressors through mass organisation and word of mouth. What's more, these laws were an extension of the Catholic Church's teachings of 'sins of the tongue', which included 'flattery', 'rumour' and the 'mocking of good people'.[22] This created an even stricter society, where questioning those in authority or talking about them in a bad light could lead to punishment.

If all this feels like familiar territory in our current times, then you would be right. History has a way of repeating itself, and today, the world has turned in an unmistakably darker direction. Those same levers that were being pulled in the run-up to the Peasants' Revolt – censorship, the suppression of people's voices and the criminalisation of protest – are being pulled now. In our recent history, we've lived through the Covid-19 pandemic; developed total distrust in political figures; seen leaders turning the poor against the poorest; witnessed a stark rise in hatred of the 'other', while traditional routes to express our dissent or hold the government to account have been increasingly prevented through changes to our rights to protest. Following the Public Order Act 2023, and the unprecedented proscription of direct-action group 'Palestine Action' as a terrorist organisation, the country has watched on as peaceful protesters are arrested for supporting the group, while white nationalist groups have been seen throwing up Nazi salutes without reprimand. All this has culminated in more civil unrest in the form of fractious protests against migrants; a proliferation of St George's flags, alongside other terrifying displays of nationalism, xenophobia, racism and misogyny – particularly directed towards Muslim women and other women of colour.

The events of the past should act as a cautionary tale for us to reflect on in today's era of post-truth, amid tumultuous civil unrest, fake news and moral panic. Repetition is history's gift and curse. We have immense power in collective action, but we must choose the side that is right, good and humane. History has shown us that what comes next is a strangulation through litigation so severe that the most maligned won't survive its clammy grasp.

We have a front-row seat to history's mistakes. In this era, we can reflect on how, slowly but surely, from century to century, what one could and couldn't say became more contentious and censored. Whatever free speech was afforded to common folk in the fourteenth century was continually eroded by legal restrictions and criminalisation.

While all this was happening in the medieval era, gossip was being associated more and more with women sharing information about their daily lives, their work, their husbands and their interpersonal relationships. This new gendering of gossip in the medieval period pointed to a fear of female friendships and the privileged information exchange taking place about mistreatment, among other, more frivolous topics.

As Dr Hetta Howes observes in her brilliant book *Poet, Mystic, Widow, Wife: The Extraordinary Lives of Medieval Women*, another motivation for preventing women from speaking to each other was shame around sex. While the medieval period was more sexually permissive than the eras to come, there was still an inordinate amount of worry concerning what women might say to one another about their husband's performance in bed. 'Alehouse poems' or 'gossip songs' were prevalent during this time, and were usually written by men about drunk women making each other laugh with stories of their husbands. Howes explains that these poems and songs fed into a broader anxiety about what women would say if they weren't kept under control by their husbands: 'It seems impossible for men to imagine women talking about anything other than them.'[23] Indeed.

The fear of what women *might* say has always been as much of a driving motivation for their subjugation as the words they *do* say. Men have always needed women to act as a mirror, reflecting back their deep-seated belief that they are all-powerful, made in the image of God himself. Men are told that they are the dominating force, the leaders. So, what happens if the reflection they see in the women around them doesn't confirm that belief? What if that reflection actively challenges men's perception of their masculinity? The result is that men feel impotent, and are driven to apply force; to silence and then control how women speak, act and live in their bodies. One need only look at the male-dominated powers of this world that continuously seek to control the female reproductive system and implement what essentially amounts to 'forced birth' policies through litigation. Patriarchy is a dogmatic megalomaniac.

While no laws were made that strictly prohibited gossip, the medieval era certainly became more serious about defamation, and as a result of the introduction of anti-defamation laws, gossip soon became easy to weaponise and criminalise under the common law.[24] Women faced charges in court for 'speech abuse',[25] something that wouldn't be abolished until centuries later in the Criminal Law Act 1967.[26] 'Speech abuse' could be a precursor to violence or revolt, which threatened political and social order,[27] but it was also weaponised against medieval women for speaking out against the wrongs and abuses that befell them.[28] Historian Vanessa Corcoran gives one example of the enforcement of the 'speech abuse' law, which took place in 1425, when Agnes Le Spenser was fined twelve pennies for yelling in a tavern about an alleged stolen pan.[29] It's hard to tell exactly how much of a blow this fine would have been to Agnes without knowing her employment or household income, but, given that most maid servants earned around 120 pennies or 10 shillings per year,[30] this could have been a devastating amount to be fined.

One of the most popular texts during the medieval period, *The Golden Legend*,[31] told the tales of the virgin martyrs. In these stories, the virgin women fall victim to sexual predation and, when they vehemently spurn the unwanted advances due to their chaste promises to God, their lives are forfeit in a display of sexual violence, rendered in graphic detail. One particularly chilling story is that of St Agatha of Sicily, who at a young age had promised her chastity to God. After refusing to submit to the sexual advances of a Roman prefect, Agatha was tortured and had her breasts removed with pincers, then was sent to the stake. Miraculously, the fires were extinguished after an earthquake was said to have occurred, arousing suspicions that she had a divine soul. She was removed from the pyre and later died in prison.[32] Only after all this horrific torture was she canonised.

These stories were used to reinforce the notion that women's suffering was best met with silence and obedience – head bent and neck exposed. It also enforced the notion that a woman's body was part of a divine sacrament and exchange. To go against that and either be raped or give in to unsolicited and unwanted sexual advances (which, in itself, can be a form of coercion, which is rape) was a sullying of a woman's purity and, by extension, her relationship with God. It shows us that for centuries women who have acted with self-determination when threatened with sexual violence have only ever been met with sexual violence so perverse it makes the teeth curl. When sexual violence happens to them despite their cries for help, women are blamed for what befalls them, for failing to be persuasive enough with their words; to impel their attacker to desist.

Despite these horrifying stories, though, women continued to gather and resist. As Howes puts it, the getting together of women, whether their husbands liked it or not, shows a subversion. The mere existence of 'alehouse poems' and 'gossip poems' shows us that women did, indeed, gather, and that it was probably a common occurrence.

> Alongside fulfilling stereotypes of wayward, gossipy women, [the poems] also show women listening to one another, offering comfort and reassurance, affection, even instruction – swapping ideas for routes they could take to and from the alehouse, so that their husbands won't guess where they're going. The loyalty of these women lies firmly with their friends, not their spouses.[33]

The weaponisation of 'speech abuse' and its legal restriction of women's voices is another example of the litigious enforcement of censorship that medieval women would have to learn to navigate. This made the parameters for what was permissive in medieval England narrower and narrower. Now, with the country enclosed by a theology that expected silence and was met with resistance, another social schism and moral panic would come to shape Europe. At the time, England was guided by Roman Catholic preachers and theologians, in addition to the monarch, who was allegedly appointed by the same strict God to rule. They monitored and regulated women's speech, often citing 1 Corinthians 14: 34, where Paul wrote: 'Women should keep silent in the churches, for they are not allowed to speak, but should be subordinate, as even the law says. But if they want to learn anything, they should ask their husbands at home. For it is improper for a woman to speak in the church.'[34]

Paul, who, when read out of context, sounds like a complete and utter misogynist, also wrote: 'Let the woman learn in silence, with all subjection. But I suffer not a woman to teach, nor to use authority over the man: but to be in silence. For Adam was first formed; then Eve.'[35]

Even today, these same scriptures are cited as reason for women's obedience and domesticity. As Beth Allison Barr observes in *The Making of Biblical Womanhood*: 'Ideas matter. These evangelical beliefs – why they argue for the immutability of female submission – are rooted in how they interpret Paul.'[36]

Barr explains how, in her class teaching history and theology, she can't count the number of times students – mostly young women – have been 'scarred' by the use of these biblical passages from Paul against them 'to be silent (1 Corinthians 14), to submit to their husbands (Ephesians 5), not to teach or exercise authority over men (1 Timothy 2), and to be workers at home (Titus 2)'.[37] Yet Barr is quick to dispel misreadings of Paul's intentions by pointing out the era of history in which they were written down, as well as Paul's counter-arguments that align him with more progressive teachings. Paul was also telling husbands in Ephesians 5:28–29 that 'husbands are to love their wives as their own bodies. He who loves his wife loves himself. For no one ever hates his own flesh but provides and cares for it …'

This message is remarkably progressive, given that, during the era when Paul would have lived, women's bodies were regarded by famed misogynist Aristotle (and indeed, everyone else) as imperfect, a type of deformed man. Aristotle wrote in his *Generation of Animals* that because females are 'weaker' and 'colder in their nature' … 'we should look upon the female state as being as it were a deformity'.[38] Whether or not we've been misinterpreting Paul's words – which is entirely possible when we take into account his good relations with other female ministers, as well as his metaphorical descriptions of himself as a mother and nurse, it hasn't stopped the words he allegedly spoke from being misused and weaponised against women for thousands upon thousands of years.

These misogynistic interpretations of Paul were good enough reasons for husbands and men more generally to enforce the mass surveillance of women. Even during communal mourning rituals, women who sobbed, cried out or writhed on the ground in their grief were often silenced by men for being too disruptive.

One prominent Christian writer of the time, John Mirk, criticised women in his anthology of sermons for whispering to one another and distracting the congregation. Mirk felt that, because of women, the Church had become a labyrinth full of vain speech and filth. These sorts of cautionary tales about women's speech and gossip were popping up everywhere.

Even those women who might have been deemed most holy were not exempt from scrutiny. *De institutione inclusarum* served as a guidebook for enclosed women, also known as anchoresses – that is, women who were often, though not always, walled into churches as part of their devotion to God. Written by Aelred of Rievaulx, the book warns in one tale of a wayward anchoress gossiping with an old woman through her window. Such windows often provided their sole glimpse into secular society and were the means through which these women would be fed, dispose of their waste and listen to those troubled by their relationship to God, 'allowing idle tales to pour into her ear like poison'.[39]

'Scolding' was another punishable mode of speech attributed to women. It was seen as a form of defamation, and being a 'common scold' was a petty crime that women were disproportionately found guilty of.[40] Women found guilty of scolding would be subjected to humiliating and painful punishments, like wearing the 'scold's bridle'.[41] A device worn over the head, with pieces going into the mouth, which often included metal spikes and prongs, this had the potential to cause serious disfigurement and damage. 'Scolds' could also be placed in the stocks, or punished with the ducking stool, a chair that the offender would be tied to before being dunked into a river.[42]

This sort of brutal sexism was rife, partially because, in the Middle Ages, women fell either into the category of saintly, virginal and 'good', or sex-crazed devil worshipper. Arguably, little has changed in our perceptions of women today. There was no in-between,[43] and women were almost always presumed to be the latter, having to continually prove themselves otherwise.

It wasn't always like this, though. Before the Middle Ages, and the cementing of crafts guilds, women in England didn't need men for much. The Crafts and Guilds were predominantly patriarchal institutions that rarely, if ever, allowed women to join, and actively prevented them from undertaking any apprenticeships that would have led to skilled labour, and by extension, fair pay. This greatly restricted women's access to paid work generally and simultaneously devalued the domestic labour expected of women and children to maintain artisanal households.[44] Women did maintain some rights in the early medieval era, however. They could own land and work,[45,46] though this varied greatly depending on marital status, class and geographical location – a world away from the housewives of the 1950s, for example, who couldn't even open a bank account in their own name until 1976. Clearly, these early freedoms weren't to last. By the time the fifteenth and sixteenth centuries rolled around, women's access to skilled and highly paid labour collapsed completely.[47] This collapse signalled a shift in the way women were valued, partially because of the way their autonomy was portrayed in the media of the time: a good old-fashioned play.

Satirical plays funded by a village, town or city's craft or guild authorities, showed women and their gossips, or group of friends, as unruly and disobedient. Usually set in a tavern, which was where many peasant women came together to discuss the day's affairs,[48] the plays would show women being demeaned and undermined for talking brazenly with one another, ignoring the demands of their husbands.[49] As a result, men were also shamed in these plays, as they equated women's matrimonial disobedience with the emasculation of their husbands, portraying them as weak and subordinate. These debaucherous depictions of working women indulging in gossip developed into a burgeoning distrust and dislike of women who might frequent a tavern and chat about the day's affairs with their gossips – as was the norm. Additionally, the subsequent shame men felt at having their masculinity threatened by the insubordination of these fictional women translated into the beginning of a social misalignment fuelled by contempt towards all women who dared to speak out of turn. Because of these plays, gossip had been successfully rebranded as idle speak in the eyes of an dogmatic Roman Catholic society. It demonised the kinds of conversations women had been relying on for news, healthcare and safeguarding, making gossip dangerous to a strengthening patriarchal, feudal society.[50] With the ascension of the Tudors to the throne in the late fifteenth century, things would only become worse for women who gossiped in Early Modern Britain.

This reframing of gossip as a sin played a powerful role in ushering in a period of 300 years where women were persecuted and murdered across the UK and Europe. Why? Because being labelled a gossip could lead to one being persecuted for witchcraft, and, conversely, becoming the subject of gossip could mean being labelled a witch too. The witch trials led to the execution of an estimated 40,000–60,000 people, the majority of them women,[51] between 1450 and 1750, across Europe. In Britain, this persecution was made worse by Henry VIII, in whose reign the Witchcraft Act of 1542 was passed,[52] which defined witchcraft as a crime punishable by death. The merciless brutality would have the biggest impact on older, working-class women; women who had a perceived standing or social influence in their community; women who rejected the advances of men; women who took on caring roles like midwifery or who were born into serfdom; those who worked in husbandry or took on property ownership; women who suffered from poor mental health, or who were simply disliked for unknown reasons.

The nature of the work that women of the age were expected to do meant they were more likely to face the 'occupational hazards' of witchcraft accusations,[53] as they would often be blamed for animal deaths, financial ruin or any harm that befell a family, even though they would almost certainly have had no involvement in the tragedies or hardships experienced by the families they served.

Interpretations of Bible passages from the Old and New Testaments warning against 'evil-speaking'[54] led to the equation of gossip with sin, defamation and slander in England, but Christianity is not alone in viewing these things as inseparable. The Torah warns against *lashon hara*, or 'malicious gossip',[55] which is prohibited by Jewish law. In Islam, *ghibah* ('gossip') is considered an enormous sin.[56] According to the Guru Granth Sahib, the central religious text of Sikhism, there is little difference between gossip and slander, and it is believed to be an addictive and dirty habit.[57] Buddhism's precept (or code of conduct), 'refrain from wrong speech', warns against gossiping and its impact on karma.[58] In Hinduism, too, *apaishunam*, or not indulging in gossip, is seen as an important quality.[59]

It is worth noting here that all religions were historically, and remain, governed by patriarchy, and those doctrines that demonised gossip could be interpreted as a means of disempowering and subjugating women. As a result, any woman who dared to contravene the values imposed by patriarchal religions would be seen as unchaste, undesirable, unmarriable and criminal. As Judith Butler mentions in the introduction to her book *Who's Afraid of Gender?*: 'Hatred is stoked and rationalised by moral righteousness, and all those damaged and destroyed by hateful movements are cast as the truer agents of destruction.'[60] Put another way, women and other marginalised folk throughout history have been blamed for the wrongdoings of those who benefit from the systems of their subjugation, which is most likely to be white, middle- and upper-class cisgender, straight men. Women can be persecuted for being too loud; too outspoken – for rocking the proverbial boat.

It's also important to note that antonyms for morality are imbued with religious meaning and connotations that feed into this shame-powered machine. For example, the word 'immoral' is interchangeable with words like 'evil', 'sinful', 'bad' and 'wicked'. The perception of gossip as morally deplorable is deeply linked with our internalised notions of purity and goodness, as well as the guilt women have been conditioned to bear for the sins of Eve; that is, Eve's act of self-determination in gaining knowledge, after God – probably a man, if we're to go by the way he is always depicted in scripture – told her not to. Simone de Beauvoir mused on this in *The Second Sex*, writing: 'For the Jews, Mohammedans, and Christians, among others, man is master by divine right; the fear of God will therefore repress any impulse towards revolt in the downtrodden female.'[61]

In de Beauvoir's words, and in the long, historical legacy of gossip as far more than just tittle-tattle, we can begin to see how the silencing and dismissal of gossip is a form of subjugation – something that Victorian women would come to know rather a lot about.

From the Regency period onwards, gossip sheets – also known as scandal sheets – were the precursors to today's tabloids. These newspapers provided insights into sexually vibrant undercurrents beneath the veneer of 'proper' Victorian society, detailing stories of prostitution, gambling and other 'sporting pursuits'.[62] However, maintaining appearances was paramount to the Victorians, and a woman indulging in too much gossip, or the wrong kind, would be considered déclassé – an ostracisable offence in certain portions of society.

That didn't mean that women *didn't* indulge in gossip, of course. Legend has it that high-society women developed a language without words so that they could gossip and communicate their intentions in plain sight. The language of drawing-room fans, or fan etiquette, played a similar role to that of parasols, and gloves, in particular. Gloves, for example, could signify so much by their positioning, whether they were being worn or not. They could denote marital status, romantic interest and social standing. People could pick up on social cues easily and gossip in full view, based on their (or someone else's) glove choreography.[63] Gestured with and held correctly, they could facilitate an entire script's worth of salacious titbits without a word ever being uttered. 'Fanology', meanwhile, was a convoluted and complicated set of rules and secret gestures, developed by dramatist-turned-fan-designer Charles Badini in 1797. In 1798, an easier language was printed on Robert Rowe's fan design, titled *The Ladies Telegraph, for Corresponding at a Distance*, which included twenty-six panels with the letters of the alphabet and an extra panel with a full stop so that women could spell out words to onlookers – rather like voyeuristic texting.

However, this means of communication required unbridled attention from your friend or love interest – not to mention good eyesight – so it's perhaps unsurprising that it was the gestures of Spanish flamenco, which were evocative and highly stylised, that were adopted by high-society ladies to convey mood and emotion, rather than these coded and fallible languages. While some of these gestures were undoubtedly known to men, the extent and complexity of the language suggest that this form of communication was for the female gaze, first and foremost – or so the story goes.

According to auction house Sotheby's, by the time fan etiquette had reached Victorian England, the language had become something of a marketing gimmick devised by Duvelleroy, a fan maker and retailer founded in Paris in 1827.[64] The company's publication of a pamphlet of demystified gestures solidified its appointment as the official supplier of fans for Queen Victoria herself. The language was adopted and used throughout the nineteenth century in heavily chaperoned environments to communicate desires, or a lack thereof. Fans remained a popular prop in the fiction of the era, such as in Oscar Wilde's 1892 play *Lady Windermere's Fan*, and no noblewoman would have been seen without one in high society. Journalist Martin Fone's 2023 article in *Country Life* magazine describes the fans of the eighteenth to the twentieth centuries as artworks and an extension of 'a woman's tastes, sophistication, and wealth, often made by workshops employing some of the leading artists, carvers, and calligraphers to produce elegant, intricate designs on the finest of materials, especially silks'.[65]

In truth, the entirety of the Victorian era was characterised by polarities coexisting in strenuous circumstances. It's easy to understand why, with the Industrial Revolution going from strength to strength, along with feminism and increasingly opposing beliefs on what womanhood ought to be. In one corner, John Ruskin posited that women were like flowers, with their inevitable fate as wives and mothers incorruptible by education, and that these roles should be embraced. Ruskin's insistence on the nature of womanhood being entwined with servitude to the hearth was at odds with his contemporaries, Harriet Taylor Mill and John Stuart Mill, whose seminal essay 'The Subjection of Women', published in 1869, eloquently opposed the 'stifling ethics of wifely subjugation'.

However, as Kate Millett put it in her 1970 essay 'The Debate over Women, Ruskin Versus Mill', Ruskin's beliefs are more representative of the 'compulsive masculine fantasy one might call the official Victorian attitude'.[66] That is to say, so long as women embodied the sentimental, matronly existence as wives or mothers in the home, they would be loved, honoured and even treated as royalty. This meant that the sexual revolution that took place between 1870 and 1910, which saw the depolarisation of Victorian ideals of morality, did little to change attitudes towards women, which were oppressive, restrictive and filled with morality policing. There also remained oppressive legislature that sought to 'regulate' sex education of any kind, using obscenity laws.[67] While strides towards progress were made during this era, they were oftentimes met with great friction and backsliding.

Despite all this, though, the act of gossip played perfectly into the Victorian characteristics of public prudery and private delights, resulting in the simultaneous denouncement and reverence of the act. To a certain extent, gossip was seen as a political device used by men to gain and wield power – while paradoxically being lamented as an ungentlemanly thing to do.[68] For a select group of men, however, the rules were, of course, different and nowhere near as complicated as they were for women. As a club or high-society man in the Victorian era, being able to entertain an audience of other elites in male-only spaces like a gentlemen's club was a signifier of status.[69] In these spaces, men would regale one another with tales about life, travels, relationships and blunders, and such social intercourse would help establish their spot in the pecking order. In other words, men would *gossip*, proving that the act itself has never been gendered. The only gendered aspect of gossip is our cultural acceptance or dismissal of it.

For Victorian women, on the other hand, gossiping – or indeed, *not* gossiping – had far more dangerous consequences. Victorian ideals placed high value on obedience, chastity and sexlessness for women in the middle classes – so much so that women were frequently praised for not knowing about their bodies, sex or childbirth.[70] Despite this, there was a flourishing underbelly of vice, temptation and hedonism being perpetuated by the same middle class that insisted on women's oppression and enforced anti-intellectualism.

On one side, societal rules were written for women to adhere to. The expectations for women were to 'pride yourself in modesty' and 'be not seen too often in public'. Reminders, advice and warnings were also shared, such as, 'Know that a man of good sense will never marry but the pious, industrious and frugal,' and, 'If you talk in society, talk only about those things which you understand,' and, 'Trust no female acquaintance, i.e. make no confidant of anyone.'[71] Indulging in a bit of gossip that broke these rules might have been seen as a little immoral, but in the worst instances, it could be interpreted as a sign of hysteria.

Hysteria, a now-debunked and controversial feminised mental health disorder,[72] was characterised by the womb 'wandering' around the body, apparently causing myriad physical and mental ailments. Today, the diagnosis has been described as a 'disguise for ignorance and a fertile source of clinical error' by researchers from the *British Medical Journal*.[73] Hysteria was characterised by everything that men found 'mysterious or unmanageable in women'.[74] As such, it was a diagnosis pointedly aimed at women who made men 'uncomfortable'.[75]

One of the treatments for hysteria was the 'Rest Cure', an intensely misogynistic medical practice created by Silas Weir Mitchell in the nineteenth century. The rest cure saw women confined to their beds, overfed like prized geese producing foie gras, and isolated with limited mental stimuli. Even writing was discouraged. Its impact on women's mental health was profound, and the unravelling it could bring about is viscerally captured in the fictionalised work *The Yellow Wallpaper* (1892) by Charlotte Perkins Gilman, who drew inspiration from her own prescription of the rest cure for post-partum depression. Even today, Gilman's book is heralded as a lasting piece of feminist literature that gives us a unique insight into women's resilience, agency and limitations of self-expression. The rest cure has been described by Joyce Carol Oates as the 'enforced infantilization of women who may have been in (healthy) revolt against the confinement of their roles in society'.[76]

Hysteria provides the perfect lens through which to view all those things that men of the Victorian era disapproved of. Symptoms of hysteria – if we can even call them symptoms – encapsulated anything that disturbed the mentality of the era that mandated that 'women and children should be seen and not heard'.[77] That's not to say that women of the period didn't suffer from mental health problems, of course, for they surely did, but many of the things that might lead to a woman being sent to a lunatic asylum had little to do with her mental state and a lot to do with her self-determination, autonomy and fertility. If a woman happened to be infertile, then she was probably suffering from hysteria. Enjoying writing a little too much? Yep, that was probably hysteria too.[78] A bit dramatic or excitable? You guessed it. Hysteria.[79]

In fact, feminists of the twentieth century noted that the pathologisation of women's mental health enforced an inescapable norm: that their health outcomes, physical or otherwise, were dependent on their purity and chastity, with their suffering perceived as a symptom of their sinfulness, or badness.[80] Hysteria was not only over-diagnosed in Victorian Britain, but also used as a method for cautioning other women against stepping out of line. As such, it became the 'bridle gag' of that era, not least because the consequence of being diagnosed with hysteria often meant commitment to a lunatic asylum. Labelling a woman as mad – or indeed, hysterical – was a way to suppress her autonomy and make her fear the repercussions of going against the grain.[81] There remain echoes of this today, with archetypes such as the 'crazy ex-girlfriend' – a misogynistic, flattening, catch-all term for a woman who doesn't behave as she ought to when faced with abuse, toxicity or sheer bad behaviour. Other known reasons for the institutionalisation of women in the Victorian era included keeping company with people who were not perceived as morally 'good'; jealousy; an overactive mind; bad habits; political excitement; dissolute habits (that is, indulging in drink and sex a little too freely) and 'female disease', which included anything to do with menstrual cycles or the menopause[82] – you know, *women's troubles.*

It's easy then to conclude that being a woman who gossiped a little too enthusiastically, emotionally or dramatically, or who upset the apple cart by talking about sex, politics and other people's relationships with those deemed unfit or improper, meant you'd likely find yourself shipped off to your local sanatorium. It was no wonder that women adhered to strict social etiquette – because slipping off the knife-edge they walked along could mean the end of them. Add to that the fact that the torturous scold's bridle was still in use until the nineteenth century as a means of punishing women in workhouses for being too 'unruly',[83] it's easy to see how gossip became a deeply private pastime, to be enjoyed only in the strictest confidence. The risks of public chastisement, shaming and potentially being quietly disappeared from social circles was too great. The gossip shared between Victorian women was an intimate pastime built on trust, but also a shared understanding of their common conditions as women, and what it would mean for their wellbeing and safety if word got out they had been breaking the rules by indulging in gossip and idle speak.

The pervading prejudice surrounding women who gossiped also meant that medical professionals such as Mary Stewart, the first appointed almoner (a hospital social worker) at the Royal Free Hospital in London, in 1895, would actively deny treatment to women she found gossiping. Why? Because 'Gossiping was not considered appropriate behaviour for a good woman,'[84] and care could only be given to women deemed worthy of receiving it. This notion of goodness, or the character of the good woman, was entrenched in every facet of a Victorian woman's education and socialisation. This imposing sense of goodness came from the ideology of 'the perfect lady', which is described by historian Martha Vicinus as a tenacious and all-pervasive feminine ideal: 'The main difficulty with the perfect lady as a model of behaviour in even the middle classes (and it came to be accepted, in an altered form, in other classes) was the narrowness of the definition. Few women could afford to pursue the course laid out for them, either economically, socially or psychologically.'[85]

And yet, despite all these deterrents of physical and mental harm – gossip persisted, amid its bad reputation and the oppressive nature of the Victorian era. Everywhere we turn, whether in history, religion or folklore, women are punished for trying to shake off the shackles of their oppression. Think of Eve, banished from the Garden of Eden for seeking knowledge.[86] Of Blodeuwedd – a Welsh princess made entirely of flowers and magic – who was chased off a cliff and transfigured into an owl, never to show her face in daylight again. Her sin? For wanting to choose who she married.[87] Even she-wolves in tales relayed by the Brothers Grimm can't catch a break. In the tale 'Gossip Wolf and the Fox', Gossip Wolf is 'taught a lesson' by a 'cunning' fox for indulging in gossip and, by extension, deceit.[88] She is lured into a trap and tortured.

For women, gossip and deceit go hand in hand, although there is no empirical evidence that it should. Studies on honesty have found men to be 4 per cent more deceitful than women.[89] Men are also far more likely to be found being selfishly dishonest through methods like gaslighting, negging and coercion for sexual and self-gratification.[90] All this begs the question then: why do we *still* associate gossiping women with untrustworthiness when it was once associated with caregivers and caregiving, and those in spiritual relation to God?

Throughout history, gossip has been tarnished by its gender-based prejudices and its adjacency to idle speak, wicked women, defamation and slander. No matter which way we turn, gossip is seen as a cultural and religious transgression, a character flaw – one that women have been, and continue to be, ruthlessly punished for. Not only has gossip accumulated an identity of deceitfulness, unworthiness and distrust, but through that, the content of what women gossip about – and perhaps a subsequent fear of what it could mean for men if the subject is believed – has resulted in a concerted effort to discredit women. We have been made out to be *unbelievable*, because, let's face it, if people started believing women, the extent of the reparations we'd be entitled to would be incalculable. Patriarchy would crumble if it acknowledged the harm it causes – a stark reason why it relies on violence to be upheld.

This is perhaps why we rely so heavily on other women to uplift us, endorse us and legitimise informal knowledge – why we lean on a sisterhood, of sorts. Despite the power of our relationships with other women, though, the sisterhood is broken and dysfunctional. It can be exclusionary and rife with internalised misogyny, transphobia, racism and classism.[91] In those circumstances, gossip becomes a tool of social control.[92]

CHAPTER TWO

Friend or Foe?

Heather, why can't you just be a friend? Why are you such a mega-bitch?

— VERONICA SAWYER, *Heathers* (1988)

I believe we're only now truly starting to appreciate the depth of magic that is interwoven with platonic and romantic female friendship. To me, there is nothing more precious than the friendships I form with other women. They are my chosen family; my secret keepers; my most trusted and precious people. I love them fiercely and unflinchingly and, for reasons I can't always see in myself, they love me back just as hard.

As part of the research for this book, I reached out to many different women, some of whom I knew and some I didn't, to ask them how they felt about the interconnectedness of women. What did it mean to them? Could they put their fingers on the rules they felt bound by? Why was it important to have a code to live by? I did this to understand what the thread that binds us together is made from, even in those instances where we are perfect strangers. Why do we feel so hyper-vigilant of one another's actions and reactions?

Over a period of months, I spoke with women over video calls, lounged on sofas, sat in cafés sipping hot coffee with frothed milk kissing our lips, and chatted over the phone for hours. Every single woman I interviewed on the topic of friendship and their feelings of belonging to a collective all shared the same sentiment: that their friendships with other women were sacred, but the bonds that tie us together are complex, nuanced and conditional.

Some referred to this as *girl code*, which we've already covered in the introduction, but the notion of being a 'girl's girl' came up time and time again while describing these bonds as an alliance, sisterhood or sorority. What I found most interesting about these conversations was that, whether we were talking about girl code or sisterhood, it soon became clear that the rules we expect one another to abide by were eerily similar, even though all the women I spoke with told me they had never discussed it or given it much thought until I'd interviewed them.

As I ended each conversation, it was evident to me that, without needing to verbalise it, women often share the knowledge that we are broadly tied by facing similar struggles – medical misogyny and the lack of education on women's bodies and health; societal and familial expectations of parenthood; enforcement of gender stereotypes both inside and outside the home; a heteronormative world view as well as a statistically high chance of being the victim of gender-based violence and, more broadly, patriarchal oppression. In fact, the commonality of the answers was stunning, all of them reflecting specific pillars around sex, vigilance, menstruation, communication and belief. These shared experiences have helped shape a set of ethical codes that many of us live by, perhaps without even realising it. Here are the key takeaways, as told by the women I spoke to:

Regarding sex: Do not sleep with a friend's ex, unless you've been given explicit permission to pursue that relationship. And, if that friend says no, then you must respect that decision. Never 'steal' someone else's partner from them.

Regarding vigilance: Look out for other women who are drunk or alone. Ask if they're in danger. When it isn't possible to ask with words, communicate with looks and eye contact. Frighten off men who are acting predatorily. Watch each other's drinks. Always text when you get home.

Regarding menstruation: Be ready to offer menstrual products to anyone who asks for them. Carry extra, even when you're not on, to share with people. Carry pain killers and share them. Tell someone if they've leaked.

Regarding communication: It's OK to gossip, but not to bitch – know the difference. What is said in confidence should remain in confidence. Secrets are safe, some are sacred. Always share information where possible and provide a safe space.

Regarding belief: Little or big, have each other's back. Believe women who come forward with stories of domestic violence or sexual abuse. Be their biggest supporter.

This list is neither complete nor exhaustive. I'm sure there will be many women reading this who will think, *Yes, and* ... or, *Yes, but* ... and perhaps some will disagree entirely. Nevertheless, this collection of answers from people who didn't know each other shows us something important about the expectations women have concerning their interpersonal relationships with one another: that the code of conduct or sense of ethics we are expected to abide by to be supported by other women are learnt through a form of social osmosis, and reflect heteronormative socialisation and an understanding of patriarchal dangers.

I visualise this as a spectrum of experiences, like a parasocial umbilical cord, tied to the shared struggles we face as women. At other times, it feels like a reciprocal alliance in the form of a secret handshake that makes life easier and more joyful.

Whatever form it takes, this conglomeration is tethered by the same basic principles: that the richness of these relationships (where they can evolve in different ways, based on how much mutual understanding and support exists) dictates how well community bonds are cherished, reinforced and empowered. Equally, when these bonds aren't nurtured, they wither, leaving the people I spoke with feeling isolated, shamed and alone, with community rules that felt oppressive or aligned with broader patriarchal ideals.

What became clear was that the connections formed from within marginalised or shared identity groups that specifically related to gender felt like an emotional lifeline to those who abided by the unspoken social rules imposed by their immediate friendship groups. What's more, these rules appeared to go beyond friendships and were applied to strangers, so long as they appeared to share in the same lived experiences. On occasion, this criteria was expanded to include those who were further marginalised by other aspects of their personhood, such as gender identity, race, religion or age. But for some groups, girl code or a shared sense of gender ethics was more complex and nuanced still. When I spoke with lesbian women, for instance, the notion of girl code seemed alien, particularly due to the heteronormative importance placed on not sleeping with exes of friends. This is because most LGBTQ+ communities are small and intimate, with most people within them knowing of one another by proximity. As a result, it's a simple fact – one that is often joked about – that most people within these social groups will share exes at some point. On the other hand, among lesbian women there remained synergy with other answers around menstrual care and belief.

It was also clear that, because of the way in which these rules are learnt – usually by witnessing what happens to someone who breaks the rules, or worse, breaking the rules yourself and reaping the consequences – that the rules themselves weren't always what we might call 'accessible', relying heavily on people being able to pick up on subtle social cues and covert language rich with subtext, implicature and inference. As such, the neurodiverse women I spoke to explained that they'd always had a problem understanding what was expected of them and had often felt confused by the eruption of sudden anger or disappointment from friends who felt they had been wronged.

Equally, for the trans women and non-binary people I spoke with, there was an additional layer of discomfort at not having necessarily been socialised as women in their teenage years. Conversely, these formative years provided a common arena for all the cisgender women I spoke with and was the period when most of them learnt, sharpish, not to kiss, fancy, sleep or flirt with their friend's ex or to spill secrets. Trans women and non-binary people explained to me that there were also scars from bullying, along with extra layers of vigilance surrounding women-only spaces such as bathrooms. There was a shared recognition of the risk that they could be turned upon, attacked and reminded of their difference, thus making them feel like outsiders – able to pick up on the broad strokes of the language, but not always having the privilege of knowing whether a cis woman would stick up for them if they were in trouble.

Similarly, the Black women and women of colour I spoke to had rules of solidarity with one another that were different to the white women they socialised with, knowing that, though they loved their white friends dearly, microaggressions and racialised topics could create unsafe spaces they would need to retreat from, instead seeking refuge in communities where they wouldn't need to code-switch for the comfort of others, or for their own personal safety. These experiences were compounded further by religious alignment and how heavily patriarchal ideals around behaviour, notions of purity and gender roles were enforced in the policing of friendships. What was acceptable to atheist women might not be acceptable to some Muslim or Catholic women. For example, while one might cheer on perceived promiscuousness, another might denounce it.

This tells us something more about these unspoken 'rules' – that the intention behind them is to have a means of navigating a society that marginalises us for aspects of personhood that are chosen and changeable, but also for those elements that have permanency and cannot be changed. By either being born a woman or becoming one, there is a collective understanding through our own experiences, and those of our mothers and our peers, that on a fundamental level, in society, the odds are stacked against us, and that it is only through banding together in whatever imperfect formation we can that we can survive systematic, gender-based inequality. Patriarchy is a predator and, as one person put it to me in a stark moment of realisation, 'Oh my God. We behave like prey.' It isn't a coincidence that they came to that conclusion, or that women, more broadly, choose to congregate and support each other under the immense social pressures that come with simply existing in the world. There is a certain degree of biological programming observed more in cis women, though not exclusively, that causes them to seek out other women and tend to those relationships as a means of survival. It is known as 'Tend and Befriend', a term first coined in a study by S.E. Taylor et al. published in 2000, which at the time identified that the underlying bio-behavioural mechanism for female stress responses was to tend-and-befriend.[1] The term describes the act of seeking community when under immense stress or facing adverse circumstances.

When humans of any gender are faced with stress of any kind, their nervous system sends signals to the brain and body that in turn send them into a state of fight, flight, freeze and/or fawn. Most of these are fairly self-explanatory: the instinct to fight could refer to a physical or verbal retaliation; flight refers to the urge to run away or behave evasively when faced with danger; to freeze is to find yourself stopped in your tracks or completely paralysed, while fawning is the act of appeasing the aggressor with a view to minimising harm caused by the threat of danger.

While these behaviours are what we commonly associate with 'fight-or-flight', the full extent of what drives these stress responses includes physiological changes, such as the secretion of catecholamines (a group of hormones and neurotransmitters),[2] especially norepinephrine and epinephrine, into the bloodstream.[3] These go on to tell our bodies that we are under stress, and we react to that stress according to our 'fight-or-flight' programming. However, the initial studies that produced the fight-or-flight theory in 1932 by Walter Cannon, after he introduced the idea in 1915,[4] were predominantly done on male rats, rather than human subjects. This meant that stress-response testing only included male neuroendocrine responses to stress for a very long time, meaning the female body's response to stress has been significantly overlooked. Perhaps this isn't wholly surprising, given that medical trials on women didn't begin until 1993,[5] and that menstrual products were only tested with human blood for the first time in 2023.[6]

While there has been some parity over the years in understanding how stress impacts male and female bodies respectively, there is still a data deficit concerning the female neuroendocrine response to stress. Historical inadequacies of female inclusion in medical research aside, this deficit is in large part due to the reproductive cycle and the complexity of the female neuroendocrine system generally. Researchers have argued that the unpredictable nature of the reproductive cycle impacts results, making them unreliable.

Dr Gareth Nye, an endocrinologist at Chester University who I interviewed about hormone testing for an article in *Women's Health* magazine,[7] once described the female endocrine system to me as operating not dissimilarly to a rail network. Each hormone is an 'independent line', he explained, and a disruption to one line could lead to disruption across the whole network.

Stress is one of the biggest causes of dysregulation to the hormonal network,[8] and women and other marginalised groups experience stress simply through being alive. This is something known as minority stress, and it is compounded by other marginalising factors such as race, gender identity, sexuality and other intersectional elements of our personhood.[9] Minority stress negatively impacts mental and physical health outcomes, and may alter biological function such as bodily inflammation, immune function, cardiovascular function, metabolic function and disruptions to the endocrine network.[10] Long periods of extensive stress are also linked to the development of autoimmune disorders, with more and more women affected every year,[11] though there is no research that has managed to connect all the dots between this gender-health disparity, and other factors like genetics and predisposition can also play a part.

Tend-and-befriend is an antidote to these kinds of stressors. According to the research by Taylor et al. and a subsequent literary review of the study in 2002, this behaviour 'appears to draw on the attachment-caregiving system', a term that describes the two complementary behavioural systems that are active simultaneously in interactions between infants and their caregivers.[12] However, as the original study by Taylor suggests, the presence of an infant isn't necessary. This is because other physical triggers can release oxytocin – that is, the love hormone[13] – in addition to female reproductive hormones, creating an urge to seek out others for survival. Gathering, forming interpersonal relationships and tending to them with care is a means of ridding the body of stress and soothing it. In short, the reason women stick together and seek out one another under immense social stress is because our bodies are telling us that if we don't, it could mean the end for us and our offspring, should we have them. What is perhaps most interesting about this study, is that the 'Tend and Befriend' hypothesis set out in 2000 by Taylor et al. didn't include the same examination and interrogation of the male stress response system. Twenty-five years later, further research into this hypothesis has revealed that 'Tend and Befriend' isn't a gendered experience, but a human one.[14] The study conducted by Jessica K. Hlay et al. in 2025 revealed that the same behavioural stress response patterns were observed across the gender spectrum, and that 'while men do report more fighting than women, both men and women use tending and befriending more than fighting or fleeing'.[15]

It makes sense, therefore, that information sharing, gossiping, bitching, locker-room talk, whisper networks and the multitude of ways people develop systems of care or social control, either for self-preservation or the preservation of others, is part of a much bigger evolutionary process. It is social grooming and maintenance, driven by generations of oral tradition and biology, which has taught us the importance of caring for one another and nurturing the development of social networks. It has also taught us how to master control of social groups and exert a specific shame-based ostracisation that relies heavily on the complicity and inaction of the wider dominant group.

This is why gossip plays such a vital role in the maintenance of these different kinds of interconnected relationships. It is a fundamental part of what makes *Homo sapiens* a more complex and evolved primate than our hairier ancestors. The truth is that gossip, and being able to keep track of multiple relationships and connections, is a sign of higher intelligence and a consequence of our evolution.[16] It is a form of social grooming that positions us as allies, or opponents, and in which we test allegiances, trust and loyalty, and learn to manipulate, expose and destroy. It's partly why, compared with other animals, even other mammals, our brains are the largest – specifically because of the size of the neocortex, where our conscious perception of sensory signals, our learning and memory centres, and our programming of goal-directed behaviour are found.[17,18] Additionally, all forms of gossip are emotionally inquisitive and built around a sense of wanting to understand complex relationship boundaries, links and alliances. People are more similar in our behaviours and codes than a gender-obsessed society might lead us to believe. Evolutionarily speaking, then, gossip is in our nature. It's only our socialisation, or other nurturing factors, that determines whether or not it is deemed valuable and excusable, or platitudinous and punishable.

In 2020, the Wellcome Collection published a series of images that demonstrate the sexism and misogyny that underpin Europe's long history of criticising or poking fun at how women talk and the subjects they choose to discuss.[19] In one etching of a meek-looking maiden with a finger on her lips and her fist full of snakes, dated somewhere between 1600 and 1699, an inscription reads: 'Prudence, bee shee maide, or wife, / Hould shee her tounge, there is noe strife.' In others, dated around the sixteenth century, the 'taming of the shrew' is a recurrent motif for an unruly wife. Illustrated as hag-like and writhing, the 'shrew' is sometimes in bed or bound to a chair, as the husband grapples with her to stop her from nagging and gossiping. During this period, wives were often portrayed as 'sheep' or 'shrews'. The sheep represented being obliging and dutiful, whereas the shrew – a mouse-like mammal that, unusually, can be venomous – denoted a wife who was shrill, nagging and untameable.

There was an immense pressure for women to be sheeplike – an attitude that hasn't totally been stamped out in our current century. According to an article published in the *Telegraph* in 2024, over half of Brits are reported to think that women's equality has gone too far,[20] which is an interesting opinion to hold when global development organisation Focus 2030 also reported that, in 2024, no country in the world had reached gender equality. In fact, one in three countries have made no progress since 2015, and it will take 131 years to reach any sort of equality at the current pace of change.[21] One year on from the *Telegraph* report, a study released by the United Nations found that a quarter of countries have experienced a regression in women's rights, with governments reporting a backlash to progressive policies. These are unprecedented, growing threats to women's rights anchored in thousands upon thousands of years of misogyny.[22]

There is a long, exhausting history of society placing an inordinate amount of pressure on women to conform to the stereotype of the 'nice' girl, which in turn positions gossip as a not-so-nice activity. However, these social constraints play another role in upholding patriarchal standards and reinforcing self-censorship. To survive the patriarchy on a social level, women need to adhere to the politics of niceness and likeability, which are themselves inherently problematic characteristics, because of their limiting, self-censoring nature, but also because they carry with them racist and homophobic undertones.

In the article 'Nice for Whom? A Dangerous, Not-So-Nice, Critical Race Love Letter',[23] G. T. Reyes questions: who does niceness coddle? Reyes gives us an unflinching lens through which to explore how niceness can be weaponised by insinuating rudeness or a lack of social class, should that niceness be questioned or challenged. This creates an arena in which niceness is expected as a reciprocation, even if beneath the niceness lies racist, homophobic or xenophobic sentiment. It is a call to heel; an exercise in obedience – one that is often deployed by those who benefit from white supremacy and colonialism.

Reyes draws attention to the win–lose situations that Black people and people from ethnic minority backgrounds encounter when they cross the imposed boundary line of niceness by demonstrating how niceness can be used defensively. Reyes gives examples such as, '*I didn't mean it that way*', '*I was just joking*', or '*I didn't know*', as well as '*Why are you taking this so seriously?*' or '*Why are you so angry?*' or '*You're being divisive*' to demonstrate how niceness can also be used to accuse others who challenge whiteness. These same responses can be used in a multitude of contexts outside of a racialised setting, to flatten and derail what might be perfectly reasonable opposition or offence to an inappropriate joke or remark. Through denial or defensive questioning, the offended party's feelings are downplayed, the problematic behaviour is minimised, and the blame is placed squarely on the person who has taken offence, positioning them as angry, unreasonable or humourless.

Most women will roll their eyes with weary familiarity at tired, sexist jokes and phrases that reduce us to stereotypical roles as homemakers, wives and mothers – phrases like 'get back in the kitchen', and references to 'her at home' or 'the old ball and chain'; the list goes on and gets darker, especially where rape jokes (if you can call them jokes at all) are concerned. The commonality of these phrases and the immediacy with which they are deployed to reassert hierarchy in both public and private settings demonstrate how ingrained this misogynistic thinking is, and how patriarchy is lacking in compassion towards women as a default setting. To make matter's worse, the more frequently we laugh at jokes made at women's expense, be the punchline about domestic or sexual violence, the more normalised and desensitised we are to the impact these 'jokes' have. Which is to programme the brain to feel happiness at the thought of harming women. These 'jokes' change brain chemistry, and researchers have noted just how dangerous this is for women's safety.

Achieving likeability is just another complex balancing act women must learn to perform. But being likeable is riddled with the same gender expectations and gender-based stereotyping we've already explored, which women are pressured to bend to in order to appease misogyny. What's worse is that women who are considered 'non-traditional' – that is, those in positions of leadership; soldiers; athletes; rape survivors; trans women; lesbians – are placed squarely in the firing line of the hateful, post-feminist backlash we are experiencing today in the modern information era.[24]

Ultimately, this culture of niceness creates impossible parameters for women and marginalised folks to exist within. How are we supposed to be nice when everything is consistently *not nice*? Why should we smile more if there is increasingly less to smile about? Considering this societal pressure to be nice, along with our desire to seek affirmation from our common experience, as de Beauvoir puts it, it's perhaps no wonder that, when we partake in gossip that's mean-spirited, it can feel like both a release and a betrayal. All too often, the line between gossiping with the intention of building closeness or finding collective experiences can become blurred into something else.

When does gossip tip over into bitchiness? I would argue that not all gossip is bitching, but that all bitching is gossip. The two words aren't interchangeable, despite both being gendered forms of speech stereotypically attributed to women. We can't, and shouldn't, shy away from the harm bitching can cause. It's corrosive, and can eat away at the material bonds of friendships and alliances until there's nothing left. It can also feel like an immense betrayal of trust to find out you've been the subject of bitching, especially if the person saying mean things about you is someone you consider a friend. It can also feel like a betrayal to have the bitching you've engaged in shared with others. Clearly, the act of bitching itself is a conundrum of social etiquette. Broadly, while we might all agree that bitchiness isn't a desirable quality or trait, the act nevertheless does serve a much broader and more nuanced purpose than simply being a display of mean-spiritedness, and most of us have indulged in it at some time or other.

It's important to note that the act of bitching carries negative connotations with a gender-specific sting. It can mean whining, whinging and moaning, minimising women's words as being unproductive and frivolous – annoying, even. But there's another side to bitching too, and that is emotional processing. Whether or not the things being said are intended to reach the person being spoken about dictates whether or not it is a betrayal or a cry for support, though this line is often murky at best, and relies on our perceptions of trust and alliances. This gives us something else important to consider in our understanding of friendship between women and the unspoken bonds between them: confidentiality. I would argue that the act of bitching can be community-driven at times, and self-serving at others, and relies heavily on perceptions of existing social bonds to denote if it's intentionally harmful or not. Sometimes, bitching can help us realise our identity in the perception of others – for better, or worse.[25]

The truth is that bitching and the unapologetic meanness that comes with it can feel so naughty and indulgent to partake in. The social rules we live by don't allow us to be so blatant with the uglier sides of ourselves – which is why a good bitch about something, or more likely *someone*, can help you let off steam, feel heard and validate your feelings with people who you trust, who might be entertained by your storytelling, and will hopefully call you out if you take things a step too far. Bitching is, to me, the most intimate form of gossip. It requires the utmost trust. Indulging in it can demonstrate that the relationship you have is safe; a place where you can show your ugliness in macro detail and not be judged for it. It also safeguards the subject of the bitching from your wrath, jealousy or sense of vengeance, hopefully leaving you room to handle things more sensitively with them in person. Is this two-faced? Yes. Is that a bad thing? Not always.

The truth of the matter is that all of us love to bitch, but few of us will admit to it. Bitching can hurt people, often those we care about. Yet it is as much a mechanism for social grooming and emotional regulation as gossip is. After all, you might not always really mean what you say, but verbalising it and discussing it with a trusted confidant can help to process emotions in the heat of the moment. Ultimately, there's nuance to be found in intention. How many times have you heard someone justify their unkind words about you by telling you, 'I only said that because I was angry,' or else that they 'didn't mean it, I was just mad'. I know I've heard that a fair few times, and, if I'm being honest, I've said it too when confronted with my own bitchiness. Very rarely are women allowed to get mean and break away from the expectations of being good, kind and likeable. The sad truth is that women and other marginalised folks are usually not afforded the grace to be anything other than obedient, subservient and obliging – or, as the Victorians would have it, seen and not heard. When we break away from these stereotypes, we are called aggressive, emotional – a *bitch*.

The bitch figure has an allure of sorts too, however. In her book, *Unlikeable Female Characters*, Anna Bogutskaya writes: 'There is something awe inspiring about a truly cold-hearted woman onscreen. It's the contradiction of desires that makes her so appealing and reviled, simultaneously. She's everything you've been told not to be – but presented in the gorgeous wrapping you've been told you should aspire to.'[26] Much like Bogutskaya's femme fatales of the silver screen, for women off-screen, bitchiness and bitching demonstrate a direct disregard for the stereotypes and gender roles society demands we conform to. It's not ladylike to say something awful about someone else, and it's undoubtedly manipulative to try to change someone else's opinion on a person based on your motives alone. It's not caring, warm, kind or motherly, but sharp and acerbic and *such an indulgence*. With the right people, in the right environment, allowing yourself to drop the facade of the good girl in favour of something deliberately naughty and menacing feels like taking off your psychological bra at the end of a long day. We can let our whole selves show, all the unfiltered elements – warts and all.

Nevertheless, there remains a negativity associated with bitching that women just can't seem to shake off, maybe in part because bitching, despite being a rejection of the good-girl stereotype, involves embracing another. The bitch isn't always a seductive siren; instead, the figure of the bitch can embody the badness women are taught to run far, far away from: the manipulator, the narcissist, the sociopath; the things that women are told they are if they are not good and meek and mild. Perhaps this is why being known as a bitch isn't something anyone would want, and why it can feel like a derogatory slight. But there is more to this story too. Being called a bitch has always been a way to disrupt self-perception, particularly if those perceptions centre around wanting more from society than being a birthing machine chained to the kitchen counter. The bitch isn't only the figure or trope of a nasty woman – she is much, much more than that.

The word 'bitch' is synonymous with women's suffrage and the fight for gender equality, after it became popularised in the nineteenth and twentieth centuries, during the first wave of feminism.[27] The term was meant to be derogatory, disparaging and offensive – an insult that could be thrown in the direction of activists with the intention of derailing gender-equality progress, by insinuating that the world would fall apart if women stopped being mothers and wives (where have we heard that before?).

This period was marked by famous abolitionists, women's rights activists and feminists. In the US, there was Sojourner

Truth, a formerly enslaved woman who, in a landmark case, won her son's freedom from slavery over a white man in 1828 and would go on to deliver her famous speech 'Ain't I a Woman?' in 1851;[28] Susan B. Anthony, an abolitionist campaigner who, in 1856, served as an American Anti-Slavery Society agent, making speeches, organising meetings and distributing pamphlets. Anthony advocated and lobbied for women's rights from 1851 to the year of her death in 1906, fourteen years before the passing of the 19th Amendment to the American constitution,[29] which promised that 'the right of citizens of the United States to vote shall not be denied or abridged by the United States or by any State on account of sex'. However promising this sounds, the vote was still not guaranteed to women or Black men and women, with state laws providing multiple obstacles such as poll taxes, literacy tests and grandfather clauses, among other imposed racist restrictions, which meant that Black women – particularly in the south – remained disenfranchised.[30]

In the UK, 1867 marked the official beginning of first-wave feminism with the National Society for Women's Suffrage. Sophia Duleep Singh, a British Indian and German Ethiopian woman who was the goddaughter of Queen Victoria, was involved in the first suffragist deputation to the House of Commons on 19 November 1910, also known as Black Friday. Singh refused to pay her taxes or sign the census in protest and was a well-known member of the Women's Tax Resistance League.[31] Sarah Parker Remond, the transatlantic abolitionist, women's rights activist and physician, was the first woman to lecture publicly against slavery in England. Famously, Millicent

Fawcett led the peaceful suffragists, and Emmeline Pankhurst rallied the militant suffrage movement. Fawcett, who became president of the National Union of Women's Suffrage Societies (NUWSS) in 1907, apposed the violent and aggressive action of Pankhurst and her daughter Christabel and would later be accused of whitewashing her government-commissioned report into the concentration camps for Boer civilians.[32] Pankhurst, who was born into an abolitionist family, founded the Women's Social and Political Union (WSPU) and brought women's disenfranchisement into the public consciousness.[33] They campaigned hard, alongside more conservative groups, for women to gain the vote, which they had famously been pointedly denied in the Great Reform Act of 1832. Despite women winning the right to vote in the late nineteenth and early twentieth centuries in other nations such as New Zealand (1893), Australia, (1902), Finland (1906) and Norway (1913),[34] it would take much longer in the UK. The WSPU focused on 'deeds, not words' and would eventually be responsible for facilitating the Representation of the People Act in 1918,[35] which gave property-owning women over the age of thirty the right to vote in the UK.

These suffragists who fought, died and never stopped campaigning for gender equality for all women, who were force-fed milk and eggs until they retched and vomited, who were held in isolation for months and tortured, were the 'bitches' that men – and some women – of the twentieth century were referring to. While there's no direct linkage between the use of the word 'bitch' and 'suffragette', in 2020, *Vox* reported on the surge in the use of the word during and after the suffrage movement, which gives us some idea of the sentiment some men had towards women taking power.[36] What's more, this pattern of trying to dampen feminist efforts to level the playing field by besmirching a woman's character is a tried and tested method used by the patriarchy for as long as records began. Even today, the act of calling someone a 'bitch' feels like an attempt at an age-old takedown that is designed to attack likeability, and subsequently, credibility. These women were labelled as unruly, disagreeable, malicious, unsexed and far worse for their attempts to change the political landscape.[37] Bearing that history in mind, then, it could be argued that to be called a bitch for disobeying patriarchal expectations is to be in excellent company.

When we call another woman a bitch, we impose on them a multilayered, gender-based shame that fails to take into account the nuances that might have led someone to speak ill of someone else in the first place. Bitches are by nature paradoxical – they represent the ugliness of backstabbing and misinformation, while simultaneously embodying a nonconformist, rebellious woman with political motives.

When we hear someone referred to as a bitch, we must interrogate the meaning behind the use of the word. Is it being used because that person can't be trusted with keeping things in confidence, or is it being used because that person challenges the norms of womanhood by speaking out loudly? There is a vital difference.

CHAPTER THREE

Locker-Room Talk

Grab 'em by the pussy. You can do anything.
— FORMER, THEN RE-ELECTED PRESIDENT OF THE UNITED STATES AND CONVICTED FELON, DONALD J. TRUMP

In October 2016, a month before the presidential election in the United States, Donald Trump's 2005 tape with *Access Hollywood* was released and reported on by the *Washington Post*.[1] In it, Trump was recorded having a conversation with TV host Billy Bush, bragging about his attempts to have sex with a married woman, ahead of his guest appearance on the US soap opera *Days of Our Lives*.

Here is an excerpt from that transcript:

Trump: Yeah that's her with the gold. I better use some Tic Tacs just in case I start kissing her. You know I'm automatically attracted to beautiful … I just start kissing them. It's like a magnet. Just kiss. I don't even wait. And when you're a star they let you do it. You can do anything.

Bush: Whatever you want.

Trump: Grab 'em by the pussy. You can do anything.

This display of misogyny was so grotesque that Trump uncharacteristically apologised,[2] releasing the following statement: 'This was locker room banter, a private conversation that took place many years ago. Bill Clinton has said far worse to me on the golf course – not even close. I apologize if anyone was offended.'

Locker-room talk, or 'banter', as Trump called it, is a type of gossip often found in male-only spaces like, as the name suggests, locker rooms. However, this mode of speech isn't limited to specific physical spaces. Locker-room talk, made up of notably vulgar and coarse language, can exist anywhere that specific environmental conditions are met. When Trump commented on sexually assaulting women during his conversation with Bush, he didn't know he was being recorded. He thought the conversation was private. Secondly, the other people with him encouraged his sexism and misogyny, at some points going along with his objectification of women.[3] Lastly, there was no threat of accountability at the time that he spoke those words.

All this tells us that, for locker-room talk to take place, the person needs to have some pre-existing gender-based discriminatory beliefs; there needs to be zero threat of a challenge from other people, and such conversations demand complete privacy. This trifecta creates an echo chamber of misogyny, where dehumanising language levelled against women and LGBTQ+ people can remain unchecked.

Interestingly, similarities appear if we apply the same lens to the environmental conditions necessary for gossip. Gossip requires those same elements of trust, secrecy and discretion, but the difference between the gossip we associate with women and the locker-room talk shared between men lies in the content of the conversation. Personally, I have never listened to my girlfriends indulge in talk centred around perpetrating sexual assault. To me, this makes locker-room talk a subsection of the broader gossip umbrella, and a deeply frightening form of social grooming. I'm right to be afraid too, as locker-room talk upholds sexism in a way that can be particularly dangerous.

In 2020, research conducted by the *Psychology of Men & Masculinities* journal found that locker-room talk often includes men's engagement in 'discussions of women as sexual objects', with 'limited attention to how beliefs about sexual violence are shaped by these conversations'. The same study also found that the pressure to participate in locker-room talk that sexually objectified women was linked to the enforcement of masculine norms, discriminatory attitudes towards women and rape myth acceptance.[4]

In 2025, another study was carried out, looking into what drove men to feel pressured to engage with locker-room talk and exaggerate their experiences. It found that men who experienced something known as masculine-contingency threat, a term which describes the feeling that their self-worth is negatively impacted when their masculinity is being brought into question by being labelled as insufficient or lacking, would often exaggerate or brag about their sexual experiences in order to appear more masculine.[5] This phenomenon occurs in men whose sense of self-worth is inextricably linked to social expectations of masculinity, the pressure of performing masculinity, and being perceived as masculine by others. Those who feel that their masculinity is threatened experience negative personal outcomes, such as increased aggression, hostility and increased prejudice towards other social groups, particularly towards trans people, who by their very nature threaten the gender binary status quo.[6] It can also lead to increases in domestic violence and intimate partner violence, which is not restricted to heterosexual relationships, but is also prevalent in relationships between 'sexual minority men'.[7] This tells us that narrowly defined and upheld notions of masculinity are harmful, not just to people who threaten masculinity, but to men themselves. There is a prevalent connection between those who experience masculine- contingency threat and those with low self-esteem, depression, or who self-isolate.[8]

Writing this reminds me of a time, a decade or so ago, when I was at university and working in a call centre. On my second or third day in the office, our boss turned around to the five of us on the phones and began talking about his sex life. He bragged endlessly about his weekly trips to the STD clinic, of passing on infections to women he called 'sluts', and of cheating on his fiancée. As he spoke, his language became more aggressive and sexually violent. He then described his perfect woman as being a torso, with a vulva and vagina right in the centre of her breasts, and demonstrated how he would have sex with this dismembered object. Then, while looking me straight in the eye, he remarked that, this way, she 'wouldn't talk', and that he would have the 'best bits of her'. Before I had time to process this deeply upsetting misogynistic performance, he left to meet with a 'booty call'. The men around me laughed while I sat there, stunned. At that moment, I was the only woman in the office. Nobody had intervened or stopped him from talking. Everyone sat quietly, occasionally laughing at the machismo caricature before us. The next day, while getting ready to return to the office, I felt frantic. I remember worrying about my clothes and wondering whether my cleavage was showing too much. The thought of having to make eye contact with my boss again brought saliva into my mouth. I decided, in that moment, that I would never go back to that job. I didn't even call to quit. I just never showed up again. This wouldn't be the first or the last time I would experience sexual harassment at work, but this experience highlighted three important takeaways for me. First, that objectification is a performance of dehumanisation that permits absurd crudity and violence. Second, and conversely, women who talk have the power to rehumanise themselves through self-determination, affirmation and community bond-building. Third, it showed me that locker-room talk, or male banter, is a key part of men's social experience in much the same way that gossip is for women. It plays a similarly significant role in how men develop social bonds and seek intimacy with other men, but this often comes at the detriment to women's physical and mental safety.

In a study of one hundred Norwegian men published in 2019 in the journal *Culture, Health & Sexuality*,[9] researchers found that, while sharing drinking stories, most men told 'animated and cheerful stories laced with erotic excitement'. There was a minority of men who also told 'sex stories characterised by aggressive, belittling and degrading language'. The researchers suggested that the men who do this do so for three main reasons: to achieve male bonding and intimacy; to explore ambiguous and confusing sexual experiences; and/or to excuse sexual events characterised by overt aggression. While you could argue that male contingency threat was certainly present within these exchanges and perhaps even exaggerated by alcohol consumption, it's also important to note that the researchers concluded that, for some men, their relationships with women are strongly influenced by their relations with other men.

For most men, then, getting together to chat about sex, their wives and partners, work and life more generally is a necessary part of establishing friendships and getting advice on how to navigate some of the more treacherous aspects of manhood and masculinity. For those who use locker-room talk as a form of bravado and machismo, it's a means of establishing themselves as manly, desirable, and dominant.

We see this in action across social media, with many podcasters and influencers in this space – the so-called 'bro-casters' – picking up microphones to spout bad and oftentimes dangerous dating advice to audiences that can reach the hundreds of thousands. From the podcasters' point of view, this posturing appears to have little to do with actually dating women, and everything to do with performing a type of machismo that is nothing more than fantasy. As such, their performances are intended to be aspirational and motivating, usually to sell courses to their audiences on how to pick up women and become a 'high-value man'. Their audience is often comprised of those suffering with low self-esteem, who might be looking for a means to break through their intense loneliness and isolation by connecting with people who appear to have it all figured out. The issue is that these charlatans haven't figured anything out. In fact, the snake oil they sell might only intensify the problems faced by their audience. The whole set-up is a scam, and it's one that women are paying the price for.

Time and time again, we see influencers in this sphere setting rules for men to follow that purport to guarantee success with women. Underpinning these rules, however, are messages that are misogynistic, violent, degrading and dehumanising – messages that indoctrinate viewers and listeners with the belief that a woman's sole purpose is to submit to men. They tell men to get women drunk, to not take no for an answer; they suggest that women only want to date men for their money and that high-value men don't date below their stations. It's a strange cognitive dissonance to watch a man demand that women 'go make me a sandwich' and then be surprised that women don't want to date him. Any woman who rejects a man or fails to submit herself to these so-called rules might find herself labelled a slut, whore or worse. As such, those watching this content seldom end up with the woman of their dreams, primarily because the woman they're imagining doesn't exist in the real world – and if she did, I doubt she'd choose them. This lack of success is perfect for the scammer, however. By placing the blame on women for exercising their autonomy, the failings of the advice these bro-casters preach are never questioned. The bro-casters are never held accountable, because they tell men who feel awful about themselves that women are to blame for the way they're feeling. Their audiences are being taught to position themselves as men of means, and to value themselves solely on their ability to accumulate. With that outlook, it's hardly surprising that they struggle to form meaningful, romantic connections. After all, their goal isn't only the accumulation of material goods, but of women too – perhaps the most capitalist objectification of women's bodies possible. You cannot collect women like dolls, treat them like dolls, discard them like dolls, and then cry when they don't say, *Thank you, shall we do that again sometime?* It is vital that we see these kinds of podcasts and the demagogues and influencers behind such content for what they really are: groomers, radicalisers and criminals. With their posts and episodes frequently going viral thanks to their outrageous hatefulness, this kind of locker-room talk finds an audience and emboldens them by reinforcing their pre-existing prejudices.

All this culminates in a culture of disrespect, either by those leading the charge, or by those who don't challenge the misogynistic language of their peers. Worse still, the impact of this kind of language doesn't stop when the conversation ends. According to a 2019 article in the journal *Aggressive Behavior*: 'exposure to peers who sexually objectify and disrespect women decreases prosocial bystander intervention'. Put simply, when people continually hear dehumanising language about women, they're less likely to intervene when they witness sexual aggression in the real world.[10] I think back to my experience at the call centre, the jovial jibing and to-and-fro at my expense. I wonder how many other women in other offices have had to sit silently and smile along when overhearing these sorts of conversations, frozen in fear and discomfort.

What makes this all the more enraging is that gossip is demonised far more than locker-room talk, which is often simply chalked up to that old adage of boys being boys. The gender-based disdain for gossip raises the question of why locker-room talk is considered more palatable than gossip, despite the fact that it perpetuates such harm. I also wonder how bad things need to get before we start talking about proactive harm-reduction strategies to prevent the radicalisation of men through this kind of speech. To answer this question, I reached out to Dr Finn Mackay, senior lecturer in sociology at the University of the West of England (UWE) Bristol. Mackay, who has over twenty years of experience in feminist activism and policy, is an authority on gender identities, particularly in the LGBTQ+ space, having published their book *Female Masculinities and the Gender Wars* in January 2024.

They agree to meet me at the Arnolfini arts centre on Bristol's Harbourside, which is stark against a moody sky as I approach it. Mackay is dressed sharply in a fitted blue plaid shirt, and their tone is warm and friendly, yet authoritative. When they speak, it is easy to listen: 'I think men's talk is seen as authoritative, purposeful and point driven,' they tell me, 'whereas I think women's talk is seen as not having a fair purpose, not being linear, being too long. The assumption is that men are some sort of machine; that their language is utilitarian. Women are meant to be objects to look at. They're meant to be pretty. They're meant to be something to see, rather than seen by what they do, so then their language is expected to be pretty; flowery. I don't think that society even necessarily associates gossip with men.'

Nevertheless, while gossiping might be thought of as a women-only sport, dalliances with gossip's history teaches us that men *do*, in fact, gossip – it's just given a different name, and interpreted as being purposeful. It places gossip and locker-room talk in inflammatory opposition. Men's gossip is branded as political and productive, whereas women's gossip is idle, flippant and indulgent, and by extension, these adjectives come to describe the gender they are attributed to. However, this widely held bias is not a reflection of the truth. In fact, it demonstrates how interwoven sexism is with our anthropological understanding of gender.

'It's easy, in a way, to "do" masculinity,' says Mackay. 'If you just observe what's demeaned, ridiculed and put down in femininity and make sure you do the opposite of that, then you're, by nature, "doing" masculinity.'

Mackay continues to explain that men and women are perceived as identity opposites, even though there is a broad and varied way of experiencing and expressing gender beyond the binary that is delightfully contradictory and without boundary. As such, women and femininity and men and masculinity are seen as interdependent yet conflicting – as unmixable as oil and water, chalk and cheese. 'They depend on each other to define themselves,' Mackay concludes.

When you are positioned as opposites, it creates an immediate empathy deficit. It stands to reason that one cannot be the other, or indeed truly *know* the other. You cannot walk a mile in their shoes. To live life outside of these socially enforced rules means to live in a kind of exile from heterosexual, hegemonic norms. This could be why trans+ people experience some of the worst repercussions of marginalisation, because their mere existence serves to break these rules. The gender binary isn't a true representation of human, or indeed animal, life. Clownfish change sex, as do bearded dragons and some species of starfish.[11] Historically, humans have always experienced transness,[12] although the word, as we know it, only became part of the popular lexicon in around the 1950s and 60s.[13]

'Man' and 'woman' as identities are, ultimately, social constructs, but they are nevertheless used to segregate characteristics and dictate life courses. The truth is that our sex – that is, which reproductive organs we're born with – doesn't dictate our gender identity. In 2020, the *International Journal of Molecular Sciences* said that when it comes to gender identity, 'many studies show how sexually dimorphic brain structures are often in line with gender identity rather than with sex assigned at birth'.[14] So, while our genitals don't necessarily confirm our gender identity by default, they seem enough to bind us to gender-based socialisation regardless: that men behave, sound and appear a certain way because they are male, and women don't, because they are female. Applying such reductive thinking to gender is enormously harmful to all parties involved. We've seen its impact stoke culture wars across the UK and the rest of the globe, with LGBTQ+ rights being repeatedly decimated left, right and centre. This has been somewhat fuelled by ignorance from people with enormous power and influence. There was former prime minister of the UK Rishi Sunak, who said 'a man is a man, and a woman is a woman', and author J.K. Rowling, who has goaded police officers to arrest her for using hate speech against trans+ people.

This is fascism in action and stoking these kinds of fires through ignorance or intent is a means of mass control we have seen before. In 1919, the Institute for Sexual Science was founded in Germany by sexologist Magnus Hirschfeld. The institute was a pioneering institution for sexual research and advocacy, focusing on issues like LGBTQ+ rights, sexual education and gender identity. In 1933, the building was burnt down by Nazi forces as part of a larger campaign to destroy materials deemed 'un-German' or 'degenerate'. The Nazis targeted the institute because Hirschfeld was openly gay and a prominent advocate for sexual minorities, which made his work a target of their ideological persecution. When the institute was destroyed, it was a significant moment in the Nazi effort to suppress scientific progress and human rights related to sexual and gender diversity. Many of the research materials, books and films collected there were lost in the fire. Hirschfeld himself had to flee Germany, and he later died in exile.

In 2025, under an executive order of re-elected president of the United States Donald Trump, the Centers for Disease Control and Prevention (CDC) has begun the same anti-science approach of dismantling institutions that advocate for minorities. Jessica Valenti, a New York-based feminist author, journalist and columnist whom I have long deeply admired, has been speaking out fervently about the detrimental and violent repercussions of these attempts at discrediting science and the resources they help to enforce. In a now-deleted Instagram story, Valenti noted with some concern that she'd found out that her work on *Abortion, Every Day* was being monitored by the government. Unperturbed, she has set up a website to archive documents being systematically removed by the Trump administration from data centres like the CDC, and to preserve the unaltered documents that pertain to abortion rights, broader LGBTQ+ identity, gender-affirming healthcare, domestic abuse and more. In her February 2025 newsletter, Valenti broke the news that the Trump administration had scrubbed information about HIPAA (Health Insurance Portability and Accountability Act) protections for reproductive rights from the Department of Health & Human Services website.[15] This is bone chilling. Since the overturning of the landmark 1973 case *Roe* vs *Wade*, which established the constitutional right in the US to an abortion before the foetus is viable, many women, primarily Black, have died from preventable miscarriage complications. Others have been arrested and criminalised. Now, in the US, there is a concerted effort to remove guidance on pharmacies' obligation not to discriminate against patients seeking reproductive healthcare.

In the UK, we're seeing a similar shift away from progressive policies, though thankfully in 2025, an amendment was made to the Crime and Policing Bill to decriminalise abortion in England and Wales. Previously, women could be charged under the Offences Against the Person Act, an archaic law left over from the Victorian era. This law criminalised women seeking abortions and the doctors who carry them out and has been used to arrest and charge women up until 2025, when Nicola Packer faced criminal charges in May 2025 following an abortion in 2020. She was subsequently acquitted.[16] The existence of this law meant that, although abortion was technically legal, thanks to the Abortion Act 1967, women and anyone found assisting them in procuring a miscarriage could still be found guilty and sentenced up to a lifetime imprisonment. In 2023, Tortoise Media reported that these types of prosecutions were on the rise.[17] Perhaps more worryingly, the law gave the police powers to seize and search through a previously pregnant person's phone records and arrest and charge women for seeking abortion healthcare beyond the twenty-four-week-limit period. Police had even been given training on how to search phones to find evidence of abortion crimes.[18] While these changes to the law have been welcomed by campaigners like the British Pregnancy Advisory Service (BPAS), it's clear that there is more to be done to unpick the systematic criminalisation of women's bodily autonomy.

In other areas, such as self-identification, the law has regressed. Now, there is more and more misinformation and disinformation surrounding the safety of women from trans women in public spaces like bathrooms and hospital wards. This is happening in spite of the fact that there is no empirical data demonstrating that women are at greater risk, and a plethora of evidence that trans women are far more likely to be the victim than the perpetrator of harm in public spaces. Meanwhile, in June 2025, the Lemkin Institute for Genocide Prevention and Home Security placed a 'red flag' on anti-trans and intersex rights in the UK, writing, 'The Lemkin Institute believes these moves are part of a broader process of erasure ... We see evidence of genocidal intent and actions targeting these communities.'[19]

It is all too easy to look at the unfolding politics of America across the pond and think that such things could never happen here in the UK. We shouldn't doubt the fact that fascism powered by gender opposition is in full motion here, and we should expect a similar dismantling of rights should a more right-wing government step into power. Elon Musk, who in 2025 did an unmistakable Nazi salute at the Trump inauguration, has offered £100 million (just 0.02 per cent of his collective wealth),[20] to the right-wing political party Reform UK – formerly the Brexit Party – headed by Nigel Farage, a fast friend of Musk and old friend of locker-room banter extraordinaire, President Trump – or, as I like to call them, three out of the four horsemen of the apocalypse. It's also worth noting that Farage, whose popularity appears to grow day by day thanks to the ineptitude of Starmer's Labour government to engage with working-class Britain, is vehemently against women's access to abortion care, calling it 'utterly ludicrous'.[21]

These men, and many more like them, are extreme examples of what happens when megalomaniacal power and dogmatic misogyny meet. But even the belief systems of these men will have started somewhere before escalating so dramatically and so publicly. It takes time to foster an environment where you can own up to sexual assault and not go to prison for it. It should alarm us all that people like Musk harp on about declining birth rates being the biggest threat to humanity while simultaneously supporting an administration that is revoking the rights to abortion and limiting reproductive healthcare access. It doesn't take a genius to see that this is a real-life version of *The Handmaid's Tale* waiting to happen. Unbending fascist beliefs, including that binary gender norms should be preserved at all costs – even if those costs go against the health and wellbeing of others – come from a rigid, misogyny-based understanding of what gender roles are. By believing in these prescribed norms, they uphold sexism and reinforce objectifying standards that disallow women's autonomy and create brittle parameters for what men should embody: a type of masculinity that is so fragile it can be shattered by using someone's pronouns correctly.

The way in which boys and men are socialised plays a significant role in building men whose identities are wrapped up in stereotypically masculine traits. To reach this idealised state of masculinity, men must be perceived as strong and productive, providers of both financial and personal safety. Their emotions should be stoic and inward, rarely expressed, with the exceptions of anger and jealousy. Such men are reliable, honourable – as good as their word. They conform to dress codes but don't wear dresses; they give strong handshakes and speak purposefully with no inflection of question or apology. They dominate politics, tech and finance, as well as more traditional trades like plumbing, mechanics and electrics. A man takes a woman to be his wife. Men take virginity. They take, take, take, but they also hold the door open, mow the lawn, take the bins out, do DIY. Men go to war. Men do not cry. Men are men. They play sports like football and rugby. Men are taught to be in their bodies, not their minds; to shake it off; to go to the gym; to drink a pint; to never hit a woman, *unless she deserves it.*

Women, on the other hand, are socialised to believe that their identity is wrapped in stereotypically feminine traits. They are caregivers with an abundance of empathy. They ask permission; they are careful, not courageous. Women are emotional, manipulative and untrustworthy, though the burden of emotionally regulating those around her is hers alone to bear. They are mothers who *can* work if they so please, but their traditional place is in the home doing domestic labour – and, no, monetary compensation will not be provided. If a woman *does* work, a caring position is best: perhaps a role in a school, like a teacher or a dinner lady, is appropriate. Otherwise, she could be a nurse; not a doctor, something with children or the elderly. She doesn't ask for promotions, because women aren't assertive – they're bossy. She wouldn't want to be thought of as pushy, or worse, a bitch. She should have her own money, but not as much as her husband, and yet she must always split the bill down the middle. She will take his last name and surrender her body to him in marriage. Women cannot exchange sex for money, but they can offer it as an incentive to get a man to pick up his dirty laundry. Women give birth. They give life. They do the dishes seven days a week. They wear dresses and make-up, and must always appear gracefully younger than they are, without falling into the pitfall of looking like mutton dressed as lamb. When it comes to casual sex, women should not have a body count that exceeds what is acceptable – or any at all. But they should also be excellent at sex. Women like to unpick their emotions. Women *talk*.

These are, of course, exaggerated, outdated views of gender roles, but nevertheless, they are stereotypes that many still subscribe to or have felt the pressure to conform to, be that due to societal expectations, or because many who are socialised in this way internalise the performance of gender and feel a great amount of shame when they can't fit into its limitations. Regardless, what remains is an expectation of opposition between the genders, and that is dangerous. To be the opposite of something places extraordinary value on conforming to a binary. It asks that you stand in opposition; to challenge the opponent.[22] So, by positing men and women as opposites, rather than as variations of the same thing that can be experienced in a multitude of ways, when patriarchal structures are challenged masculinity feels the earth move beneath its feet. This also goes some way towards understanding how modes of speech like locker-room talk are upheld and strengthened.

According to an article written in 2020 in the *Current Opinion in Behavioral Sciences* journal, fragile masculinity – a term that refers to the anxiety felt by men who believe they are falling short of cultural standards of manhood – can 'motivate compensatory attitudes and behaviours' to 'restore the threatened status of "real" manhood'.[23] There is no one right way to express masculinity. What rules there are, are open to interpretation. Sometimes this can be joyfully found and expressed, particularly among the LGBTQ+ community. In their blog titled 'Who's Afraid of Female Masculinity?' Mackay notes that 'too many men are not facilitated or encouraged to have this chance, [whereas] butches[24] do have time to reflect on the type of masculine they want to be and become'.[25]

One of the many problems that arises from this is that, generally, men learn about masculinity from their peers – fathers, uncles, brothers, friends – and broader representations in media, meaning that the identity is not 'God-given', but inherited through a narrow lens, which has the propensity to 'manifest certain recurring characteristics such as homophobia, power and dominance over women'.[26] Heterosexual men characteristically *don't* embrace femininity, because embracing femininity when you're a heterosexual male carries a stigma imbued with homophobic and misogynistic rhetoric. To understand why this stigma exists and the impact this has on women's and men's use of gossip, we must examine two things closely: men's historic entitlement to women's bodies, and homophobia.

We're all no doubt familiar with the phrase 'Men are from Mars, women are from Venus', but we're perhaps less familiar with the mythology that underpins it, so here's a quick shakedown: the goddess Venus was synonymous with love and beauty. She was symbolic of Roman power throughout the empire, with Caesar, the famed general, and his adoptive son and the subsequent first emperor of Rome Augustus, forging explicit ties to her to cement their authoritative power.[27] Mars, on the other hand, is the Roman equivalent of Ares, the Greek god of war, and stands as Venus's counterpart in the Dii Consentes, the Roman equivalent of the Greek Pantheon of the Gods. Unlike his Grecian ancestor Ares, however, Mars's identity is embedded in sexual violence. With such powerful representations of the feminine and masculine divine, interweaving love and beauty with the brutality of sexual violence and war in myth and religion, it gives us an early example of how some of the groundwork was laid for today's misogynistic culture.[28]

This story begins in antiquity, and it goes a little something like this: once upon a time, Rhea Silvia (sometimes known as Ilia) – a direct descendant of Aeneas: son of Venus and Trojan hero of legend – was held in servitude in the ancient kingdom of Alba Longa.[29] After Silvia's father was usurped by her uncle

Amulius, Silvia was sworn as a vestal virgin, ensuring that no heirs would be born that could challenge her uncle's rule. It was said by the Latin poet Quintus Ennius that a dream came to Silvia that foretold she would experience suffering at the hands of the war god Mars, but that this suffering would lead to greatness. Then, one night, as she lay sleeping, Mars raped her. As the prophetic dream promised, Mars's sexual assault on Silvia resulted in her pregnancy with twin boys, Romulus and Remus, who went on to found Rome, and therefore the Roman Empire. So, all's well that ends well – right? After all, according to the writings of Roman historian Livy,[30] Silvia's confinement to perpetual virginity was to 'deprive' her of the 'privilege' of bearing children and heirs, and now she had produced two sons who would one day usurp the king and reclaim the throne.[31] As a woman, as a *vessel*, she had fulfilled her only purpose. The story of Romulus and Remus's conception and their subsequent myth as the founders of Rome cemented Roman culture as being masculine, dominant and war-proud, like Mars. Rome was underpinned by a divine right to sex, heirs and legacy at the expense of women's (often) virginal bodies. The trickle-down impact of this myth into Roman day-to-day culture meant that rape as a tool of war, along with other dehumanising practices, was a common weapon against the civilisations they colonised. Rape was also a real, everyday threat to non-citizen and non-elite women, who were not protected from predation by law.[32]

This doesn't mean that rape was seen as socially acceptable in Roman society; quite the opposite, in fact – while there were no explicit laws against rape, people could be found guilty of '*stuprum*'. *Stuprum* was a Roman civil law referring to a shameful act of sex outside of marriage with a widow or a virgin. It was also used to describe homosexual relationships and sexual acts between men and boys, both of which carried harsh punishments.[33] Further examples of gender discrimination at the heart of the Roman justice system include it being the marital status of the woman in question that determined whether or not a man would be found guilty of adultery,[34] which weighted the severity of the crime on the perceived value of the woman in question, based on her chastity and socio-political identity.

It is laws like these, with their inherent, in-built slut-shaming and victim-blaming, that went on to influence legal systems across the West and in some parts of the East,[35] including our judicial system in the United Kingdom – which hasn't changed its format of hearing, ruling and sentencing for centuries.[36] This presents an interesting dichotomy of opposing and contradictory beliefs that are mirrored in our world today, because, in many ways, Roman culture set the stage for our model of civilisation in Western Europe. We can't place the full blame on Rome for the inherent disregard for women's autonomy when it comes to seeking justice against sexual abuse and violence, however, and nor can we blame it for the enforcement of machismo-infused masculinity.

In early history, rape would have been defined as the defilement of a man's property as opposed to a violent crime against women and girls, an approach that was echoed globally, according to an article published by the Centre for American Studies department of Columbia University.[37] In the Code of Hammurabi, a Babylonian legal text dated 1755–1750 BCE, the rape of a virgin was punishable by death, and the virgin was held blameless. If a married woman was raped, however, this would be considered adultery, and the woman was held equally responsible, with sentences of execution by drowning handed out to both rapist and victim. On the plus side, if you can call it that, the victim's husband did have the option of rescuing his wife by pulling her out of the river, if he wanted to. This trend of protecting virginity is present throughout other ancient civilisations too. Hebrew laws dictated that virgins were only protected if they were raped within the city walls, because *theoretically* they could cry for help. If they were betrothed – that is, promised to another man – and were raped before the marriage took place, they would be sold at a low price. And, if they were raped outside a city wall, they would be forced to marry their rapist. If the rapist was found guilty, he would be stoned to death, and if the victim was married, she would be stoned beside him for adultery.

The ancient Assyrians kept things somewhat simpler with an 'eye-for-an-eye' law, which gave the husband of the raped woman the right to rape the rapist's wife. Much like the ancient Babylonians and Hebrews, there was no legal protection for unmarried women or widowed women.

When it came to the Celts (various tribes who inhabited Britain during the Bronze and Iron ages, before the Roman invasion of 43 CE), the law was slightly more discerning, with two different kinds of rape recognised: forcible rape, and the rape of a woman who was incapable of consent due to intoxication or mental illness. While this might on the surface seem more progressive when compared to other ancient civilisations, there were still deeply troubling elements to this law that placed the burden of responsibility on the woman. For example, if you were a 'promiscuous' or 'adulterous' woman, or if you didn't cry out for help during the incident, you were not protected by the law.

This focus on virtue and the defilement of property is still present in our culture today on a global scale, even though the laws have arguably moved on to be somewhat more protective – though, according to Rape Crisis UK in 2023, only 3 out of every 100 rapes recorded by the police ended in a charge that same year,[38] let alone a conviction. Additionally, it wasn't until the Sexual Offences Act 2003 was passed that a more nuanced understanding of consent made it more difficult to use defences like 'I thought she said yes' to escape prosecution (yes, this really was a defence and, yes, it did work).[39] This 2003 law requires men to take reasonable steps to ensure a woman's consent, and the defence must prove an absence of reasonable belief in consent.[40]

What we see time and time again, both in our world today, and in global culture for centuries, is that, if a woman is raped, it is all too likely that she will be disbelieved and discredited because of the number of sexual partners she might have had and her virginal or marital status, and ultimately, the chance of her seeing any meaningful justice is slim to none. This way of thinking has been embedded into the way we think about rape and sexual assault for millennia, creating a hotbed of distrust in women who come forward with accounts of rape, sexual violence and abuse. When it comes to women's voices, they are systematically disbelieved because, since records began, women have been perceived as unbelievable.

The only reason locker-room talk exists in the way that it does is because men have historically always participated in women's subjugation and oppression, either politically, financially, legally or socially. Locker-room talk is seen as unserious, a bit of fun, *banter* – because women aren't regarded as equal to men or valued in society in the same way. Between some men, it's socially acceptable to use dehumanising language to talk about women, and, despite the repercussions that locker-room talk can have on women's and men's physical safety and mental health, there is still resistance to it being challenged. We see that lack of challenge still more online, where locker-room talk is bandied about freely in ways that have made my skin prickle with anger. While we aren't always privy to men's private conversations, we don't need to look too far to find examples of locker-room talk on the internet, where it flourishes, particularly on social media platforms like X (formerly Twitter), Meta, Reddit and 4chan. Scratch the surface and you'll reveal the manosphere, a world where sexist beliefs and anti-feminist rhetoric are alarmingly commonplace and familiar.

The MANTRaP research project at Lancaster University aims to explore misogyny and anti-feminist language found in male-dominated communities on various social media platforms. It describes the manosphere as 'a network of online men's communities against the empowerment of women and who promote anti-feminist and sexist beliefs. They blame women and feminists for all sorts of problems in society. Many of these communities encourage resentment, or even hatred, towards women and girls.'[41]

Men's involvement in these online forums and manosphere spaces that are devoted to misogyny is partly due to a widening gap between the sexes when it comes to political belief systems. This gender divide is happening everywhere, and it is particularly notable in countries like the UK, the US and Germany, but none is facing such extreme polarity as in South Korea.[42]

In South Korea, women are taking a hard turn left, while men are taking an unprecedented swing to the right. Feminism in South Korea is seen as something of a dirty word,[43] so much so that journalist Catherine Kim reported for *Politico* that Huh Yun-jin, a twenty-two-year-old member of the popular South Korean girl group LE SSERAFIM, had come under fire on social media for visibly reading the acclaimed book by Japanese author Mieko Kawakami, *Breasts and Eggs* – a novel that portrays women's lives in Japan. Kim lists some of the comments Huh received for being perceived as a feminist: 'If a girl group is tainted by feminism, you've got to send them to hell,' one person wrote, while another, more alarming comment read, 'Feminists, if I see you, I'll beat you up and make you crippled.' This is just a taste of some of the extreme misogyny present in South Korea, which was exploited and stoked by a staunch anti-feminist government during the election in 2022. Young South Korean men cheered as the then elected president Yoon Suk Yeol tore apart the Ministry of Gender Equality and Family, a body dedicated to gender equality in all forms – echoing the Nazi burning of the Institute for Sexual Science.

What Korea teaches us, and what we can only hope America and Britain will learn from, is that the dissemination of gender rights isn't instilling trust for South Korean men, neither is it improving their mental health or career prospects – all it is doing, in spades, is leading to more disdain for women. This means that, for women, this ideology-based gender divide has resulted in increased intimate partner violence so extreme that every nineteen hours a woman is killed, or almost killed.[44]

At the heart of so much of misogyny is a sense of shame at not adhering to the narrow constraints of masculinity. This is what makes boys and young men so vulnerable to escalating radicalisation. They are emboldened by the locker-room talk they perpetuate and engage with, despite the inferiority they feel at traditional notions of idealised, machismo-led physical traits. It is a moment of great pathos to consider that, if misogynists weren't so burdened by their inability to conform to perceived notions of masculinity and instead chose to embrace their differences outside of the binary, they might find peace and pleasure. Just as shame is a powerful motivator, hope can be too, which may explain why many choose to grasp at masculinity instead if rejecting it, in an attempt to combat that shame they feel for not feeling good enough, or 'man' enough. As a result, we are witnessing the impact of this radicalisation and misplaced hatred of women on gender equality on a global scale.

Just as locker-room talk tests alliances and pushes the boundaries of what is acceptable within a social setting, it also creates an ambiguity around the women they're referring to. In non-extreme or casual examples where family or friends make sexist comments, we're conditioned to grin and bear it. It's easy to give them the benefit of the doubt, to presume that they're a good person, if perhaps a little ignorant. This permissiveness is a sliding scale, however, and one that can lead to a complete dehumanisation of women from the perspective of the offender. Calling out such comments when we hear them (and, indeed, when it is safe for us to do so) is one way that we can interrupt a slide into more radical ways of thinking.

To paraphrase Margaret Atwood, who published an essay titled 'Writing the Male Character' in 1982, 'Men are afraid that women will laugh at them. Women are afraid that men will kill them.' I'm reminded again of Mackay and our meeting at the Arnolfini: 'All of us have had experiences of being dumped, feeling bitter not going out with the person you wanted to go out with,' they said. 'And what I always think is quite shocking is that young women have all these experiences too. Young women get told they're unattractive and too ugly to go out with; they fancy this boy, and he puts them down in a public way, or their boyfriend cheats on them and everybody knows apart from them and it's embarrassing. Or they apply for a job, and they don't get it. And yet, we don't see young women going [and] shooting up their entire school the next day.'

Incels – heterosexual men who blame women and society for their lack of romantic success (a subject which we will explore more thoroughly in the chapter on social media) – cannot consolidate the dissonance between desperately wanting to be desired by attractive women and the unbridled hatred they feel towards females who they believe are denying them their entitlement to sex, even though these two entities are more often than not the same person. Perhaps it is this ability to see them as separate entities that enables them to detach their humanity, meaning that those women that they both desire and hate are not considered human to them at all.

In a 2023 article in feminist journal *HYPATIA*, Filipa Melo Lopes calls this a desire incels have for 'The Other', women who are 'without the capacity of choice' – this is, of course, a form of objectification and dehumanisation, a theme that runs solidly through this touch with locker-room talk and misogyny at large. Another side of this 'Other' identity is the sense of entitlement incels have. Lopes writes, 'Incels see women as loyal servants who owe them sex and love.'[45] She argues that this creates a false expectation, that the women incels choose should be 'picked off the shelf' like a doll, which in many respects men were able to do until women had the right to work, have bank accounts in their own name and get a divorce. And women were only able to do this because they fought tooth and nail, protesting, marching, campaigning, organising, signing petitions and sharing information – *talking*. It shows how much power there is in community bonds that rely on building trust and rejecting exceptionalism. It also explains why there is such an appetite for suppressing and muting the voices that speak out against it.

However, it is the additional element of ambivalence, the dichotomy of love and hate, the obsessive desire and world-ending rejection that reaffirms blame on women for causing such a Sisyphean struggle for incels when it comes to forming romantic relationships. You might be wondering how these men end up believing in incel ideology – which has the propensity to spew out some of the vilest vitriol against women and girls – in the first place. Lopes argues that only focusing on the objectification element of incel behaviour lacks nuance and depth, especially as it fails to recognise the hangover of chivalry, the 'good' or 'nice guy' identity and frightening ambivalence.[46]

In the West, chivalry is the religious, moral and social code that places great importance on honour and, ironically, being kind to women.[47] Knights were a major part of the European feudal system. Their duties were broad, from fighting in wars and conquests and riding horses, to escorting services and guarding castles. But one might argue that these macho, highly respected roles helped to further embed some of the gender inequality we face today. More specifically, upon these foundations we see the building blocks of how early-stage capitalism favoured men and laid the groundwork for the modern-day wealth gap, bestowing land and status on them in favour of military service.[48] Again, we find an association with war and violence; with men women should swoon for, or risk being taken by. Unlike the women of the era, knights could accumulate immense wealth and power for their adherence to gender roles, whereas women would be burdened and oppressed by theirs. The ideology of the perfect knight's identity was very important in the Middle Ages. However, rarely did a knight's behaviour actually match up to their persona.[49] This didn't stop the Church from capitalising on their brutality, though. They are described as being 'heavily armed and prone to violence' in historical archives,[50] and chivalry was a measure adopted by the Church to try to keep them in line. This created an honour-bound class system that elevated knights in social and spiritual status, which was instrumental in the crusades that waged holy wars against followers of the Islamic faith as it settled across the Mediterranean.[51] The knights' adjacency with the royal family, majesty, God and godliness cemented their identity as a powerful one that commanded respect in the feudal hierarchy. This meant that knights could take advantage of the power structure that favoured them. In short, they benefited from the establishment of patriarchal societies, which had been taking root globally since before the Bronze Age.[52]

In contemporary society, being able to take advantage of social status, while wielding weapons and being backed by an institution that dictates cultural scruples, is still a perfect storm where power and oppression can exert control on a disadvantaged and marginalised population. It could be argued that this is broadly the modus operandi of politicians and others who hold celebrity of some kind. After all, great wealth and power is a social and political currency. Time and time again, we've seen that the more you have, the less accountable to justice you have to be, no matter what era you live in.

If you're a cisgender man, it pays to be surrounded by equally powerful people who share in your privilege and belief system – a member of 'the old boys' club', as it were. Defined as 'the male-only network of social and business connections among the elite',[53] 'the old boys' club' not only contributes considerably to the gender pay gap by favouring male colleagues and their promotions over their female colleagues,[54] but also shows us that male camaraderie can gatekeep access to wealth and power by punching down with intent. That has dangerous consequences when the entry fee for many men's membership to this club is complicity – turning a blind eye to the sexism and misogyny they witness.

This begs the question, then: when it comes to calling each other out for their sexist beliefs and misogynistic actions, why are men so bad at it? The beginning of this answer lies in the relationship men have with their emotions. Take this study published in 2023 in *Sociology of Health & Illness*, titled 'Masculinities and men's emotions in and after intimate partner relationships'.[55] The study asked thirty Canada-based men to explore their emotions pre- and post-break-up. Many resorted to stoicism to cope. During this phase, the men did not express themselves, denying and downplaying their turmoil. What is most interesting about this study is that the discordant emotions men felt when their relationships ended – emotions such as 'sadness, shame, anger, regret and guilt' – called into question 'men's rationality for deciphering and expressing what was concurrently but inextricably felt'. They reported being 'overwhelmed by mixed and weighty break-up emotions', with shame and anger being the most dominating and demanding.

That word shame, *again*. But it's worth us drilling down into its insistence on repeating itself, because that in itself is telling us something, loudly: that if we don't try to remove shame, then we are destined to be ruled by it. Shame is a socially charged, motivating emotion, as our look at incels (see pages 93–4) – and everything else for that matter – has proved. Biologically speaking, shame is an important part of our evolution, which signposts to a time when we would have been hunter–gatherers, relying on group dynamics to stay fed and watered. Shame would quickly teach us what was and wasn't acceptable in our tribes – and quickly serve to secure hierarchies of dominance. In its most basic form, shame as an emotion was our social safeguard from behaving in a way that could damage our chances of social (and literal) survival.[56]

The problem now is that men who display the utmost hatred towards women appear to feel no shame for their belief system, only for themselves. If shame is not acknowledged and disbanded, then people become ruled by it. Where that shame is drawn from and where the blame is placed is vital.

When it comes to gender threats and shame, another study published in the *Journal of Experimental Social Psychology* in 2021 found that gender threats (versus assurances) led to emotionality in men (but not women).[57] In essence, this means that when men's sense of self – that is, their masculinity or masculine identity – is threatened, it can lead to public discomfort and an increase in feelings of anger, guilt and, of course, shame. Soberingly, this results in compensatory displays of dominance. The study noted that these reactions weren't only reserved for physical outbursts and altercations like punching, but also extended to social and economic punishment.

Plainly, as this chapter has demonstrated, when masculinity is threatened, women suffer, but so too do people who exhibit feminine traits that they stereotypically wouldn't. Homophobia, and more specifically the fear of being perceived as homosexual, is one more part of the picture, as is latent homosexuality – a term that describes underlying homosexual arousal that the person is unaware of or wilfully ignores. Finally, there is also the fear built on the notion that a person might somehow unwillingly become homosexual, either by proximity to LGBTQ+ people, objects or spaces that are inherently made for and by the queer community. To be clear, you can't 'catch' gayness, and neither can you 'turn' gay. Take it from me, you are born this way, and being part of the

LGBTQ+ community is nothing to be ashamed of. There is a reason why the LGBTQ+ rights movement is called Pride. Nevertheless, a 1996 article titled 'Is homophobia associated with homosexual arousal?' stated, 'When placed in a situation that threatens to excite their own unwanted homosexual thoughts, they [heterosexual men] over-react with panic or anger,'[58] which partly explains the exaggerated presentation of machismo and misogyny in the podcasts of pick-up artists.

Another theory is that heterosexual men are afraid of being sexualised by homosexual men in the same way that heterosexual men non-consensually sexualise women.[59] This makes it clear that men understand how detrimental unwanted sexualisation can be, which brings with it an additional layer of perversion and violation. In addition, because of the historical societal shame attached to homosexuality, the fear of being wrongly thought of as gay might generate enough inward panic to lead to outward homophobic tendencies, resulting in violence and hate crimes.[60] Evidently, heterosexuality is not only perceived as being fragile, but as an identity it is more threatened by homosexuality than homosexual identity is by it.[61] Simply put, heterosexual men rely on masculinity and gender roles as integral to their identities, but masculinity has no one fixed point. As a result, when people who are homosexual go about their daily lives, it can bring chaos to the heterosexual man's perceived sense of self, because by their very existence, gay men challenge the masculinity myth.

I can think of few people who fit this summary of fragile masculinity more perfectly than Andrew Tate. Tate, whose extreme misogyny has resulted in the radicalisation of an untold number of men and boys, relies on a dogmatic subscription to masculinity. Speaking of subscriptions, Tate's business model is a tiered coaching programme that, at its most affordable level, clocks in at £40 per month. The target demographic is boys aged twelve to eighteen,[62] and the programme teaches its audience how to become a 'high-value man', i.e. a man who has an abundance of money, power and dominance over women.

In the UK in 2023, around 6 per cent of men agreed with Tate's views on women. These men were found across age groups but were more commonly found between the ages of eighteen and thirty-five. Of those who have a favourable opinion of Andrew Tate, 54 per cent say they agree with his views on how women should be treated, compared to 64 per cent for his views on masculinity and 78 per cent for his views on work and success.[63] This becomes more alarming still when we consider children's opinion of Tate, with one in six holding an unfathomably positive view of him. It is worth stating here that this is a man who has been charged with rape, human trafficking and forming an organised crime group with his brother to exploit women sexually. Tate is the model for machismo gone wrong, but the problem with models is that they are replicable. So, while Tate might be the first podcaster and influencer to create a following so hell-bent on accumulation in this way, he's far from unique, as copycats have sprouted up across the internet, microphone in hand, misogyny on their tongues, ready to cash in *big* on the pull of capitalist exploitation. Tate's biggest amplifier? Social media.

CHAPTER FOUR
Social Media

I think it's worse for women online. It's part of an old tradition of misogyny, but more for young women because they are objects of desire.

— MARGARET ATWOOD, Wired

The concept of social media began way back in the 1940s, when computers as we would recognise them today were invented and the idea of connecting them with one another began to be bandied about. However, it wasn't until the internet became available to the masses in 1991 that social media, as we know it today, began to reach its networking potential. First came a site called Six Degrees, which started the ball rolling in 1997. Then came MSN Messenger in 1999, an instant messaging service where I spent hours after school online speaking with people I'd spent all day with – much to my parents' dismay. These sites were fertile ground for gossiping and providing an opportunity to nudge that person you fancied, if only you could pluck up the courage. Even then, we knew that being behind a screen could imbue us with a sense of bravado and charisma, which also made it easier for bullying behaviours to spout.

In the early 2000s, platforms like LinkedIn, Bebo and MySpace started gaining in popularity, connecting people around the world. MySpace was a particularly important social tool for me, growing up in a pretty rural area in North Wales. All of a sudden, I was speaking to people in other schools, comparing my looks and outward presentation with theirs. I remember learning basic code to enhance my profile, adding music, animated GIFs and photos, all with the intention of outlining my identity and letting people know who I was. I believe this early form of curation and self-promotion paved the way for the type of influencer culture we've come to know intimately in the mid-2020s. The boom of platforms like Facebook in 2004, and Reddit and YouTube in 2005, created spaces where people could share information and create echo chambers of opinion in an unprecedented fashion.

But amid the rise and fall of these social media platforms in the noughties, something else was also brewing. It's believed that the manosphere first rose in popularity in around 2009, on a social media platform called Blogspot. This could be imagined as a digitisation of the men's rights movement (MRM), which, although it had originally supported feminism in the early 1960s, grew to oppose it in the 1970s, becoming increasingly conservative and concerned with the rise in women asking for autonomy, which, by extension, was perceived as resulting in men having less power over, and access to, women's bodies.

This is a pattern that would be repeated time and time again throughout modern history, where a step towards some form of parity or gender equality leads to an enormous backlash. By the time the internet rolled around and somewhat democratised access to communities and information, this movement had metamorphosed into men's rights activism, or MRA. As time has gone on, these transformations and reimaginings of manosphere groups have become more misogynistic,[1] from the milder communities like pick-up artists, to the black-pilled incel groups, who are considered to be the most extreme incel belief system, compared to red-pilled incels, who are still regarded as an extremist group, and the acts of terror committed under their influence. If you're wondering what black, red and blue pill mean, or what it means to be 'pilled' at all, let me explain. The terminology is derived from the 1999 film *The Matrix*, where the main character wakes up in a world ruled by machines and automatons. He is offered to be sent back to the world and life he knew, one you and I would recognise as 'the real world' by taking a blue pill, or to take the red pill and know the secrets of the Matrix. The appropriation of this metaphor by incels ignores the original intent of *The Matrix* creators Lana and Lilly Wachowski, who have explained since their transition that the film is intended to be an allegory for the trans experience, in particular, coming out.[2] However, incels have adopted their own metaphor for the allegory, and instead relate the awakening of the red pill as their realisation of their position as 'beta males' – secondary to the dominant 'alpha male' – and a resulting warped rationale for the sexual strategy they have developed to outsmart 'manipulative' females.[3]

Combining the accessibility of the internet, the history of misogyny and the rampant sexism of the 2000s, the Wild West of social media sparked a particularly grim conversation around women, their bodies, sexuality, identity and class.

There was something else tying these social media platforms together too: they were all developed by men.

'Given how blatant the media was in the early noughties, especially around its treatment towards women, people started creating their own blogs dedicated to hating on women, sexualising them in ways that were reminiscent of the circle of shame that the magazines would come to have,' Robyn D'Arcy, data scientist and gender equality activist, tells me over a video call. D'Arcy and I worked together in 2023, when allegations against the comedian and TV presenter Russell Brand were aired on a Channel 4 *Dispatches* documentary episode, 'In Plain Sight'. D'Arcy's data fluency meant we could see in real time how many posts about the documentary across social media contained misogynist language.

Four days after the Channel 4 documentary aired, I reported for HuffPost that 1.8 million posts were made across social media reacting to the news, and 59 per cent of those posts used misogynist language[4] – a sobering percentage, and a sign of things to come in the new era of Elon Musk-owned social media. D'Arcy explains that the 2000s remain a horrifying case study for blatant and overt sexism and misogyny in media, where online hate gained enormous traction thanks to the way in which algorithms reward engagement.

'The noughties were a time of "the game", "Tucker Max" and then – one of the worst people on social media I've ever heard of – Roosh V,' D'Arcy goes on. Both of us wrinkle our noses remembering the names of these notoriously vile pick-up artists of the early noughties.

Daryush Valizadeh, also known as Roosh V, ran a manosphere blog up until 2018, when he finally shuttered it indefinitely. The campaigner describes himself as a neo-masculinist,[5] and during the six years his blog was running, articles and posts written by him and guest writers mused on the pros of dating women with eating disorders, lengthy explanations on why women shouldn't be allowed to vote, and why homosexuality is similar to Nazism.[6] Here is an extract from his self-published book, *30 Bangs: The Shaping of One Man's Game from Patient Mouse to Rabid Wolf*:

> No means no – until it means yes. The sex was painful for her. I was only the second guy she'd ever had sex with. I didn't think she was lying, because pumping her was like jamming my cock through a medieval keyhole. She whimpered like a wounded puppy dog the entire time, but I really wanted to have an orgasm, so I was 'almost there' for about ten minutes. After sex, she sobbed for a good while, talking about how she had sinned in the eyes of God, but in an hour, she got horny again and we went at it once more.[7]

Despite his views, Roosh V's online presence fading from prominence didn't happen because people stopped believing his message; it happened because he was deplatformed. Even on Musk-run X, V's account was suspended. For believers in the manosphere message, however, bans are a badge of honour, and V was being kicked out of everywhere, including his own events.[8] 'What he was able to do when he got kicked out of these places was turn it into a good thing,' D'Arcy says, going on to explain how these bans were twisted by V to reinforce his message around being so truthful that 'they' – whoever 'they' might be – just wanted to censor him because he was too strong, and because people just hated masculinity. 'He was like Andrew Tate, before Andrew Tate,' D'Arcy states.

Today, though, V has found God. In an interview with the Muslim Skeptic on YouTube in 2021,[9] he explains to host Daniel Haqiqatjou that in 2019, one year after his X deplatforming, he had felt the urge to reach out to God, feeling that there was more to life than satisfying his body, ego and pride in this life. He even nods along while host Haqiqatjou affirms that he now views fornication as evil, as a place of darkness, and asks the question we're probably all asking: *what changed?* Brace yourselves. V tells Haqiqatjou that he is no longer red-pilled, in the same way as an incel might claim to experience, but *God-pilled*; that he has seen the proverbial light and recognises that he had put time and effort into faithless women, only to get cheap sex back.

It never ceases to amaze me how men find God and faith after they've been outed as monstrous, and how the blame for their indiscretion rests solely with the temptation women exude. The use of 'faithless' to describe the women in question here is interesting too, because his earlier writing suggests that the woman he had sex with felt shame and remorse for going against her faith. Then there is the usage of 'cheap sex', which is a loaded term. It implies that cheap sex is sex for pleasure, and not reproduction – and therefore not 'good' sex, or at least, sex that would be acceptable in the eyes of his God.

Nevertheless, in his new Christian world view, V says that there was truth in what he said while red-pilled, although it was 'wrapped in garbage'.

'I would see it as an insult now if someone today called me red-pilled. That pill is gone. I'm God-pilled now,' V tells the host, who is smiling back at him while he continues. 'My faith doesn't have to have a cool, modern, trendy term. You know, I'm not a red-pilled guy – I'm a Christian man … I want to own the Christian term.' *Sigh*.

Before we break this down, it's important to make clear that I am in no way undermining faith or religious beliefs. Despite being what people like V might call a godless feminist, in no way do I want to suggest that turning to God, or whomever you might believe in, is an eye-roll-worthy act. It is not. To have faith in a higher power, a deity, a god or gods, can be a beautiful, healing thing. What I take umbrage with is this predator-to-godly-man pipeline – a familiar route for celebrities and public figures accused of and found guilty of truly awful abuses. To me, these actions mock the forgiveness that religion preaches, and are called opportunistic proselytising – that is, taking advantage of certain opportunities that come with faith, such as gaining power, influence or personal benefit. This behaviour is driven by self-interest rather than a true desire to spread the word of God.

If, like me, you've ever wondered how people could be sympathetic to those who use this pipeline to excuse their actions and receive some form of public redemption, we need to look at the circumstances that make it easy for fascist and totalitarian views to start making some sort of sense. In this information era, we cannot look away from the impact of the financial crash of 2008 on male disenfranchisement. That year, unemployment was the highest it had been in the UK since 1995,[10] and amid the more competitive job market, sexism abounded, particularly among young men, who could point to the advancement of women's rights as the reason for their hardship and lack of opportunity.[11]

A few years later, in 2012, when popular media was congested with sexist tropes, the No More Page Three campaign was launched, which fought for the removal of photographs of topless glamour models in the *Sun* newspaper. Additionally, the Lose the Lads' Mags campaign by Object and UK Feminista in 2013 was perceived as a war against 'the average bloke' and a direct attack on masculinity.[12] It's worth noting that these campaigns weren't driven by a desire to shame the women involved, but rather to express a concern for the degrading content of the magazines, like this line: 'I think girls are like plasticine, if you warm them up you can do anything you want with them.'[13]

By the early 2010s, the forum-style social media platform Reddit had been around for a couple of years. 'You find a lot of subreddits for these sorts of male-centric grievances,' D'Arcy says. 'And we saw this again during the Covid-19 pandemic and everything that's happened since.' D'Arcy draws attention to Trumpism, explaining that any kind of economic, political or social instability is met with an immediate response to revert to traditional gender roles. 'It creates a nostalgia for a period that never really existed, or existed in ways that only benefited straight, white cis men; middle-class men, at that,' she states.

Nevertheless, the addition of social media and its propensity to propel and promote networked misogyny has had truly devastating consequences. The rise of incels in 2010 created a new outlet for men who felt wronged by society and by women, but, surprisingly, the origins of inceldom were actually made with good intentions. The word 'incel' came from a well-meaning project by a woman known only as Alana, who described herself as a late bloomer who wanted to help lonely people struggling to find romantic connections. Speaking with Anna Foster from Radio 5 Live in 2018,[14] Alana said, 'The word [incel] used to mean anybody of any gender who was lonely, had never had sex or who hadn't had a relationship in a long time. But we can't call it that anymore.'

The website she created, Alana's Involuntary Celibate Project, in the nineties, grew to become what we recognise today as the extremist group inciting terror against women and girls. Alana is, of course, blameless in this – there are multiple threads that have compounded one another to create a tapestry of hate that she could never have prevented from forming. Speaking on this, Alana says that when 'angry men' decided to 'hijack' the word, it caught her by surprise.[15] Following an attack in Toronto where a man ploughed into a crowd of pedestrians, Alana, who is also from Canada, told the *Guardian*, 'It feels like being the scientist who figured out nuclear fission and then discovers it's being used as a weapon for war.'

'It's another form of male martyrdom,' D'Arcy tells me as we discuss the Greek-style tragedy of Alana's well-intentioned attempt to connect lonely people. 'The evolution of incel encompassed this real sense of, "We are being downtrodden.

The norms have changed. We're the real victims. Why do we focus on women when we should be focused on looking after men?"'

This is perhaps why, when a multitude of celebrity women had their nudes leaked in 2014, an event known rather grossly as the 'Fappening' or 'Celebgate', there was little sympathy for the women at the centre of it, who had had their privacy breached in such a public way, despite the arrests of multiple men for their roles in the scandal. In the past, when nudes of celebrities have been leaked to the public, it has been the women who have had to make the apology for their 'indiscretion'. For example, in 2007, when nudes of Vanessa Hudgens – who was just eighteen at the time – were leaked, *she* was blamed, with the Disney Channel releasing a statement, which was later reported in *People* magazine, saying, 'Vanessa has apologized for what was obviously a lapse in judgment. We hope she's learned a valuable lesson.'[16]

When Jennifer Lawrence denounced the 2014 hacks as a sex crime in *Vanity Fair*,[17] it created a vital shift in the conversation around shame, victim-blaming and slut-shaming. Despite this, though, the victims of this sex crime still weren't taken seriously. 'It was this idea of women's bodies as public property, and people would be like, *Well, nothing's happening to them, like, they're not actually physically being hurt, so, what's the problem?*' D'Arcy reflects.

The nudes were leaked to 4chan, first and foremost, which was described appropriately by the *Washington Post* in 2014 as the internet's 'bogeyman'[18] and as one of 'the darkest corners of the web' by the *New York Times*.[19] It was, and *is*, a shock site where one-upmanship is currency. It blends juvenile jokes, lad culture and trolling, with little regard for the personal impact it might have on those it mocks and jeers at, arguably going so far as to revel in it.

The site was created in 2003 by then fifteen-year-old Christopher Poole for Americans to discuss anime. However, the site mutated and evolved, much like Alana's Involuntary Celibate Project, to popularise memes like Pepe the Frog and LOLcats (you had to be there), but also to spawn Anonymous, the hacker group who took down PayPal, Visa and Mastercard when they blocked donations to Wiki-Leaks through their organisations. It was also the birthplace of QAnon in 2017,[20] the conspiracy-theorist group who believe that Donald Trump is waging a secret war against an evil cabal of cannibalistic paedophiles in Hollywood.

'Then you have a fish-rots-from-the-head situation,' D'Arcy explains. 'This is the post-truth era, where someone like Trump, who is not only a public figure, celebrity and presidential candidate, [but] embodies, neutralises, glorifies sexist and misogynist things other men are talking about on social media.' D'Arcy explains that this is why, in any other era of social media, saying things like 'grab 'em by the pussy' (see page 68) would have been bad enough to get users taken off any sort of political platform. 'People have been taken off for way less violent and obvious statements,' she says.

This post-truth era has made the truth malleable and deniable. You might recognise the phrase 'alternative facts', used by counsellor Kellyanne Conway in 2017 to defend Sean Spicer's false statement about the attendance numbers of Trump's inauguration as president of the United States. Then there is, of course, the phrase 'fake news', used liberally by Trump himself.

Online, this thinking – and sometimes the very same phraseology – is used as an anti-elitist, anti-women, misinformation-driven clapback to discredit reported-on phenomena by credible institutions on the gender pay gap, health gap, orgasm gap, education gap, violence gap and so on and so forth. This adds to the simmering anti-education and anti-intellectualism sentiment that is fuelling fascism in the West, empowering people with existing prejudices to use their opinions as fact. It discourages fact-checking altogether, in favour of emotionally driven opinions that discredit factuality.

Misinformation and disinformation are used as propaganda to discredit feminism and gender-equality activism. This is a tried-and-true tactic that uses notions such as the sexualisation of children through sex education, anti-abortion rhetoric and positioning LGBTQ+ folks as predatory and perverse as ammunition to prevent the advancement towards parity and gender equality.[21] This time around, though, they have the power of social media amplifying these messages in a way that's unlike anything we've ever seen before. The proliferation of anti-women, anti-homosexual, anti-trans+, anti-Black, anti-Muslim and antisemitic hate speech – which, in theory, should violate community guidelines – isn't being taken down, in favour of preserving a without-consequence version of free speech.

Meanwhile, sex workers, sex educators and content creators, as well as folks who are Black, of colour, women or LGBTQ+, face losing accounts due to mass reporting and coordinated attacks from online groups. Others are simply being flagged for using basic terminology to describe identity. For example, on the X platform, Musk has flagged non-slur words like 'cisgender'. This all feels like an attempt to censor left-leaning voices and marginalised people and to amplify fascism. I'm eager to understand how social media platforms with community guidelines against hate speech and violence have normalised misogyny and in the same stroke censored activism against it.

'What we have to remember is that platforms like Meta, in particular, are born within the space that is Silicon Valley,' says Dr Carolina Are, Innovation Fellow at Northumbria University's Centre for Digital Citizens and social media and platform governance researcher. Dr Are explains how the technical workforce – that is, the people who create the algorithms that often moderate social media content – are predominantly cisgender, white men. 'Sadly, still, when it comes to STEM, these positions are quite male dominated. So that is then reflected onto the type of detection that these algorithms carry out.'

It's sobering to think that, despite the policies and rules that exist to protect against misogyny and hate speech in general, a lack of diversity in tech correlates to a lack of empathy towards gender-based violence and struggles. This deficit in care results in women feeling less empowered to use social media as a tool for activism, community and intimacy, for fear of undeserving retribution from unchecked and emboldened voices from the manosphere, in addition to a biased collective of social media users who either haven't done anything to unlearn their internalised misogyny, or feel righteous enacting sexism, victim blaming and slut-shaming.

Dr Are explains that part of the reason why there is this lack of accountability for misogynist language and action on social media platforms is the way platforms are expected to mitigate against sex crimes and pornography.

'[Social media platforms] define pornography in their policies as anything that elicits sexual arousal – "arousal" because this is the legal definition.' While this is fair enough in theory, the lack of nuance and guidance in the enforcement of these rules means that anything considered arousing is in the firing line to be flagged. 'You may be aroused by a woman sitting on a chair in a bikini, even if she's not performing a sex act,' says Dr Are, before highlighting that this isn't the only problem broad policies create: 'In general, their policies tend to blend nudity with sexual activity,' Dr Are explains. 'That means that nudity is viewed as sexual by default, therefore any type of expression surrounding women's bodies or health is flaggable. Queer expressions are often moderated this way too, but this also applies to discussions around sexual violence and domestic abuse.'

The picture is becoming clearer, even though the answers I've been hoping to find bring little comfort. According to Dr Are, the policies social media companies have in place surrounding violence and sexual abuse means that the algorithm doesn't have enough nuance to understand when discussion of these issues is not about perpetration, but rather, about survival and building community and safe spaces. By grouping everything together, the algorithm is bound to make mistakes, making it very difficult for human workforces to undo the machine-driven decision-making.

'A lot of these moderators are outsourced to Global South locations, where workers have to make split-second decisions over content, and they're often traumatised because they see horrible stuff,' Dr Are tells me. This creates a multi-faceted problem, where traumatisation becomes part of the job description, with dangerous consequences for the individual moderating and being moderated. The people in these job roles are likely to sacrifice huge portions of their mental health for, in some cases, less than $2 per hour.[22] Additionally, according to a 2024 investigation by the Center for Democracy & Technology, dozens of reports have shown that, in many cases, human moderators are inexperienced, untrained and underpaid, and work under inhumane conditions.[23]

'Incorrectly blending things like enacting sexual violence with survivor testimony and then again with the technology, which is targeted and created by a largely male-dominated workforce, with the moderators that are meant to be undoing those tasks, but that are traumatised, underpaid and overworked – well, you can see why it's a system that doesn't really create the premises for effective content moderation,' says Dr Are.

This calls into question the ethics of social media moderation and the use of digital sweatshops to police the overconsumption of social media content. This cost-saving exercise, which takes advantage of a disadvantaged workforce, also has ripple effects across continents in the way that society is metabolising misogyny and sexism. This knock-on effect is one that emboldens places like the manosphere, because there is a lack of accountability from the platforms they use to subjugate, objectify and oppress, which creates a perverse engagement-based reward system for those who trade in negative comments and trolling. There are multiple ways that misogynist groups mobilise against pro-feminist, victim, survivor and body-positive content. One such way is by weaponising the flagging tool, which is designed for community moderation at a peer-to-peer level.

This is called user-generated warfare, or UGW, and when it's used against marginalised people discussing what might be considered thorny topics under social media's community guidelines, it wreaks havoc. So much so that I'd go as far as to say that it is a direct attack on the human right to free speech. This is because of the disproportionate way these attacks are moderated and policed by social media platforms themselves, which are not accountable, legally speaking, for the kind of activities their users get up to on them. 'The flag tool is important,' Dr Are states. 'It does need to be there. It's a tool that platforms like to say empowers users and fosters community moderation.'

However, she explains that the flagging tool is easily weaponised by mobilised misogynist groups, as well as white-supremacist, sex-worker-exclusionary radical feminists (SWERFS), and homophobic and transphobic groups, to discredit and silence people for their identity, lived experience or educational content. 'Whether it's one user constantly reporting, or a user-coordinated effort to report a lot of things with a crowd of users, then that means that they are harnessing the tools that are meant to protect users, to actually do users, and particularly women, harm,' says Dr Are.

This is often in addition to flagging misuse, explains Dr Are, who continues to tell me that 'because policies and platform automated structures like algorithms are already being weaponised against content that is deemed controversial ... it's super-easy for this to result in wrongful takedowns'. Not only does this mean that people who are looking for community, or to contextualise their sexual-assault experiences, are left without the type of content online that could support them, but it limits the potential for true discourse on societal issues and structural imbalances that reinforce oppressive pressures.

A study conducted in 2022 by Lund University in Denmark found that many manosphere users felt that the MeToo movement was akin to a terror organisation and that, in a post-MeToo world, men generally felt as though their rights had been stripped back by women disclosing 'false' abuse accusations. What's more, the same study also found that women and discourse surrounding feminist topics are portrayed in the manosphere as inherently untrustworthy.[24] 'It's the same inequalities that we see offline, but perpetrated to a much bigger extent online,' Dr Are states.

To me, it feels clear that there is an undeniable link between the stigmatisation present when women speak and the manner in which social media platforms operate that's keeping that same stigma alive. What's also clear is that aspects of our digital world can be weaponised in insidious ways to discredit and tear people – especially women – down. One internet tool that can be used to tear down not just people but entire governments is a bot. Bots themselves are automated tools used to get a specific task done and, chances are, you've probably spoken with one in the chat box of a website. These bots aren't a form of artificial intelligence (AI), however, though they might use AI to perform their designated tasks. In short, bots are programmes with pre-determined outcomes, whereas AI seeks to mimic human intelligence without pre-determined outcomes.

The programmers who run bot accounts, like most of the moderation services we've already encountered, are based in the Global South. This means that the working conditions for the people in the organisations responsible for creating bot accounts are dubious, at best, but they're also outside the legal jurisdictions for the UK, US and Australia, which all have protective laws against spreading misinformation. In the UK, new offences were added to the Online Safety Act 2023 in January 2024, criminalising the spread of fake news intended to cause non-trivial harm or online abuse, in addition to cyber flashing.[25] In the US, it is a crime to be found guilty of imparting or conveying false information.[26] Even with these laws in place, though, the use of bots is a legal grey area, if not a morally grey one. This is why the Office of the Attorney General in the US has put together motions to make fundamental changes to Section 230 of the Communications Decency Act, a law that protects social media platforms from civil liability from third-party users.

The act is antiquated, having been made law in 1996, and I'd argue that it is no longer fit for purpose due to its ambiguities in moderation requirements and the potential risk of handing over too much power and not enough accountability to social media platforms – something we've watched play out in real-time with the re-election of Trump, the temporary ban on TikTok and on Musk's X. Nevertheless, while it is good that there is some recognition of how harmful programmes like bots can be on businesses and individuals, it hasn't stopped people from using them to discredit women in the public eye.

Amid the post-MeToo backlash, which hit something of a peak in 2022,[27] bots have become the weapon of choice when it comes to fomenting public dissent and discreditation against women and left- to centre-leaning governments.[28] This is exacerbated by the rampant misinformation and disinformation of the digital world, which is creating a 'truth gap' that has enormous real-world consequences on gender-based violence.

The phrase 'truth gap' itself was coined in a 2021 report by Plan International,[29] which surveyed 26,000 young women and girls across twenty-six countries, only to find that 87 per cent of respondents were negatively impacted by mis- and disinformation. This resulted in girls and young women lacking the confidence when it came to sharing their views online, which is compounded by the fact that 85 per cent of women worldwide have seen violence enacted against other women, as reported in Rutger's 2024 report, 'Decoding Technology-Facilitated Gender-Based Violence',[30] or 'TFGBV' for short.

Gender inequality and violence is simply inescapable, especially as, according to Tech Policy, 'TFGBV amplifies existing inequality and is part of a recurring continuum of abuse in women's lives across online and offline spaces.'[31] Even the UK

Government recognises that women are disproportionately more likely to be victims of TFGBV.[32]

To make matters worse, University College London (UCL), the University of Kent and the Association of School and College Leaders (ASCL) have found, in a collaborative report into the spread of misogyny on social media, a 'fourfold increase in the level of misogynistic content in the "For You" page of TikTok accounts over just five days on the platform, in an algorithmic modelling study'.[33]

Bots used to discredit women are yet another extension of this recurring continuum of abuse. To make matters worse, the widespread and interwoven nature of this cultural misogyny is being powered by disempowered communities experiencing further marginalisation through digital colonialisation, in addition to their integration into a disconnected global network of inequality. To understand how using bot farms in poorer nations is contributing to networked misogyny online and offline, we need to revisit the trial of *Depp* vs *Heard*. In 2024, Tortoise Media launched an investigative podcast, *Who Trolled Amber?*, which sought to identify the root of the trolling of Amber Heard, following her abuse allegation against actor Johnny Depp,[34] a man who has since claimed to be a 'crash test dummy for #MeToo'.[35] Tortoise Media's investigation found that Heard was being trolled by hundreds of bot accounts, apparently based in Saudi Arabia, and that Depp's latest movies (the period drama *Jeanne du Barry* and a biopic of Modigliani, *Modi: Three Days on the Wing of Madness*) were also being funded by Saudi money. Over and above that, Tortoise Media contributor Bradley Hope, author of *Blood and Oil: Mohammed bin Salman's Ruthless Quest for Global Power*, reported that Depp is personal friends with Crown Prince Mohammed bin Salman.

The report claims that 'manufactured online hate against Heard could have jeopardised her right to a fair trial', and that according to the disinformation and computer experts Zhouhan Chen and Kaicheng Yang, who Tortoise Media employed for the investigation, over 50 per cent of the tweets in the 2020–2021 database, which contained around a million tweets – all critical of Heard – were from inauthentic accounts. All this evidence culminates in a damning picture that means online trolls in the guise of bot accounts played a significant role in the hate directed at Heard throughout this period. Additionally, they discovered 'a coordinated network of Twitter accounts', which sent 'more than 100 identical messages at exactly the same time to any brand which had worked with Amber'. These tweets sent the following message: 'This brand supports domestic violence against men.'[36]

In the cold light of day, and in the excellent post-mortem investigations that have looked unflinchingly at what went wrong for Heard, it's easy to see how this malicious, concerted effort to discredit her and her accounts of abuse have resulted in her losing $50 million in TV, movie and endorsement deals,[37] and having to change her name and move to another country. What's more, the same investigation found that comparative tweets made by inauthentic accounts promoted Depp.

To the average person witnessing the orchestrated downfall of Heard, it would be incredibly difficult to discern an individual spewing vitriol about her from a bot spewing vitriol.

Bots are remarkably impactful and effective when deployed to infiltrate and change public opinion due to their ability to disperse sentiments and incite engagement, creating a feedback loop that aggrandises negativity. By doing this, bots are uniquely formidable in being able to diffuse both influence and information. Bots also aren't operating in isolation to interfere with public opinion. In 2016, Russian bots were able to sow the seeds of right-wing propaganda. A subsequent report in 2022 found that, alarmingly, these same bots had become so enmeshed within user discourse that the data suggested people were treating these fake accounts as credible sources of information.[38] You might only need a few bots to 'exert significant impacts on user network structures and opinions'. If bots have been proven to impact elections, it's fair to assume that they influence our opinions on perceived behaviour, which is why the case against Heard is so tragic.

'Amber Heard wasn't her best advocate, and I'm just going to make this very clear: when you've been traumatised, you're not your best self,' stated Laura Richards on the *Should I Delete That?* podcast. Richards is an award-winning criminal behavioural analyst, and a former New Scotland Yard and international expert on domestic abuse, coercive control, stalking, sexual violence, homicide and risk assessment. In 2022, speaking on her own podcast, *Crime Analyst*, with special guest, journalist and author Lucia Osborne-Crowley, Richards noted how Heard's defence failed to interrogate just how manipulative bots were in destabilising her credibility in the eyes of public opinion, but also how they infiltrated the courtroom and brought with them the vitriol that was being stoked online. From the jury not being sequestered and having access to social media, to the availability of court footage that spurred a torrent of hateful videos about Heard fuelled by a radicalised, rabid anger, as well as an algorithm that rewarded and pushed pro-Johnny Depp content while pushing negative content about Heard, it seems inevitable that public opinion swung so violently in favour of Johnny Depp, resulting in internet pile-ons and a 19-billion-strong JusticeForJohnny hashtag percolating online. When you combine a mechanism that is hell-bent on discrediting you and built on pre-existing misogyny, a fanbase with unshakeable loyalty, plus money, power and something of a home-turf advantage, it doesn't matter that a court halfway around the world was able to determine twelve instances of domestic abuse. You're already facing a dogged scrap against the odds. Add on a mountain of public dislike, distrust and a stark empathy deficit for your side of the story and you're destined for a fall. 'We need to get over this idea that what happens online doesn't spill over into the justice system, because that is happening,' says Osborne-Crowley.

Alarmingly, in 2022, the same pattern of social media hatred was observed by *VICE* in an article titled: 'Amber Heard's Vicious Online Trolls Are Coming for Angelina Jolie Now'.[39] Journalist Anya Zoledziowski highlights the vilification of Angelina Jolie by some portions of the internet, following her disclosure of allegations of abuse by her former husband Brad Pitt against her and her children. Zoledziowski explores the way in which the Depp–Heard trial created a 'playbook' for online hate against women, which can be used against other women in the public eye, like Jolie. Such behaviour also gives courage to non-celebrities to mistreat women – so much so that the escalating severity of misogynistic and sexist language used on social media has reached a crisis point. This is in part because of how cases like those of Amber Heard and Angelina Jolie normalise hate speech through the lack of responsible moderation by social media platforms in favour of preserving 'free speech'. In turn, this lack of moderation demonstrates that language that historically might have been confined to more covert online spaces like the Dark Web can now be spoken freely without any risk of repercussions from the owners of social media platforms. If anything, your words are more likely to be amplified than censored.

Robyn D'Arcy goes further. 'Algorithms and the censorship benefit from being as misogynistic and as awful as possible,' she says, explaining that this is one of the driving forces of engagement. Additionally, the overtly misogynistic and hateful language we're seeing regularly on mainstream sites now bears striking resemblance to the types of discussions that D'Arcy would historically have associated with the Dark Web: 'The top search on Google about rape isn't "rape case", it's not "rape charities", it's not "support a friend who's been raped" – it is "rape porn"; 38 per cent of all searches in the UK in 2024 about rape did so in the context of porn. So, "rape", "kink", "rape porn", "rape hentai", "gangbang", "rape tape", that kind of thing. That search data, it's not from incognito search, it's not a search on Reddit, it's not the Dark Web.'

While fantasy and intent are not interchangeable, and some kinksters may consensually explore rape fantasy, it's hard to imagine that the regular person using Google in this way is aware of the extent of the planning, trust, respect and aftercare that goes into this more extreme kink fantasy. As such, the weight of what these searches mean is heavy and, I fear, something that has been compounded with the complicity of social media bosses, who have chosen to look away from the worsening usage of these platforms, while lining their pockets with advertising revenue built off the engagement driven by intensifying hate speech.

What seems clear from the growing prevalence of searches for terms such as 'rape porn' is that there is a desensitisation to misogyny taking place, and that darker corners of the internet and human behaviour are seeping into our normal everyday experiences. It shows us that there is a permissive brand of radicalisation taking place that is giving rise to more extreme and more violent depictions of crimes against women. The very idea that 'rape' is becoming a popular search term for your average man is a bone-chilling thought – one we're perhaps too overwhelmed to fully acknowledge the impact of. Combine that with how quickly the comment sections and private inboxes of women can be inundated with rape threats or violence, and it becomes clear that we must come to terms with the terrifying idea that rape is being normalised.

Rape carries a maximum term of life imprisonment, and it is generally perceived to be one of the most shameful crimes you could commit against a person, echoing the ancient civilisations that condemned the act but did little in providing access to justice or fair penalties for the harms caused. Victim blaming seems to be the trend that has persisted for millennia, and not, as one would hope, believing women who come forward to accuse. Despite this, 798,000 women across England and Wales will experience rape and sexual violation each year on average, and one in five women will likely experience sexual violence or rape in their lifetime.[40] Perhaps this rising tide of searches for 'rape porn' only demonstrates what women have intimately known for generations: that men feel an inherent sense of entitlement towards women's bodies. The difference is that, now, the shame of wanting to rape might have lessened, because there likely isn't even a slap on the wrist waiting for someone who chooses to voice such things online.

The knock-on effect of this is that women – particularly Black women and other marginalised folk – are facing greater difficulties in congregating and talking online in plain sight without encountering death and rape threats, cyber flashing and unsolicited commentary on their bodies and features, let alone in feeling supported enough to use social media as a tool for change. In her seminal book, *The New Age of Sexism: How the AI Revolution Is Reinventing Misogyny*, author Laura Bates tells us that women simply have a different experience of technology to men. She reports that nearly nine in ten women say that they restrict their online activity in some way as a result of online violence, and that a third of women think twice before posting any content online, while half of women don't consider the internet a safe space at all.[41] This creates a unique threat for women who need to talk and find community. Of those who do choose to share their lived experiences online, whether regarding sexual assault, rape, harassment, intimate partner abuse, parental abuse (and, specifically, paternal abuse), many are met with thunderous claims of false accusations from men amid an increasing distrust of women.

The 2014 film *Gone Girl*, based on the 2012 book by Gillian Flynn, had a significant impact on the backlash women experience from speaking out. Even though *Gone Girl* is a complete work of fiction, the book and film perpetuated the idea of women making false accusations, which then fed into the broader backlash against the MeToo movement and women speaking out about abuse. This myth of the 'real-life *Gone Girl*' became a way to discredit women's experiences and testimony. Speaking with Robyn D'Arcy, it's clear that *Gone Girl* did in fact give men an alibi, though I'm positive that its author had zero intention of creating a means for men to sidestep accountability for rape. What the book does so effectively is to build on a pre-existing stereotype: that of the crazy ex-girlfriend, or the crazy woman; someone whose credibility is immediately brought into question because of how easy they find it to manipulate men and the world around them. *Gone Girl* is a parable that has become synonymous with victim blaming, with many incels and those adjacent to the extremist ideology using the lead character's name, 'Amy', as a catch-all to signal that a woman shouldn't be believed. They suggest that, like Amy, women are likely manipulating situations to make it appear as though they are being abused when they aren't. The more we come to understand about sexual violence and the circumstances that can lead to it, the more men may look back at their own sexual history and realise they have likely committed acts that might today be perceived as a crime. Instead of bearing the brunt of that shame and making amends or accepting accountability, a defensiveness arises – one that justifies certain behaviours in an attempt to conceal their own transgressions. They might defend other men because they themselves feel accused. If we begin to turn the tide on these 'grey' areas, how long will it be before we come for the average man? The direct or indirect fear men experience when survivors of sexual violence come forward, whether they're famous or not, is part of the reason why we see such attempts to discredit and silence those survivors.

Creating a caricature of the wronged woman isn't only reserved for fictional women: Amber Heard has become a symbol of a woman who lies about her experiences and cannot be trusted, even though Heard's testimony against Depp in his defamation case against the *Sun* was proven to be credible enough to have lost Depp the case, and strong enough for her to counter-sue Depp for a considerable sum. The mass online discrediting through caricature is a meme-ification that makes fun of women's struggle to be heard and believed. Creating something that mocks what that woman or group of women are saying sends a very clear message to those who might be thinking of doing the same: *Don't do it. You won't be believed. And if you do, we'll make fun of you for it by likening you to a person ridiculed for trying to do the same. We will shame you into silence.*

'"Heard 2.0"; "learning from Amber"; "another Amber"; "Amber in the wild",' lists D'Arcy. 'These are all ways of discrediting women.' D'Arcy pulls up a social listening tool on her computer. 'Any female celebrity you can imagine, who's done anything, even if it's nothing to do with feminism or men's rights, will have probably been referred to as an "Amber Heard 2.0" at some point.' Sure enough, the list of those referred to as an 'Amber Heard 2.0' includes every famous woman you can think of: Hillary Clinton; Kesha; Lil' Kim; Ariana Grande; Stormy Daniels; Amanda Knox; Monica Lewinsky; Greta Thunberg; Jill Biden; FKA twigs; Olivia Wilde; Angelina Jolie; Rihanna; E. Jean Carroll; Keke Palmer; Julia Fox; Rebekah Vardy; Megan Thee Stallion; Hayley Bieber; Taylor Swift; Selena Gomez; Greta Gerwig; Demi Lovato; Miley Cyrus; Meghan Markle; Nancy Pelosi; Liz Cheney; Cassidy Hutchinson; Sophie Turner; Evan Rachel Wood; Yoko Ono; Megan Fox; Michelle Obama; Virginia Giuffre; Cassie Ventura; Beyoncé and Alexandra Ocasio-Cortez. It's worth taking a second here to process the breadth of women who face such criticism and disbelief. Regardless of their social or marital status, their career success, their wealth, whether they're a parent or not, nothing disqualifies them from the firing line. They all have the potential to be labelled an 'Amber' because, as a society, we have come to expect that women lie.

In short, calling a woman an 'Amber Heard' has become locker-room slang for a woman who makes men uncomfortable. This is destructive gossip. This is gossip that ruins lives, careers and livelihoods, and it's not the only way that such speech can be weaponised online. There are entire forums dedicated to gossiping negatively about people, and Tattle Life is one such platform. Here, you'll find a deluge of posts, all dedicated to ripping chunks out of people in the public eye, from A-listers to micro influencers, where slut-shaming, victim-blaming and body-shaming proliferate. It's the ultimate mean-girl platform, built for tearing other women down – although the platform has in the past disputed this reputation. While it's believed that the majority of the users on the site are female, the anonymous nature of it makes it near impossible to discern the gender split.

Originally, on the site's 'About' section a moderator, identified only by her username 'Helen', had created a lengthy statement about what Tattle Life is for: 'Tattle Life is a commentary website on public business social media accounts. We allow commentary and critiques of people that choose to monetise their personal life as a business and release it into the public domain.' Helen's post goes on to explain that Tattle Life has a 24/7 moderation service that seeks to remove 'abusive, hateful and harmful' content. Helen states that the purpose of the forum is to allow people to have their opinions as part of a 'healthy and free society'.

Despite this apparent moderation, however, when I visited the homepage, I was immediately met with a thread calling former glamour model Katie Price a 'hag', and it took mere seconds to find even more repulsive language: posts calling her 'skanky'; making fun of her regional accent and claiming that her son, Harvey, who is disabled by a range of medical conditions, as well as having autism, is being drugged while Price 'enjoys a bouncy blow dry' and a 'night on the town'. Whatever your opinion of Katie Price, it's hard to see how these comments help to contribute towards a 'healthy and free society' when they are steeped in classism, sexism and misogyny. It suggests that Tattle Life is hardly the idyll that moderator 'Helen' claims to be striving for. I'd argue that the comments made against Price are a clear breach of community guidelines, though at the time of writing this book, they remain live, in addition to some 400 other threads dedicated to Katie Price, with the earliest dating back to 2018, which all appear to lack the moderation Tattle Life promises to provide.

Katie Price is one subject of many to be found on this forum. Any brush with fame, no matter how fleeting, is enough for someone to find themselves in the firing line of Tattle Life users. This is something that Lauren, a UK-based influencer and writer, has experienced first-hand. Lauren is not her real name, as she is choosing to remain anonymous. In 2020, while searching for something she'd written online, Lauren noticed that a Tattle Life sub-thread had been published about her. She explains that, in many ways, it felt like an inevitability, having sensed that it would only be a matter of time before she found herself there.

'I was like, *Oh, God – here we go*,' she remembers. But as she read on, the language used against Lauren became more and more personal. 'I was absolutely heartbroken, because I know so many of my content-creator friends and acquaintances who are also on that website [as victims], and it's some of the most soul-destroying content you could ever come across.' Lauren and I are speaking on a Sunday afternoon in late September. Her voice is calm and composed, but it's clear that this is a difficult and sensitive subject. As we continue to talk, I begin to appreciate just how awful the past four years have been for her.

'They will just make up really weird scenarios and run with it as if it's fact,' says Lauren. 'They talk about my partner, my body, my clothes, my parents ... It got to the point where I had to shield the screen when I googled my name; it was detrimental to my mental health, seeing new things written about me, sometimes on a weekly basis.'

The comments on Tattle Life took such a toll that they started to impact how Lauren worked. 'I noticed that I was beginning to tailor my content based on what they were saying. So, for instance, if I had gone in there and I had noticed that they said, "She's doing too many Instagram stories where she's talking to camera and she looks ugly," or something like that, I would stop,' she recounts, before continuing. 'If they said something about the way I was dressed, I would stop buying from that specific store in order to appease them and not have them talk about me. It got to a point where it just felt like it was dictating my everyday life.'

This desire to conform went against Lauren's character, and she describes herself as having developed a resilience to people discussing her body. 'Existing in the body that I do ... has always attracted trolls, specifically fatphobic men who don't like listening to a larger, plus-sized, dark-skinned woman being very vocal about body image and desirability,' she explains. Despite this, it was comments about Lauren's personality that chipped away at her self-esteem the most: 'I really try to pride myself on being a nice person and being kind to people and being very honest as an influencer as well,' she says. 'And when they started calling me annoying, or that I seemed like a nasty person, and when they began talking about my parents

– that's when I became defensive.' Lauren realised that one of the people writing about her on Tattle Life must have been someone she knew, further deepening the betrayal. 'I have had to put a lot of distance between me and a lot of people, because it's really shown me that I can't trust anybody.'

Tattle Life is a stark reminder that not all gossip attributed to women is good; neither is it wholly a force of resistance or inherently feminist. While gossip is a mode of speech, its goodness or badness lies in the way it is utilised to navigate relationships, be those in-person or parasocially. It is a chitter-chatter powered by intent to uplift or destroy, making it a deeply complex aspect of human nature, particularly as herd mentality can quickly turn to mob mentality when it comes to punishing people online for behaviour that doesn't fit within a moral value system, causing untold upset and harm.

Tattle Life has been labelled a 'troll's paradise' by the *Guardian*, and the site has been linked to doxing, cyberbullying and other antisocial online behaviours – so much so that research into the motivations behind the site show that this online community 'legitimizes itself by deploying a feminine gender identity in three overlapping and internally contradictory ways': to 'minimise the power of their community to do harm', to 'provide moral justification for their actions' and 'to claim the status of persecuted victims'.[42]

There are hundreds of thousands of posts and threads that exist for the sole purpose of tearing other women down. The idea that this brand of bitchiness is an inherently female trait, or that threads scrutinising and harassing celebrities and influencers should be shrugged off as nothing more than 'mean-girl' behaviour seems absurd. For years, Tattle Life was believed to be a site made by women, for women. In 2025, however, it was revealed that the site had been founded by Sebastian Bond, a forty-two-year-old vegan food influencer,[43] who had been using the false name 'Helen McDougal' – the moderator behind the 'About' page.[44] In a landmark case that saw Neil and Donna Sands, two of the site's victims, sue Tattle Life for defamation and harassment, anonymity would no longer shield people from culpability. The couple were awarded £300,000 in damages and Bond was named as a result.

The idea of outing someone for misbehaviour and malicious intent could look like cancel culture, although I'd argue it's only ever women who face the permanency of cancellation, as many men are still able to return to work, fame and fortune, even after being accused and found guilty of the most heinous abuses. Just look at disgraced comedian Louis CK, a man who had a decade's worth of sexual misconduct allegations levelled at him before finally admitting to them in 2017. He promised to step back from the 'public spotlight', a promise that had an expiration date of just nine months. In 2018, CK was back to performing his stand-up routines to sold-out shows, with audience members laughing along as he joked on stage about the charges against him.[45]

CK is joined by actor Kevin Spacey, who was charged with nine sexual offences against four men between 2004 and 2013 (but was subsequently cleared of all charges),[46] and who is returning to play 'The Devil' in Italian film *The Contract*.[47] We also have musician Ryan Adams, who faced multiple allegations of sexual harassment but enjoyed a return to music in 2022, with four sold-out shows.[48] Next, there's Arnold Schwarzenegger, who was pressured by protestors not to attend an awards dinner following multiple sexual-misconduct allegations against him, which he admitted to and apologised for. Schwarzenegger has since released *another Terminator* movie. Chris Brown, who infamously punched his partner and fellow musician Rihanna and split her lip in 2009, and was charged with felony assault for the crime, reached chart-topping success in 2012 for his album *Fortune*.[49] Brown recently toured the UK, despite being on bail on assault charges after allegedly bottling someone outside a club in Manchester. Ahead of one of his shows, the *National*, a Scottish newspaper, interviewed audience members to ask what they thought and knew of Brown's convictions and his history of violence against women. Alarmingly, the majority were happy to continue lining his pockets despite having knowledge of his charges, helping him acquire still more wealth and power that could arguably be used to help him sidestep accountability for any further harms he might commit. If a man is perceived as being 'likeable', then there is every chance that he will be welcomed back into the fold, especially if his crimes – or alleged crimes – aren't perceived as being violent or forceful.[50] If anything, the person who pays the greatest price is the person who pointed the finger in the first place.

According to research published in the *Journal of Personality and Social Psychology* on the virtues of gossip, 'Reputation systems promote cooperation and deter anti-social behavior in groups.'[51] In other words, being aware and concerned about the way the group perceives us can have an impact on our behaviour, knowing that our place in the social hierarchy could be influenced – whether that group is comprised of our peers and contemporaries, our family members, our friends or work colleagues. This particular research showed that people who observe antisocial activities were negatively impacted by it and felt 'compelled to share information about the antisocial actor with a potentially vulnerable person'. By sharing the information, it reduced the negative effect created by observing the antisocial behaviour. What's most interesting is that the people who behaved with more pro-social orientations – that is, people who chose to act in a manner that benefited society, rather than adhering to their own individualistic desires – were more likely to engage in gossip of this nature, even if it was at a personal cost to them. These people – the gossips – exhibit 'the greatest reduction in negative affect as a result'. This highlighted that those who were the most motivated to help others by sharing information about people's reputations are integral to the maintenance of cooperation in human groups.

In short, gossip keeps us in line by threatening to reveal the good, bad and ugly sides of our reputations. If you do something untoward, nasty or mean, people will know about it and that will have a direct impact on your reputation and how you're received in group situations. A Dutch study in 2021 found that people who gossip often shared information about the cooperativeness of the third person or subject of gossip. Gossip in this context, which would fall into a sort of 'word-of-mouth' category, was overwhelmingly believed, resulting in the reputation of the person being elevated if the gossip was favourable. The study also found that the gossip shared by the participants often comes from first-hand experiences (75 per cent), was communicated face to face (68 per cent) or between two people (74 per cent). To me, this shows that gossip isn't simply a case of 'he said, she said'. Rather, gossip is an intimate act that relies on an existing relationship where trust and belief is unquestionably established. The reputation of the subject of the gossip is measured by how they fit into these pre-existing relationships and how they contribute towards the common goal of the social group.[52]

Reputational perception is a critical element of surviving human society. We are time-poor, and our attention is commodified, which means we tend to make snap decisions based on limited information about a person, experience or object. Our digital footprint is often all that stands between us and a potential employer, new friend or romantic relationship, showing how essential it is that we present ourselves in a good light to the world,[53] and how important it is that the people who talk about us primarily have good things to say. I can't help but feel a visceral sense of injustice when someone goes viral and finds themselves on the wrong side of the internet, with trolls and real people piling on the hate for something they couldn't change about themselves in five minutes, such as their race, their size, their accent and so on. When the internet decides to attack one person, it can be a devastating thing to experience and to witness, and you don't need to be a celebrity or someone in the public eye to go through it – though, depending on the virality of the moment, it might propel you into some form of recognition.

But why are people quick to denounce actions without reading too deeply into the facts? Why is it so easy to jump on the bandwagon? There are several ingredients at play here.[54] The anonymity afforded to us by the internet, and the subsequent ability to protect your identity from the person you're communicating with, gives rise to dehumanisation. This lack of face-to-face contact amplifies the level of dissociation from the person on the other side of the screen, further disconnecting people from the real-world impact of their words or actions. There is also the fact that many of us operate within echo chambers online – that is, a curated experience of the internet based on, and reflecting back, our own opinions and beliefs, whether cultural, political or religious. Because of this, mob mentality is often rife online, with users conforming to group behaviour, even if that behaviour is wrong or harmful, and can lead to groups or communities mobilising to defend or attack another person. Social media is also the ideal platform for virality, with content spreading and being consumed quickly, by vast numbers of people. Finally, there are online trolls – those who take pleasure from participating in nasty commentary, encouraging mob mentality using fake accounts in a way that's not dissimilar to bots, except that trolls are people, not programmes.

When gossip enters the digital space, on social media, online forums or, frankly, anywhere with a comments section, its propensity to do harm as well as good is multiplied by the permanence of the words published, shared, read, agreed with, liked, reposted and engaged with. This means that the mental and physical health impact of being on the receiving end of this level of negative attention can be catastrophic, even when the claims made against you aren't true. It seems that gossip cannot and perhaps shouldn't be fully detangled from its reputation as something career-ending, reputation-destroying or cancel culture worthy, because ultimately, gossip isn't always truthful, even though it can be a mechanism for truth. The other issues with this entanglement between gossip and the internet is that it is almost always negatively weighted towards women – there is a clear gender disparity in the type of gossip we read online and choose to participate in when it comes to celebrities, influencers or people we think owe us their world and their pound of flesh.

Would we ever speak about men in the same way we do women? Would we call them skanky? Would we talk about their parentage, their bodies, clothes and personality in the same way? I don't think so. So, why is there this compulsion to speak about women in the public eye like this? Why does celebrity, or a celebrity on the rise, fortify people's sense of entitlement to speculate about and pull apart the most tender and private details in their life? In short, why do we love to gossip about the rich and the famous, and what impact does this have on credibility, both for them and the rest of us?

CHAPTER FIVE

Whisper Networks

I'll get libelled if I say it ... If Harvey Weinstein invites you to a private party in the Four Seasons, don't go.
— COURTNEY LOVE, 2005

It's 3 p.m. in Bristol when I make the call to Dr Carrie Ann Johnson, associate director at the Center for Women and Politics and postdoctoral research associate with the Women's and Gender Studies Department at Iowa State University. I've been meticulously combing through Johnson's 2023 research paper on whisper networks all morning and am fizzing with excitement to speak with her. Johnson joins the call, and with immediate enthusiasm we jump headfirst into the topic.

'A whisper network is an informal communication system that people use to protect each other,' Dr Johnson explains, 'but, you know, gossip is just the way people have always taken care of each other.' Dr Johnson's latest research into whisper networks tells us that, not only is this a gossip-based care system, but that the language used is purposefully coded to avoid suspicion. In her research paper titled, 'The purpose of whisper networks: a new lens for studying informal communication channels in organizations',[1] Dr Johnson explains that entry into a whisper network relies on a pre-existing understanding of sexual harassment, in addition to being able to interpret or decipher the coded messages people use to communicate within the network itself.

How someone responds to this coded language determines whether or not they'll be seen as an insider or an outsider to the whisper network. This means that, for those who don't pick up on the subtleties of the social cues, it's likely that they'll remain on the outside and be more vulnerable to known predators. Dr Johnson notes the prevalence of phrases like 'handsy', or that someone might flag that a colleague likes new girls 'a little too much'. Other adjectives that ranked highly were 'creepy', 'slimy', 'overly friendly' and 'problematic'. Warnings consisted of phrases such as 'weird vibes', 'avoid being alone with him' and 'take someone with you'. Each one of these is chilling in their familiarity. The phrases used are all suggestive of a deeper meaning, without being overtly accusatory or directly pointing the finger towards criminal activity or misconduct. This form of communication – the art of referring to something indirectly while still clearly offering a warning – relies on a collective experience in which there is the risk of running into some form of sexual misconduct, like some perverse cultural obstacle course. The fact remains that, statistically speaking, one in three women will experience sexual violence in their lifetime,[2] so it is no wonder that this shared knowledge is easily alluded to.

One of Dr Johnson's case studies refers to a feeling of needing to have some sort of sixth sense; to be vigilant, wary, 'on your toes'. The implication behind these words and phrases is clear to anyone who has ever had a friend pull them aside and mutter, 'Just be careful.' There is a deep sense of knowing and foreboding contained within those words, which does away with a need to go into any detail or relay a personal experience. Much like gossip, then, the coded language of the whisper network is representative of intimacy and comfort, but it can also be indicative of the fear and secrecy associated with speaking out.

Women who choose to warn via the whisper network need other women to read between the lines for everyone to remain safe. This can often lead to the use of minimising language that feels more socially acceptable and vague. Speaking in this way strikes an important balance in a world where justice is statistically unlikely if a crime should occur and accusation carries great reputational and personal risk. This balancing act provides enough 'common knowledge' that the likely targets are aware they could be in danger, but it also allows for perpetrators of sexual misconduct or harassment to continue their abuses unchecked. Meanwhile, nobody risks being discredited or brought into disrepute.

Discreditation can take any number of forms, and it relies on social stigma and the oppressive nature of gender roles to be effective at silencing women or branding them as unbelievable. One such form of discreditation is because of the stigma attached to emotionality. Being labelled as 'troublemaking', 'hysterical', 'over-emotional' or 'hormonal' when something upsetting happens can mean being treated as though you're crazy or making a mountain out of a molehill. This is in part due to the legacy of the now-defunct diagnosis of 'hysteria', but thankfully, we've made *some* progress since then. However, the hangover of these stereotypes, and how quickly women's emotionality can be pathologised into flattening and socially damning stereotypes has, sadly, stuck around. If you've ever had someone ask, 'Time of the month?' in response to an effort to be assertive or set a boundary, then you'll know exactly what I'm talking about. The knock-on effect of this is that, rather than expressing their negative emotions,[3] women instead intellectualise and discuss them,[4] leading many to develop depression, eating disorders and self-harming behaviour in a bid for control and to restore emotional regulation.[5] My conversation with Dr Finn Mackay echoes in my mind: 'Women are meant to be objects to look at. They're meant to be pretty. They're meant to be something to see, rather than seen by what they do.'

For Black women, this discreditation is compounded by other pejorative stereotypes like the trope of the 'angry Black woman', which characterises them as hostile, aggressive, overbearing, illogical, ill-tempered and bitter.[6] Hypocritically, displaying emotions like rage or anger, which are celebrated and normalised parts of masculinity, is enough to condemn Black women and ethnic minority women as being too loud, or untrustworthy.[7] This stereotype has historical roots in American culture, dating back to chattel slavery,[8] and continues to hold Black women back in the workplace by paradoxically ascribing power while simultaneously taking it away.[9] It's important here to note that, for Black and ethnic minority women, traditional whisper networks don't always transcend racialised prejudices. This inconsistency is why the solidarity we believe underpins 'sisterhood' is predominantly flawed, because for many, solidarity is contentious. Mikki Kendall, author of *Hood Feminism*, explains that calls for solidarity from some white feminists mask the undertones of privileged entitlement, as they ignore the capacity and struggle of those who are more marginalised and oppressed.

The co-opting of grassroots movements is an understandable pain point for many Black activists. Take the fat rights movement, which began in 1969 and subsequently became the body positivity movement, which, in today's era of Ozempic and #SkinnyTok, feels like a faraway dream. The movement was pioneered by fat, Black and queer people as a form of liberation and protest against patriarchal, neoliberal, capitalist and colonial ideologies,[10] to challenge what a 'good' body should be or look like. Once the ideology went mainstream in 2012 on Instagram,[11] however, the message became watered down and commercialised beyond recognition from its radical activist roots.[12] The solidarity that activists had been asking for was taken as an invitation to participate in the conversation, rather than simply a call to support and uphold the message. This resulted in a toxification of the 'fat liberation' message, which is not very 'sisterhood' at all when you think about it. But this is far from the only movement started by Black women that has ended up being co-opted, colonised and subsequently policed by white people.

The origins of the MeToo movement were wrongly attributed to Hollywood A-listers like Alyssa Milano, whose viral post on Facebook with the hashtag 'MeToo' amplified the call to take seriously the testimony of sexual-assault survivors in the wake of multiple allegations levelled at producer Harvey Weinstein and, more broadly, to hold perpetrators of sexual abuse in Hollywood accountable. While this was, of course, a vital message, it piggybacked on the pre-existing, hard-fought campaigning of the original MeToo movement without acknowledging those roots. This hashtagification, if you like, erased the original message of Black social worker and activist Tarana Burke, who had been campaigning and advocating for young Black women for almost a decade before the movement she began was co-opted. As such, it took weeks for Burke to be credited for the movement and the work she put into fighting sexual violence against women and girls in the Black community.

In 2017, the Associated Press reported that, in the first twenty-four hours after Alyssa Milano's post, the celebrity-driven message was shared in over 12 million Facebook posts, comments and reactions by 4.7 million users around the world.[13] Speaking with the University of Chicago in 2023, Burke explained that, understandably, she still felt agitated by the en-masse social media co-opting of her work: 'When people hear me, they want to talk about court cases and Harvey Weinstein and R. Kelly, and I'm like, "That's b—t y'all. That's just smoke and mirrors to confuse you." I am hoarse from yelling at the top of my lungs, "Stop being diverted. Stop being confused." They put a hashtag in front of the s—t I've been doing for 20 years and told y'all something else and y'all run behind it.'[14]

Social media has become a sandpit where we can watch the colonisation of activism fronted by marginalised people play out in real time. Centring white voices in Black struggles is dangerously distracting, as it pulls focus away from people in more need of support, who are less likely to be helped. The hashtag BlackLivesMatter and the accompanying, utterly redundant and performative black square on Instagram acts as a case in point – it was a form of virtue signalling that demanded nothing further from the poster. Even though white people might see their struggles partially mirrored in marginalised experiences, and white voices might want to show some sort of misplaced solidarity that signals to other folks that they themselves are, in fact, not racist, this performativity ultimately minimises what it means to carry out anti-racist work. This sort of colonialist thinking doesn't only exist in the activism space – it happens *everywhere*. For marginalised women, therefore, there is a deeper need for interactive care within the whisper-network mechanism, something called 'whisper care'. Whisper care is a relatively new term introduced by researchers in 2024 as part of an article titled 'Confronting *Mean Girls* Niceness: Conceptualizing Whisper Care to Disrupt the Politics of Niceness in Academia'.[15]

The term describes a theoretical construct and a practical approach to challenging and dismantling systemic racism, specifically as a response to racism and colonialism within academic circles, though it can be applied to any number of social situations where racism and colonialism are present. Essentially, whisper care challenges the 'politics of niceness', a term that describes coded language that conceals demeaning and prejudicial intention beneath compliments and niceties. Niceness in this case operates as a proxy for whiteness, which is why it can be difficult to discern if you aren't socialised to pick up on the cues. It can also make these cues seem invisible enough that any form of confrontation could lead to negative repercussions, giving false confirmation of stereotypes like 'the Angry Black Woman'. How can you ask for accountability from someone who was 'just being nice to you'? Dr Johnson suggests that, if you want to act with anti-racist intentions, then the more open you are to listening, the better, as well as emphasising the importance of 'thinking critically about your privilege'.

The social barriers faced by those who are marginalised on the grounds of gender, emotionality, race – or all these factors – make it enormously challenging to navigate upsetting or difficult situations in any number of social settings, but in particular those that occur within the workplace. Once one's character has been brought into question, a mark is made against our person. We become disparaged through prejudice, which is why, when a rumour about sexual assault is dispelled as being nothing more than just gossip, three things happen. First, it immediately genders the experience in a stigmatising way, leading to the complaint being filed away and labelled 'untrustworthy source' or 'trouble-making woman with nothing better to do than ruin a man's life' – so much so that a 2020 study conducted by the TIME'S UP Legal Defense Fund found that 70 per cent of women who had complained about sexual assault or harassment in the workplace were retaliated against in some way.[16] This is in part because of gossip's gendered history and its association with idleness and sinfulness. The other part is down to the aggrandised nature of masculinity, and centuries of men's reputations and their 'potential' being put ahead of women's safety.

Take the case of Brock Turner as a prime example. Turner was a student athlete at Stanford University, who one evening was found sexually assaulting an unconscious, partially clad woman behind some dumpsters. Passers-by intervened and restrained Turner until police came to make the arrest. When the case came to trial, Turner was found guilty, but he received a light sentence, serving only six months in jail, despite the fact that the crime he was found guilty of carried a maximum sentence of fourteen years. This begs the question, then: why didn't the judge make an example of Turner and his abhorrent crime? Addressing the court, then-residing Santa Clara County Superior Court judge Aaron Persky said that a term any longer than he had given 'would have a severe impact on him [Turner]'. Persky put Turner's potential above the impact of the crime he was found guilty of. The judge's ruling sparked tremendous outrage, particularly as the sentence given to Turner by Persky evoked a certain brand of white male privilege. This was further exacerbated by the fact that the victim of Turner's crime was an Asian American woman, and, as research shows us, women of colour are less likely to be believed than their white counterparts when reporting sexual assault.[17]

When complaints of this kind are labelled as gossip, the person making the claims can be put under intense scrutiny designed to bring them into disrepute. This includes questioning that person's sexual history, their clothing at the time of the alleged assault and their previous relationships. It can also mean interrogating their perceived promiscuity or provocativeness. This is a form of slut-shaming and victim-blaming, which means that, bit by bit, if a victim has been brave enough to come forward, they will have pieces of their character chipped away. This scrutiny is designed to instil doubt in the person's 'quality', as well as their credibility. It also leads to a devaluing of the bonds that women form with one another – bonds that are often built on a combination of instinctive and historical knowledge that accounts of sexual violence are disbelieved and go unpunished. We've witnessed this play out publicly and loudly in recent years, particularly with the case of Harvey Weinstein. Weinstein found himself at the centre of the MeToo movement after Alyssa Milano tweeted, 'If you've been sexually harassed or assaulted write "me too" as a reply to this tweet.' Milano's tweet soon went viral, with dozens of allegations against Weinstein.[18]

Prior to 2017, when these fresh allegations brought this whisper network, or 'Hollywood's open secret', into the light, any accusations that had been levelled against Weinstein were met with punishment for the accuser, as were any successful avoidances of his non-consensual sexual advances. Weinstein removed many actresses from projects, with American actress and activist Ashley Judd filing a defamation lawsuit against Weinstein, saying, 'I lost career opportunities. I lost money. I lost status and prestige and power in my career as a direct result of having been sexually harassed and rebuffing the sexual harassment.'[19]

Judd was far from alone, with eighty women coming forward in October 2017 alone. As that number began to rise, the breadth of harm that Weinstein was alleged to have committed became nothing short of soul-destroying.

When Katherine Kendall, actress and survivor of Weinstein, spoke about why she didn't come forward at the time, she said, 'This is Weinstein … I'll never work again, and no one is going to care or believe me.' Kendall wasn't wrong. But it wasn't just that people didn't care about her, or what had happened to her. It was that people were complicit in moral muteness, with actors like Matt Damon and filmmakers like Quentin Tarantino making very public apologies and admitting to turning a blind eye. 'I knew enough to do more than I did … There was more to it than just normal rumours, the normal gossip. It wasn't secondhand. I knew he did a couple of things … I wish I had taken responsibility for what I heard,' Tarantino said, following the outpouring of claims against Weinstein.

Moral muteness is a form of complicity that is similar to that of a passive bystander – someone who doesn't intervene when they witness wrongdoing. It is easier, some say, to turn the other cheek, to look the other way, to be safe rather than sorry. And in some cases, where personal safety is at risk, intervening directly can have adverse outcomes. Yet, to not act at all is unconscionable to me – though I have never stood in the room with a 'Weinstein'. It's important to remember that those in his inner circle and outside it, such as his peers and employees, who witnessed the harm he carried out, would have been influenced by the same threats that kept his victims silent, dissuading them from intervening. 'If Harvey were to discover my identity, I'm worried that he could ruin my life,' one anonymous former employee said. The secrecy at work to conceal Weinstein's perpetual, unforgivable cruelty towards women and girls wasn't to last forever, though, and in the cold light of day, the well-guarded whisper network was brought to public attention.

Dr Johnson explains that the creation of whisper networks is a consequence of inherent, deep-seated distrust in formal reporting systems, coupled with a feeling that the information they have is unsafe to share publicly. This creates a sense of intimacy and trust between the person receiving the information and the person disseminating the information. In short, we know what's at risk by alluding to a colleague's inappropriate behaviour, yet we trust that the person receiving the message is glad to be warned and would hopefully do the same for us.

'It is because of the case involving Weinstein that there is probably less stigma attached to the term "whisper network", because we saw very clear implications of how it was working, and that the whispers held a lot of truth,' Dr Johnson says. That said, whisper networks, or 'gossip circles' – the term used by the HR team at Uber in the case of Susan Fowler – can also be a bone of contention. Fowler, who was an engineer at the then start-up taxi firm Uber, wrote a blog about her time working for the company in 2017 titled 'Reflection on one very, very strange year at Uber'. The blog quickly went viral and spoke of the sexual harassment Fowler had experienced working at Uber. According to Fowler, during her time at the company, Uber didn't have the appropriate processes and structures in place to deal with complaints of a sexual nature. When HR at Uber addressed her complaints, they accused her of being an 'instigator', asking her 'if women engineers at Uber were friends and talked a lot'. You could suggest that this is an example of an institution telling on itself a little here. Why would a group of women talking a lot be a problem? What's that about? The remark heavily implied that female engineers were coming together to disrupt the company, with Fowler as their leader. The conclusion that Uber's HR team reverted to illustrates a point that researcher Alexander Rysman made years ago. Rysman, who published his paper 'How the "Gossip" Became a Woman' in 1977, wrote that women who cause trouble are immediately punished with the stigma of gossip, which discourages other people from associating with them or following their example.[20] This is yet another example of shame being weaponised to prevent other women from feeling safe and comfortable supporting other women. So, when women who come forward about sexual abuse in the workplace are labelled as gossips, there is an attempt at discrediting, which is exactly what Fowler experienced.

Following her selection as one of five people of the year dubbed 'silence breakers' by *TIME* magazine, Fowler stated that she knew her credibility would be attacked when she came forward, and had even gone to the lengths of intentionally removing emotionality from her blog post, describing this as a sort of 'emotional detachment' so that she might avoid being disbelieved by being labelled as 'too emotional' or 'irrational'. This anticipation that her credibility might be called into question because of 'emotional language' demonstrates that Fowler not only understood the potential risk of being branded hysterical or emotional, but she also understood that, in order to be believed, every single accusation she made would have to be backed up by physical documentation, 'so it couldn't be "he said, she said".'

In the case of Weinstein, a similar pattern of discreditation took place. Whisper networks were formed between women working in the film industry in Hollywood, New York and London to help shield one another from unwanted sexual advances, but once accusations were made public, the 'quality' of those women would then be brought into question. Weinstein, who has always maintained his innocence, was accused of multiple sexual-assault crimes. During his first trial in October of 2020 at the Manhattan Supreme Court, his criminal-defence lawyer, Donna Rotunno – described by the *Guardian* as a legal Rottweiler[21] – resorted to tactics of sex-based shame and victim-blaming to discredit, disgrace and demoralise the women who had come forward.

In her opinion piece, published by *Newsweek* in February 2020, Rotunno urged jurors to 'look beyond the headlines',[22] something she would later be chastised for by presiding judge James Burke. However, this wouldn't be the only time Rotunno's conduct played on gender-based stereotypes to defend Weinstein. In an article for *Advocate* magazine in 2020, Shannon H.P. Ward, a partner and trial lawyer at the Aarons Ward law firm, where she specialises in sexual harassment and assault cases, pointed out that the defence's tactics, while skilful, were not new. She wrote:

> For as long as there has been sexual assault and survivors brave enough to object publicly – defendants and their lawyers have made the same arguments. These

arguments can be effective and persuasive, in part, because the average person does not understand the mindset of a sexual-assault survivor. Also, because not every survivor responds the same way. Unless one is a survivor or works closely with them, some things don't make much sense at first glance.[23]

Ward points out that the defence implements this strategy with a number of different attack tactics – by attempting to prove that the victim had a 'friendly' relationship with the defendant; by bringing into question the victim's own personal accountability and forcing jurors to consider whether or not Weinstein had been 'led on' by their approachability or misinterpreted their openness to sex based on their previous sexual history; by putting the onus on the victim for not preventing the attack from taking place – that is, the 'why didn't you fight back harder?' defence (which fails to acknowledge one of the five major stress responses: 'freeze'); by drawing attention to the time that's passed between the alleged event and the victim coming forward, as well as alluding to ulterior motives the victim might have for making the claim, like gaining access to money, notoriety or fame – a trope that, frankly, belongs in the bin.

Each one of these defence tactics relies on the idea of the 'perfect' or 'ideal' victim narrative, which are necessary for a victim to follow in order to be believed: they must appear weak, defenceless or vulnerable; they ought to have been doing something respectable or associated with goodness at the time of the assault; the victim must be completely blameless at every level of the interaction, so that it would be impossible to allude to some sort of seduction; the accused must fit the preconceptions of what an abuser looks and behaves like (in and of itself, a problematic and limiting profile); and, finally, the victim must not know the attacker.[24]

Straying outside of these societal expectations results in distrust, doubt and intense questioning designed to pick apart a person's character. If, for instance, the victim and attacker knew each other and had enjoyed a date with some alcohol, a defence attorney might suggest that the prosecutor cannot prove beyond reasonable doubt that the person committing the offence wasn't aware that consent had been withdrawn. This is victim-blaming, although it's not its only form. In truth, victim-blaming can happen in a variety of different ways, whether through comments made directly to or about a victim, via the perpetuation of rape myths, or through the concept of a stereotypical perpetrator or perfect victim. It's worth stopping here to note that in the majority of rape and sexual-assault cases, the victim knows the perpetrator, who is, more often than not, a friend, ex-partner or family member.

You have likely heard, or even used, some of the more common phrases, such as, 'Why didn't she just leave?' during discussions of domestic-violence allegations, which place the emphasis and responsibility on the victim, rather than on the abuser.[25] But statistics show that the point of leaving is the time when a woman's life is in the most danger. This is partly why many women refuse to come forward about assaults, either because they believe they have not behaved in a way that is characteristic of a victim, and have therefore internalised the blame and shame, or because they know how their failure to conform to a 'perfect victim' profile will be viewed and subsequently fear how they may be perceived by authorities and how their cases will be handled. Returning to or resuming a relationship with a partner who has been accused of abuse can also create a 'cry wolf' scenario, where the myth of 'they're just as bad as each other' begins. Empathy for what a victim has gone through circles the drain. People might question the legitimacy of the victim's claims, but we must remember that traumatised people who have suffered emotional, sexual and physical abuse are not rational in their behaviours. They are stuck in a loop, trying to regain control and to understand what is happening to them. We must also remember that we are not privy to the persuasion that often happens in these situations of abuse. A perpetrator might cry, beg and plead, offering up promises of change, sorrow and remorse. They might dangle the positives of a relationship – the love and the good times shared – before the victim, in order to win them back. That promise of love and care instead of abuse and anger can be a tremendously powerful proposition. I know intimately how easy it is to push past the harm when those sorts of promises are made. It's all too easy to believe that you've finally got through to them, that they see you and how their behaviour impacts you. It might be affirming, but it's also disorientating. You let them back in, the pattern repeats, the trauma deepens and becomes more complex, except this time, when you try to leave, those who were there the first time around are exhausted by the back and forth and their compassion has run dry. It's isolating, confusing and dangerous. You feel shame and stupidity for believing them and blame yourself. The cycle continues until you either leave or are killed.

According to Rape Crisis England & Wales, five in six women don't report rapes to the police,[26] citing 'embarrassment', that they 'didn't think the police would help' and that they 'thought it would be humiliating' as reasons. It's understandable why women who have been attacked might feel this way, when fewer than three in one hundred rapes recorded by police between April 2023 and March 2024 resulted in someone being charged that same year. Additionally, survivors in the UK face long wait times for cases to come to trial. For adult rape cases, it can take an average of two years – sometimes longer. This comes at a time when the UK criminal courts are yet to try over 10,000 sexual offences cases, and almost 3,000 cases of adult rape, both of which are record highs.

Witnessing cases of sexual violence play out in the media, like that of Weinstein, can act as a sobering reminder that being believed isn't a given, no matter how truthful you're being. In 2024, Weinstein's charges were overturned, on the basis that he had not been given a fair trial. The decision to overturn the guilty verdict was down to the judge's decision to allow for a cross-examination that painted Weinstein in a 'highly prejudicial' light, and that the prosecution had called upon witnesses whose accusations were not part of the charges against him.[27] In 2024, it was reported by the BBC that Douglas Wigdor, one of the lawyers who represented eight of Weinstein's accusers, had called the decision 'tragic' before going on to explain that, 'Courts routinely admit evidence of other uncharged acts ... the jury was instructed on the relevance of this testimony,' and that the decision of the judge 'will require the victims to endure yet another trial'.

For powerful, rich monsters like Weinstein, justice comes in the form of technicalities in how the law is applied. But for the victims who have suffered his sexual violence, reliving some of the most traumatic moments of their lives – *again* – will be the price they pay for a shot at lasting justice and peace. Even without these obstacles, demanding legal accountability requires mental fortitude, resilience and stamina, because statistically speaking, the journey towards conviction is an impossible struggle.

Just ask Christine Blasey Ford, who, in 2018, came forward to allege that the then Senate candidate Brett Kavanaugh had sexually assaulted her at a house party during his college years at Yale.[28] There were months of marches and protests at Capitol Hill, untold pressure from the public – many of whom identified as survivors of sexual assault, imploring the Senate to vote against Kavanaugh's confirmation. However, the FBI investigation on Kavanaugh was nothing more than a sham.[29] In August 2022, an exchange between US Senator Sheldon Whitehouse and FBI director Christopher Wray revealed that the complaints against Kavanaugh were presented to the White House without any further investigation. Despite his actions, Kavanaugh enjoys a lifetime position at the US Supreme Court to this day.

This is perhaps why women rely heavily on the bonds of 'sisterhood' and whisper networks as a preventative measure to stay safe from predatory and sexually violent behaviour in the workplace and beyond. It also explains why women still rely on gossip, rumour and, *You didn't hear this from me, but ...* to sidestep gender-based violence. We know the default is not to be believed by taking the formal route, and yet, there is a readiness to believe women in these whisper networks that is not present in wider society. This tells us that we are bound by the common experience of sexual violence.

Dr Johnson believes that women choose to put their trust in the whisper network rather than in formal reporting channels because of a shared understanding of privilege and marginalisation. 'I think when you have to learn the language of the superior and the language of the less privileged group, that language of the less privileged group will always feel slightly more authentic to you,' she says. 'And I think everybody understands that the risk of getting asked questions that are inappropriate and getting retraumatised is really high, which is disturbing.'

This was the case for Jade Blue McCrossen-Nethercott, who in 2024 was awarded £35,000 in compensation from the Crown Prosecution Service (CPS) after her sexual assault case was dropped by the CPS because of a 'sexsomnia' defence – that is, the alleged perpetrator claimed that McCrossen-Nethercott had a rare sleep condition that causes a person to engage in sexual acts while asleep. Following extensive efforts on McCrossen-Nethercott's part to disprove the claim that she had sexsomnia, she submitted her appeal. A chief crown prosecutor reviewed the evidence and concluded that the case should have gone to trial. While the CPS has 'apologised unreservedly', it cannot give back the seven years she has been fighting for justice,[30] nor can the case be reopened, since the defendant has already been found not guilty.

This is yet another example of how hard the system works against women who come forward. Time and time again, police forces have failed in their duty to uphold the law – so much so that in 2023, a report commissioned by the Metropolitan Police found it (the Met Police) to be institutionally misogynistic, homophobic and racist, following the death of Sarah Everard at the hands of one of their serving police officers.[31]

The realities of women's experiences of reporting sex-based crimes to the police echo what is happening behind office doors. For many women, feelings of malaise are conjured at the very thought of having to go through the formal reporting systems in the workplace. Nevertheless, sexual harassment in the workplace is common, even if reporting it isn't, and mimics the same trends we see in wider society when it comes to sexual violence.[32] A survey of 2,000 employees conducted in 2024 by Personio, an HR software company based in Germany, found that 10 per cent of employees had witnessed sexual harassment, but of that 10 per cent, just under half (49 per cent) had reported it. Speaking with People Management in 2024, Pete Cooper, director of people partners and equality, diversity and inclusion (EDI) at Personio, said that, while the extent of workplace misconduct revealed by the study was worrying, the rate at which incidents go unreported was 'even more so'.[33]

This sentiment was echoed in Deloitte's annual report, 'Women @ Work 2024: A Global Outlook'.[34] In this survey, women cited similar reasons for not reporting sexual harassment, micro-aggressive behaviour or other forms of misconduct, like bullying, repeating that they didn't think any good would come of reporting; that they could be risking their jobs and careers; that they didn't trust their internal systems to keep them anonymous; and they feared the abuse would get worse. For more marginalised women, these experiences become more complex. For example, disabled women and LGBTQ+ women reported higher experiences of sexual harassment than their heterosexual and/or non-disabled colleagues.

This also points to a disquieting trend whereby predators seek out people who are less likely to report sexual harassment and abuse because of their identity make-up, preying on vulnerable people with the intent to cause harm. Speaking with the *Guardian*'s Lucy Webster in 2022, Amy Kavanagh, who is blind, explained that men often targeted her under the guise of assistance: 'A typical experience is that someone offers to help me cross a road and, whether or not I accept, they grab me by the arm and refuse to let go. Often, they will use this opportunity to touch my breasts, make inappropriate comments about my sexuality or physical appearance, or ask me personal questions about my body.' Kavanagh is certain that men target her because she is blind, saying, 'I can't easily identify them, I can't see them coming or know if they are following me or watching me.'[35]

This is something that Sarah, who I spoke with as part of my research for this book and who is using her first name only, has experienced too. Sarah tells me that she is autistic, and that she isn't very good at picking up on subtle social cues, taking every gesture and action in sincerity and good faith. 'I'd just started my first role in what would become my career, and the head of my department took a specific shine to me,' she begins, explaining that the man would compliment her hair and ask for hugs, then linger for too long.

'Knowing about my autism, an older member of staff took me aside and asked if I fancied lunch with her and a few other women.' This lunch would be Sarah's welcome to the fold, where the women brought her up to speed regarding her colleague's behaviour. 'They warned me that he often would take a "shine" to new staff members, often resulting in sex and then them being fired,' Sarah recounts. 'These women protected me.'

Later, when a new staff member was hired, Sarah herself made a conscious effort to pull them to one side and warn them about their predatory colleague. I ask Sarah why she didn't go to HR, or the police, to report her head of department's behaviour. I suspect her answer will be similar to those of the many other women I've spoken to over the years as a health, sex and relationships journalist with a focus on gender equality and sex safety. I'm not wrong; Sarah's response echoes all those I've spoken with about formal reporting systems. 'While these logically seem like the better option, they very rarely are,' she says, explaining how in her previous (non-sexual) complaints to HR, when it came to her wellbeing or that of the company's, it quickly became clear which side they were on.

It's a bitter reminder of my own experiences. In 2018, I was working as a contractor for an architectural firm in London. The Christmas party was jungle themed, so I wore a leopard-print jumpsuit. It ought not to be relevant, but the jumpsuit had sleeves and a high neckline. While on the balcony with a colleague, I asked to pinch a cigarette from an older man already smoking. He gawked at my chest before making an inappropriate comment about my breast size. I told him he could keep his cigarette and made to leave the party. My colleagues insisted I stay, and, concerned that perhaps I was making a big deal out of nothing, I joined them on the dance floor. In front of our entire staff, the same man groped at me, swung me around and made repeated attempts to touch me, despite me telling him to *fuck off*. No one intervened, and no one asked if I was OK. A few awkward jokes were made, and I left. I made a complaint to HR, but without me waiving my anonymity, they wouldn't do more than make a note against his profile. My colleagues told me that the man had 'a bit of a reputation'. He'd been at the company for over a decade, while I was temporary. The following week, I had to share an elevator with him. I quit the same day and threw the jumpsuit in the bin.

Sexual harassment is one of the most prevalent forms of discrimination,[36] with 81 per cent of women and 43 per cent of men experiencing sexual harassment and/or assault in their lifetime.[37] According to research by the Trades Union Congress (TUC) in 2023, incidents of sexual harassment aren't a one-time event, either. In fact, 43 per cent of women experience sexual harassment incidents at least three times.[38]

'Authority very rarely protects women. We see it time and time again. We need each other,' Sarah says defiantly. She's right, of course. How can we expect women to come forward with stories when they are repeatedly treated so disrespectfully? It seems that reporting workplace sexual harassment and abuse means making peace with the risk of retaliation, whereby you either risk your job and career, or else face the potential for continued abuse. So, to report, or not to report – either way, it can feel like a lose–lose situation where you're damned if you do and damned if you don't. With this in mind, it's perhaps easy to see why women rely on other women to safeguard them against sexual harassment and abuse. Whisper networks, aside from creating communities built on trust and care, plug the gaping inadequacies in our problematic reporting systems and legal frameworks.[39]

This is something that Rooster, who has been a sex worker since 2016, understands intimately. Their experiences with whisper networks in the sex industry have provided safety and information, but they have also found that these networks can be places that are biased and harmful. Rooster found that whisper networks in different areas of sex work had varying implications, and the types of communications shared between these networks was dependent on the type of employer or client. It wasn't until they were assaulted on a feminist porn set in their mid-twenties that they realised that whisper networks existed to warn against working with the person responsible for their assault.

'I wouldn't have expected anything bad to occur in these spaces. But unfortunately, it did. Even in feminist porn, assaults happen.' Rooster's assault opened them up to the complicated dynamic between employer and whisper networks and those that access them, mirroring the experiences of many others who find themselves sexually harassed and assaulted in the workplace. However, what separates and compounds Rooster's experience further is the stigma attached to sex work and the marginalisation of their identity as a Black person in that space. 'There's pressure to brush things off and not share the harms that are perpetrated with whisper networks within those marginalised spaces, because the harm comes from other marginalised identities themselves,' they explain. 'It can be difficult to even access whisper networks and the information because you don't want to be seen as bad-mouthing someone else.'

Rooster explains that the MeToo movement opened the conversation around sexual abuse within the porn scene, whereas prior to the movement, those discussions were much harder to have. However, these conversations and whisper networks were already accessible for escorts, who frequently share information freely about clients and prospective clients. I ask Rooster why they think there is such a difference between these spaces, and why information-sharing feels less restricted as an escort than as a porn performer. They note that, in porn, networks are often more guarded due to higher risks of defamation – organisations and brands that have reputations to uphold usually have greater access to power and resources than those speaking out against them. 'Within escorting, you don't usually have clients who have access to your whisper networks,' Rooster explains, 'while within the porn circles, the information you're trying to share – there's a high chance it's between colleagues and directors and production companies who might have access to the same whisper networks, or networks and groups you're part of.'

So, why not just go to the police – or follow any other sort of formal reporting route? A study drawing on a 2020 survey by National Ugly Mugs (NUM), an organisation fighting to end violence against sex workers, found that 'sex workers feel alienated and untrusting of police and courts', and this signals 'significant flaws in our legal system regarding safe and inequitable access and pose dangers for all of us'. What's more, in 2012, only 28 per cent of those who chose to report incidents of sexual violence to NUM chose to then engage with the legal system; eight years later, in 2020, this was down to 7.7 per cent among off-street independent workers.[40] This downward trend demonstrates that mistrust is growing among sex workers, mirroring the statistics from workers outside of the sex industry who experience sexual violence in the workplace. There is no silver bullet that will solve this, but some researchers and activists have put forward calls to decriminalise the sex industry, while also supporting action to improve procedural justice.[41]

The criminal justice system isn't just a large ship that turns slowly, to which we need to give a bit of grace, though. Nor is it an organisation in need of a change in management. They are gatekeepers to justice, yet the Metropolitan Police have been found to be institutionally racist, misogynistic and homophobic by the Operation Hotton Report and the 2023 review conducted by Baroness Casey.[42] This isn't just a London-centric issue either, with the chief constable of South Wales Police (SWP) accepting that institutional racism applies to his force in 2023,[43] in addition to having the worst record of violence against women and girls of all Welsh police forces.[44] In a similar vein, the Greater Manchester Police issued an apology following the release to the public of Dame Vera

Baird's report, the Baird Inquiry,[45] which found that officers had unlawfully arrested and strip-searched victims of abuse.[46] It goes on and on like this. In fact, you'd be hard pushed to find any constabulary without similar claims made against them. The statistics aren't much better globally. A study on the challenges police investigators in Australia and New Zealand face when interviewing adult victims of sexual assault, published in the *Violence Against Women* journal in 2024, shows that both forces are steeped in a failure to determine victim credibility.[47] In short, the police lack the ability to believe victims, but are perfectly capable of assaulting them. The lack of care for women, particularly sex workers and Black women who experience sexual violence and victimisation,[48] results in further degradation and traumatisation, as well as a deepened sense of distrust. It's the embodiment of rubbing salt in the wound, and proves just how important whisper networks can be, despite their imperfections.

There is also a case to be made for how integral the work of citizen journalists is. Citizen journalism relies on gathered knowledge, community action and a whisper network connecting the dots to uncover crimes and other wrongs in order to bring about justice and even help find missing people.

You might remember the Netflix documentary about internet sleuths called *Don't F**k With Cats*, a show that detailed the work of a community hell-bent on exposing a serial killer. Through tenacious information-gathering across a network online, a group of people were able to gather enough evidence to convince police that a series of murders had taken place. However, while reporting on online communities is very much within the realms of traditional journalism, there are also citizen journalists to be found across social media platforms. But what happens when you build a career commenting on people's feuds, missteps or criminal behaviour to an audience of tens of thousands, possibly millions, of people?

I'm talking about a very niche area of the internet, where content creators are journalists and documentarians. Their subjects of interest? Each other. I've been following reports on one particular YouTuber since around 2012, Onision (real name Gregory James Jackson). Jackson has long been the subject of many popular YouTube accounts seeking to pinpoint some accountability on his alleged abusive behaviours. The rumour and speculation surrounding Jackson is alarming to say the least: primarily that he allegedly sexually abused some of his ex-girlfriends, and that his spouse, Kai Avaroe, had participated in grooming and coaxing underage girls across county lines to engage in sexual activity. This isn't the half of the allegations, neither does it represent the depth of the potential criminal activity Jackson and Avaroe have been accused of by their peers. But the rumour and gossip surrounding the two have resulted in many YouTubers producing discursive and evidence-based content to disseminate information to other people in the community and their respective audiences.

It should come as no surprise that eventually, after more YouTubers began creating content around Jackson and Avaroe, the story piqued the interest of journalist Chris Hansen, of reality TV series *To Catch a Predator* fame. In 2024, Jackson and Kai faced the real-life consequences of their alleged actions, when a lawsuit against the couple began in earnest. This is far from the only incident of citizen journalism on a social media platform. There's the *Swoop* documentaries and exposés on Colleen Ballinger, another person who was recently exposed by the YouTube community for allegedly engaging in inappropriate behaviours with minors, as well as the videos detailing child abuse by family YouTuber Ruby Franke, who was recently sentenced to four prison terms between one and fifteen years, on aggravated child abuse charges.

There is an undeniable legitimacy to the work of citizen journalists, who listen to rumour and gossip and spend the time gathering evidence in order to protect vulnerable communities and people from further harm. That's not to say that citizen journalism isn't flawed, though. Often, it is wholly unregulated, and the people who undertake investigations are untrained, even if they set out with the best intentions. There is also the attention economy to contend with. Even well-meaning people can get sucked in to capitalising on the ad revenue of particularly salacious stories. I'd argue that digital journalism is in a similar pickle, however. The difference is that most, if not all, publishing output is expected to adhere to a code of ethics and legal best practice. Citizen journalists who create online content and comment on community happenings aren't necessarily held to those same standards. Equally, the rate at which misinformation can spread because of careless reporting and a lazy approach to fact-checking brings with it another dimension to the necessary but error-prone style of community management.

There are other ways in which whisper networks are utilised as a form of community safeguarding. They're deployed frequently in our dating lives too. Online, you can be whoever you want to be, which means you can hide the less appealing sides of yourself. So, while you might not put in your dating profile, 'Snores loudly after consuming one sip of wine,' omitting this sort of information isn't likely to cause serious harm to a prospective partner. Leaving out that you have a criminal background or are already in a monogamous relationship might, however. For those looking to avoid relationship hardships, many turn to the Facebook community group Are We Dating the Same Guy? (AWDTSG) to find out if the men they are dating, or interested in dating, really are who they present themselves to be, as well as warning other women of their bad experiences. These digital whisper networks are split by geography, with users posting names of men, dating profiles and profile pictures – though the rules differ from group to group, both in the way that they are written and how they are enforced.

Unlike traditional whisper networks, these online groups have a tangible visibility because of their digitisation. That visibility has positive and negative consequences – on the one hand, it keeps track of alleged serial daters doing harm, but on the other hand, whether you agree with these groups or not, there's no denying that they *do* infringe on people's privacy. Posts usually comprise pictures of men's dating profiles and their first name, often accompanied by red-flag emojis, with details of bad behaviour in the comments. These warnings can range in severity, from the more minor offences of being stood up or ghosted to suspicions of someone they've been speaking to already having a partner, stories of sexually violent run-ins, and accounts of stalking and harassment.

Some of these posts gain enormous traction, with commenters jumping in to share their own similar experiences, offering advice on how to contact authorities, as well as sharing how to go about using Clare's Law – under which you can request information about a current or ex-partner if you suspect they may have previous domestic abuse convictions[49] – alongside more general emotional support and shows of solidarity. 'Groups like these exist for a reason,' Dr Carolina Are tells me. Dr Are continues to explain that the intention behind online forums like AWDTSG is to create a place where information dissemination can take place with a level of discretion. They are, like whisper networks, informal places to warn women of predatory, toxic and abusive behaviour. She explains how trust in dating has decreased for many people, and that faith in dating apps in particular is at an all-time low. As a result, the strength and importance of gossip, and the ease with which you can screen potential partners, is massively important for those from marginalised groups who have always shared gossip to protect each other from dangerous situations and dangerous people.

Femicide rose globally in 2022, according to a YouGov survey by UN Women UK. The survey reported that, 'Globally, nearly 89,000 women and girls were killed intentionally in 2022, the highest yearly number recorded in the past two decades,' and that most of these killings were 'gender motivated'. In 2022 in the UK, 97 per cent of women aged eighteen to twenty-four experienced sexual harassment,[50] which points to a commonality of experience so universally understood that it is then reasonable to assume that these UN Women UK figures ring with alarming truth in many women's minds. In addition, women are constantly and systemically victim-blamed for the sexual and gender-based violence they experience. They are questioned about what they were wearing; how many drinks they had; whether they'd been leading the guy on; whether they were already naked when the assault took place. This could be why there is a compelling need to make sure that you have done everything in your power – of which there is little – to protect yourself from predation. Because women know intimately that you don't need to look like a monster to be capable of monstrosity, as well as the stark fact that, most of the time, women are killed by the people who are supposed to love them the most – their intimate partners and family members.[51]

Statistically speaking, when it comes to domestic abuse – which is defined by the National Centre for Domestic Violence (NCDV) as physical abuse, sexual abuse, violent or threatening behaviour, controlling or coercive behaviour, economic abuse, psychological, or emotional or other abuse where the victim and perpetrator(s) are aged sixteen or over and are 'personally connected' to each other – it does not matter whether the behaviour consists of a single incident or a course of conduct. Women are more likely than men to experience repeated victimisation, to be physically injured or killed, or to experience sexual violence.

That's not to say that men *don't* experience domestic abuse. The NCDV reported that one in six to seven men will experience domestic abuse during their lifetime. The reason *why* domestic abuse is often referred to as 'gendered' is because of the differences between male violence against women and female violence against men – namely, the amount, severity and impact. Additionally, Women's Aid, a UK national charity working to end domestic abuse, state that 'men do not experience domestic abuse as part of embedded structural inequalities against their sex'.[52] Office for National Statistics (ONS) data collected from the year ending March 2023 revealed that the victim was female in 73.5 per cent of domestic-abuse-related crimes.[53]

Alongside the statistically higher risk of domestic violence within heterosexual relationships, there's also a general disdain for modern dating fuelled by swipe culture, ghosting, performative male trends and overall dating fatigue, which may lead single women to wonder if it's worth it at all. In 2024, *Forbes* published an article on the state of dating fatigue, which claimed that, for Gen Z, 79 per cent reported experiencing dating-app burnout. According to *Forbes*' health advisory board member and sex therapist Rufus Tony Spann, this is because of frequent encounters with disappointment and lies, and constantly meeting new people – which takes an enormous amount of emotional energy. It's easy to see, then, how a distrust in dating, combined with a sense of malaise at the thought of having to utilise deeply flawed formal methods of reporting sexual violence and domestic abuse, has caused women to organise themselves in the digital sphere in a collective and proactive protection measure.

That said, such whisper networks are not without their shortcomings. The line is somewhat blurry when it comes to people's privacy in these spaces, and even though community rules might strictly ban using full names to identify the men in question or doxxing them by publishing their place of work or home address, that doesn't mean the rules are always enforced or adhered to. Moderators also don't have complete control when it comes to leaks – that is, where the men in question are alerted to the fact that they've been posted on community groups. I've witnessed anonymous posters having to remove their post completely in order to placate someone they've been dating. The worry is that these groups can't guarantee the safety of women who post about the men they are dating online. It can put them in harm's way, potentially exacerbating abusive behaviours.

There is also no way of telling whether the posts are entirely truthful. They act as bulletins, warning of bad behaviour, abuse, toxicity and more – but posts don't always necessarily include examples or proof. It's worth remembering that these groups are not formal reporting methods, and as Dr Johnson remarked, 'Whisper networks are about creating a sense of emotional safety … most women actually are out to help other people.' These groups are often infiltrated by 'moles' too, which means the presence of both fake and real accounts that report back to the men who have been featured. In one case, in the Bristol/Cardiff/Swindon Facebook group, an anonymous member posted on 15 July 2024 about her experiences with a man identified only as Tobi. They claim their dating experience consisted of '18 months of lies' where Tobi had lied about his existing child and slept with sixteen other women while the anonymous poster was pregnant. She also claims to have been labelled as a 'crazy baby mamma' for confronting Tobi about her suspicions. Then, on 26 August, the original anonymous poster returned, informing the community that there was 'no girl code in this group whatsoever', pointing to four members who had 'taken it upon themselves' to tell Tobi he had been posted about.

It seems that community groups built to protect women from mistreatment from men rely on the unspoken code of ethics we've been socialised to embody – that of girl code. However, as we've already explored, not every woman adheres to girl code – either because they have no use for it and have not been conditioned by their socialisation to rely on it, or because they lean into internalised misogyny, or 'pick me-ism'. There is a grey area, of course – nothing in this world exists in binary forms – but the impact of women and men joining these community groups to report back on people who have been featured can be potentially catastrophic. I'm not being hyperbolic when I say that, without the wrap-around care that a formal reporting system is supposed to provide, the consequences can be life-threatening.

In response to AWDTSG, revenge Facebook groups and Reddit threads have sprouted up across the globe, playing on the original title – Are We Dating the Same Girl, r/AWDTSGuyExposed and r/AWDTSGisToxic, to name a few. These groups mirror the 'About' sections of AWDTSG, bastardising them to proclaim 'empowerment for men' and 'protecting men' from 'gold diggers' and 'toxic women'. These descriptions range in severity with their use of sexist language. In my local (now deleted) Are We Dating the Same Girl? Facebook group, for instance, the language is particularly coarse, stating that the group exists to 'expose slags and dirty jaybags in their rags'. Charming.

There's a reason why there's such a profound and alarming response to women creating groups that men feel humiliate them and question their masculinity. Findings from a 2023 article titled '"It's Getting Difficult to Be a Straight White Man": Bundled Masculinity Grievances on Reddit' suggested 'that criticisms of social equality are embedded within a discourse of threatened masculinity, straightness, and whiteness'.[54] Within this, it seems that women taking action to protect each other from sexual violence leads to a far bigger and greater reaction from men who feel like their masculinity, entitlement and privilege has been called into question. Once again, men are in fear of reputational damage, while women are in fear of their lives.

In Reddit threads, there is a general consensus that the AWDTSG Facebook groups are geared towards man-hating, describing them as being 'all about gossip and revenge', with some making claims that women are 'addicted to gossip', rather than recognising the need for this primary social-care mechanism. The irony isn't lost on me that these threads act like a reverse (and perverse) whisper network, where rather than exposing misogyny, they provide information on how to sue women for speaking out,[55] how to shut down women-run groups, and how to go about getting posts removed,[56] among many other things.

The (since deleted) 6,000-plus-member Reddit thread AWDTSGisToxic claims to have been set up as a response to AWDTSG, calling it a 'toxic', 'one-sided gossip group', with the main gripes pertaining to the lack of a right to reply, fake scenarios and malicious posting about over-exaggerated behaviour. These are not unreasonable complaints, but when belief in women is already low, the knee-jerk reaction to distrust and discredit women who come forward in any capacity with stories of abuse is symptomatic of the broader societal issue of networked misogyny.[57]

Networked misogyny is a term that describes how our traditional and digital media, especially the tabloid press,[58] along with social media – particularly Reddit, Twitter (X) and 4chan[59] (all three of which have reputations for being drivers of inceldom, hate speech and the worsening treatment of minoritised people, including women) – have become tools for networked harassment channelled towards women and their rights, with the aim of inciting violence or dismantling credibility. Nowhere is networked misogyny more rampant and overt than in manosphere spaces, like the AWDTSG revenge groups. It is evident in everything from the posts to the 'About' sections. Although they state that abusive men should be exposed, in the same breath they continue to claim that the mostly women-run community group has become a 'gossip mill' where women bully and shame men. Because of the anonymous nature of AWDTSG, the Reddit group discredits them by claiming that these stories are 'often exaggerated' and 'vicious', immediately making clear the reasons why so many women might rely on informal groups like these to warn of bad behaviour.

This simultaneous agreement that causing harm to women is abhorrent while doing everything in your power to discredit women who have been harmed by men is another example of how those arcane laws from our ancient history are just as relevant today. Centuries on, we have still not escaped the dilemma of the blameless infallible man, the 'white knight', and the blameful, flawed woman. Eve, Lilith, Lavinia, Ilia and all those who have gone before us would no doubt sympathise with the plight of women today.

There's more to these threads and sub-threads than just anti-feminist rhetoric, however. These groups mobilise by identifying men who have already been posted on AWDTSG Facebook groups across the world, through the deployment of 'moles' who purposefully break the community guidelines and share the posts with the men being spoken about. Often, these men then label themselves as victims, saying they feel part of a 'witch hunt'. If this sounds a little incel-like to you, then you'd be right. There are multiple cross-posts about AWDTSG to threads on Reddit's MensRights group, a known incel forum. You will also find a lot of incel colloquialisms and slang used to describe and degrade the women making the posts. Some members refer to these women as 304s, shorthand for a promiscuous woman. If you're wondering why this is, you only need type 304 into a handheld calculator and hold it upside down to see that it spells out the word 'hoe'. This is one of many, many examples that point to a level of playground juvenility that would be laughable if it weren't for the fact that the existence of these groups is so dangerous. As such, turning to one of these groups to find out if you've been posted about could be an entry point for radicalisation. News in the manosphere also travels fast, working quickly to discredit women – something I experienced first-hand. As part of the research for this book, I created a public call-out for anybody who had experience with AWDTSG to reach out. My inbox and DMs quickly began pinging with messages from people wanting to talk – then, one email in particular caught my attention.

The sender, Anna, who asked to remain anonymous, admitted to being a woman who would report back to men about their inclusion on the social media group. She went on to say that she had ended up choosing to no longer 'snitch'. I found myself immediately filled with questions – *Why on earth would she choose to do something like that?* Anna went on to inform me of a Reddit sub-thread discussing my call-out, and signs the email off: 'I Have Learned If A Man Is Posted He Deserves It. [sic] Please Contact Me And I Can Share Specific Details.'

Intrigued, I searched my name along with AWDTSG on Reddit and, lo and behold, there I was – with the dubious honour of having my very own sub-thread on r/AWDTSGisToxic. Quickly, it became clear that the actions of this sub-thread were somewhat hypocritical of the broader group ethos – when it came to my call-out specifically, they were quick to exhibit the same behaviours they themselves found repugnant in the AWDTSG group. They trawled my social media accounts, citing that I wrote editorial content 'largely about how awful and violent men are' – a bit hyperbolic but an otherwise astute observation; that I was out to get a 'sensationalist' angle, and that my intentions were to twist, manipulate and dismiss what men had to say on the matter. I was also often referred to as 'that woman'; and they claimed that my journalism would be 'laden with lies and exaggerations'. When I went back the next day to see if the post had gained any more traction, it had disappeared. This reaction is hardly surprising. Women are often called liars and manipulators, and Reddit is a well-documented social media platform where masculine-coded language is structured to pack together salient, interlocking themes that uphold gender inequality and toxicity – the more negative, the better, as these posts draw engagement quickly.

With this in mind, I set up a Zoom meeting with Anna immediately. It was clear that we had much to discuss. When the day arrived, I was nervous to meet her and hear her story. I worried that it might not be Anna at all. The thought sent a chill down my spine as I waited for her to join our call, scheduled for 12 p.m. At 12:05 she joined, and I was immediately relieved to find that she appeared to be legitimate.

'Have you heard from Henry?' is one of the first questions she asks.

'Henry', whose name I've changed to help protect Anna's identity, is a convicted felon and Anna's ex-partner. During our email exchange, prior to our meeting, Anna shared police reports, news cuttings and a message, the content of which was vile and violent. I reassure her that I have not heard from him, and no suspicious accounts have tried to contact me about her or this book, beyond the sub-thread. Her shoulders lower almost immediately and her face softens. She speaks softly: 'That man is a murderer and a felon. He is the reason groups like these were made.'

Anna tells me the story of how she met Henry. 'It was a time in my life when I was very vulnerable,' she says, explaining how, after a series of heartbreakingly traumatic events, she found herself speaking to him on a dating site. Anna describes Henry as persistent, but despite this apparent enthusiasm, something in her gut was telling her to be wary. 'If I hadn't been in such a vulnerable place ...' She trails off. It would be years until Anna actually became involved with Henry romantically, but once they were together, things soon began spiralling out of control.

Anna had used the AWDTSG Facebook group to warn of a man with a criminal record working for a roadside recovery company, who she describes as 'getting fresh' with her. Then, one day, up popped Henry's name on the group. Her face drops as she remembers reading the post for the first time. 'I wish I would have listened to his ex then – she told me exactly what he was.' Over the course of their relationship, Henry became obsessed with AWDTSG Facebook groups, constantly asking Anna if he had been posted in them. After months of love-bombing, breadcrumbing and dehumanising interactions with Henry, Anna found herself longing for affection. 'I just wanted more attention from him,' she says nervously. 'I'm so disgusted with myself.' I reassure her that I'm not here to judge, and that I understand how complicated abusive relationships are – the way that they can twist us into someone we barely recognise anymore.

Anna relaxes a little before detailing how she would take screenshots from the group and send them to Henry whenever he asked. He would then threaten lawsuits and cease-and-desists towards those that had posted about him. In time, Henry went on to buy historic Facebook accounts to join the groups (an act which, while not illegal, goes against the platform's rules), which changed their dynamic. While he no longer relied on Anna to inform him of what was being said, he would still come running to her if he was posted about. 'It got to where I was his confidante, like he was contacting me every single day,' she remembers. 'But, I felt dirty and unclean that he would only contact me about these groups and not about other stuff.' Anna kept asking Henry why they couldn't talk about other common interests – but Henry's behaviour in the relationship didn't improve.

He refused to let Anna use walking aids for her disability because he was 'embarrassed' by her and wouldn't pick her up from hospital appointments. Anna continues to detail other, more disturbing actions and behaviours, before stating, 'Henry is a narcissist.' The term 'narcissist' is appearing more and more frequently in dating discourse, both on and offline, as a means of pathologising and labelling behaviour, as therapeutic and psychiatric terms become ever more mainstream. While 'narcissist' is a descriptor that is often levelled at anyone who appears selfish, it's important to pause here to note that narcissistic personality disorder, or NPD, is not as common as it might seem.[60] Symptoms of NPD can manifest through a sense of grandiosity, a need for admiration and a lack of empathy for others. While diagnosed narcissists can exhibit abusive behaviours, it's important to remember that abusive or problematic behaviour doesn't automatically equate to narcissism. NPD is a mental health condition and should be treated as such. That being said, while the weaponisation of therapy speech has been a concern for some psychotherapists, when

Anna refers to Henry as a narcissist, I'm inclined to believe her. From the transactional nature of their relationship to his emotional manipulation, as well as the threats of violence and suicide when Anna would pull away from him, it all seems to add up. Being able to label behaviour is an important part of coming to terms with what has happened in an abusive relationship. It can anchor us in reality and help us to shed some of the blame and shame we've internalised.

With the realisation that Henry had been using her throughout their relationship beginning to sink in, Anna turned to his friend for clarity. Upon reaching out, Henry's criminal past came to the fore. After this, she finally ended the relationship for good. Accredited British Association for Counselling and Psychotherapy (BACP) psychotherapist Kamalyn Kaur tells me that therapy speech has become an empowering tool for women to talk about abuse, trauma, emotional distress, boundaries and self-care. It provides women with the language to articulate their experiences and how they feel – something that may otherwise have been difficult.

'To a certain extent, therapy speech can help women validate their feelings and experiences, because it enables abusive patterns to be identified and acknowledged, rather than dismissed or minimised,' she says. However, Kaur recognises that therapy speech can be misused in certain situations. 'Doing this can run a number of risks, such as pathologising normal relationship behaviours or challenges. Not every conflict is a sign of emotional abuse, and not every partner who displays frustration or a lack of understanding is "gaslighting",' she explains, before continuing. 'Overuse can lead to individuals misinterpreting typical relationship challenges that most couples will experience as being more severe than they are.'

Kaur explains that this can result in situations escalating very quickly, when they might otherwise have been managed with conversation and compromise. However, the more dangerous outcome of therapy speech misuse is weaponisation. 'An example of this could be someone who is themselves controlling and toxic accusing the victim of being "toxic", "narcissistic", "controlling", or "gaslighting" if they try to set a boundary or challenge the abuser's behaviour,' Kaur explains. 'The language of therapy, while empowering, can be weaponised by abusers to manipulate, control, and undermine the credibility and experiences of their victims.'

Ayo Adesioye, a BCAP-registered integrative psychotherapy practitioner, echoes Kaur, adding that pathologising behaviour without the knowledge of mental health disorders and how to treat them can be a dangerous game to play. 'What you don't want to be doing is policing your partner unnecessarily,' she says, explaining that when it comes to labelling behaviours without appreciating the weight of the words, it can shut down communication pathways, block accountability and prevent honest dialogue.

AWDTSG isn't the only space where women have congregated in good faith to share information and protect one another. The social media app Tea, one of the fastest-growing dating apps on the Apple App Store, was one such space. Taking the concept of AWDTSG to new heights, Tea, which was founded in 2023, provided a forum-like space where users could share information about their dates and experiences with men, connect on private chats and upload personal content. The app claimed it had amassed 2 million new users with the tagline 'Helping women date safe'. The app asked for gender verification in the form of a photo, meaning that an estimated 72,000 images, including 13,000 verification photos and photos of government IDs, were held in its database. Once verified, users could access the global network as well as tools to do background checks that looked for criminal records or sex offender registration.

As part of the research for this book, I reached out to them in their infancy, ready to discuss how their app would help women, but also how it might put women at risk. I was keen to understand what safety protocols they had in place, how they would protect user information, if they understood the ferocity of the manosphere in relation to AWDTSG Facebook groups and the legal proceedings made against some of their members. After a video meeting, off-the-record conversations and some emails back and forth, they turned down the request to contribute. Fast-forward two years to 2025, and Tea experienced a data leak. Journalist Arwa Mahdawi summed up my thoughts succinctly in her article for the *Guardian* in July 2025: 'An app designed to protect its users from dodgy men has been hacked by dodgy men. I wish I could say I'm surprised.'[61]

This 'leak' isn't your average kind of data breach, however. The hackers came from 4chan, the popular trolling site and home to numerous right-wing misogynists and incels. This attack wasn't about justice, but about enacting revenge and humiliation on women. In the words of Faith Hill, journalist for the *Atlantic*, 'First Came Tea. Then Came the Male Rage'.[62]

The hackers exposed the app users' photos and personal information, creating a map that claimed to link Tea users to locations with the chilling accompanying message, 'Enjoy.' A rating site has also been created where men can comment on leaked Tea users' photos, calling them 'whales' and 'ugly bitches' who deserve 'all of this'. Sensitive conversations have also been leaked, including social media handles and phone numbers.

There were undoubtedly good intentions behind Tea, something that was confirmed in my own conversations with them. Its flaw lay in its attempt to streamline the digital whisper-network experience. A spokesperson for Tea told the *Atlantic* that the company is 'investigating the issue' – that is, the leaked conversations between members – and it has responded by taking down the direct messaging feature. They also claim that there is no evidence of further exposures and that they are 'working to identify affected users and offer them free identity protection services'.

Nevertheless, what Tea has exposed is yet another example of the vitriol women face when they reject men, or warn one another about dating experiences in a world where there is so much gamification of the dating experience. It also contributes to the growing list of shortcomings that tech companies are stacking up when it comes to protecting women. It is ironic, then, that so many people – millions, in fact – came to Tea expecting a sanctuary where they could mutually support one another in the absence of a care and criminal justice system that does. Instead, they have been left exposed and in danger. Aside from the wrath users are likely to experience at the hands of these men, who will see their 'conquering' of Tea as a win on their misogynistic campaign of hatred against women, it is what happens next that will likely set the precedent for how the digitisation of whisper networks are to be handled legally.

The risk facing members of whisper networks, both online and offline, is a defamation lawsuit. You'll remember the outcome of the *Tattle Life* founder, a man posing as a woman whose anonymity was waived in favour of identifying his role in a defamation lawsuit, or the plight of Amber Heard. After Heard testified as a witness for the *Sun* in Johnny Depp's libel case against them, following their reports that Depp was a 'wife beater' – a case that Depp lost – she chose to write a (if you ask me) relatively tame op-ed on domestic abuse and was subsequently sued for defamation by Depp. It should come as no surprise then that any woman seen to be making accusations against men runs the risk of facing some form of punishment, especially in a culture with a history of silencing women with ducking stools, scold's bridles and the mantra of being 'seen and not heard', while war, rape and brutish conquest are celebrated across the earth and in the digital sphere. Now that these whisper networks are tangible, they are provable, which can only spell danger.

Traditional whisper networks rely on word of mouth, which is hard to prove and, at best, might land you in trouble for slander – the action or crime of making a false spoken statement damaging to a person's reputation. Now that these networks exist in the digital sphere, however, cases of defamation – the action of damaging the reputation of a person or group by saying or writing bad things about them that are not true[63] – are beginning to rise.

In theory, if what you're saying is true, then you have nothing to worry about. However, using a justice system made by the most privileged group of people in society isn't always as simple as it seems. In 2024, Dr Stewart Lucas Murrey brought a legal case against fifty women who he claims have made defamatory statements about him on an AWDTSG Facebook group. In a video shared to his Twitter (X) account,[64] Murrey states that these women stalked and harassed him. This video is one of three, where Murrey addresses questions from Manosphere Highlights Daily, a YouTube channel with over 220,000 subscribers.[65]

During the video, Murrey states that 'among the most dangerous issues was matching with women who manifest psychological disorders', followed by a clip of a witch-like bog creature accompanied by eerie music. It's interesting that Murrey should choose this depiction of a woman as a monster, given our exploration of Lamashtu and hysteria in earlier chapters. Make no mistake, choosing this image is done on purpose to stoke the ancient fear that women who assert their desires and boundaries are monstrous and mad, and therefore fundamentally untrustworthy and unbelievable.

He continues to allege that women he would match with on dating apps would conceal neuroses and psychoses, 'behind a deceptively positive image of themselves', an act he refers to as 'catfishing' to reassert this belief. It's worth pointing out here that Dr Murrey is not a psychiatrist with any medical training. At the time of writing, he is a PhD at Yale with a post-doctorate in German studies, according to the Amazon 'About the Author' segment for his book about Nietzsche,[66] a philosopher often pedestalled by the far right.[67] Dr Murrey also has a track record of suing his exes for defamation and slander.[68] In 2023, Dr Murrey's self-published papers, 'Are We Being Murdered By The Same "Intelligence" Mafia? From Epstein's Pedophile Network to Facebook, United States and Israeli Cyber-Criminals',[69] and 'Who I am, and what I suspect happened to me' in 2025,[70] reveal a babbling narration filled with right-wing buzzwords. He introduces himself as a 'victim of a cyber-attack' after 'Hundreds of *anonymous* Facebook accounts had been working in secret to ruin my life'. After misspelling YouTube as 'YouTulbe' four times, he announces that anyone who is 'actually intelligent' would know that private Facebook groups aren't actually private, while stating that 'One theatre in their "intelligence" war on truth are "private" Facebook groups.' He accuses AWDTSG groups of being fronts for 'military cyber units', 'military click farms' and 'criminal cyber fusion centres' that have, so far, been 'successful' in providing evidence that users have published material that has caused harm.

All this is presented without evidence or data, of course, ahead of a launch into a tirade about AWDTSG, stating that 'AWDTSGuy? is just a front for the real goal of the Epstein 2.0 scam'. Yes, according to Dr Murrey, groups of women coming together to share vital information with one another to try to prevent harassment, abuse and sexual violence is a sign that the QAnon paedophile cabal are up to no good again. I, for one, can't imagine why anybody would claim to have a terrible time with Dr Murrey on a date. He sounds like a delight.

Dr Murrey's account, as reported by *Daily Mail+*, attacked the appearance of the women he was suing, stating that, 'These two women are uneducated, lack class, lack sophistication, look unhealthy and simply do not compete in a city like Los Angeles,' before directing readers to his GoFundMe account.[71] This playbook is a highly familiar one, in which mental health, attractiveness and emotionality are weaponised to discredit women as fundamentally unbelievable, conniving and manipulative. In this instance, such wrath was provoked simply because the women in question discussed their own negative dating experiences with Dr Murrey. As of April 2024, the first of Murrey's fifty defamation cases has been thrown out of court,[72] but nevertheless, actions like this are inspiring men to mobilise against groups like AWDTSG in a bid to seek revenge against the women they perceive to have wronged them. There are multiple threads online dedicated to sharing legal advice and emotional support and more in the pursuit of a defamation lawsuit. Is it really that simple, though? Defamation is a complex legal issue with a multilayered history – one that relies largely on perception, precedent and prejudice.

CHAPTER SIX

Defamation

And who will believe a group of women over a man's word?
— DAPHNE BRIDGERTON, *Bridgerton*, SEASON 1

'Why does "innocent until proven guilty" translate to "lie until proven true?"' reads the Post-it note that I've ceremoniously pinned to the shelf above my desk. It's a thought that's stuck with me throughout my journalistic career as I've reported on stories relating to sexual violence.

Time and time again when someone – usually a woman – makes a claim that something terrible has happened to them, the response – usually from men – is that they're lying. The truth isn't as black and white as we're led to believe. Social ethics dictates that there are many kinds of truths.[1] There is objective truth, which relies on something being correct or incorrect. Then, there's subjective truth, which relies on a person's morality, opinion, culture and other competing factors – that is, the truth is what you believe it to be based on your lived experience and held belief system. Basically, you can believe what you see, but others might see it differently. Finally, there's relational truth, which sits somewhere between the subjective and objective truth, relying on sound argument for the arrival or revelation of the truth.

Whether or not something really happened is secondary to establishing a truth that fits a belief system. After all, if we're to follow the broadly accepted definition of the truth, it is nothing more than a collective agreement of an idea or outcome.[2] As such, the truth is a belief, but it is not always a fact. Further, establishing the truth can't be done without interrogating moral credibility, in an environment where collectively held beliefs are a broadly agreed-upon reality. All this leaves room for interpretation, prejudice and bias.

Perhaps this is why oaths are taken in a court of law as a means of pledging ourselves to truth and honesty. We swear to tell the truth, the whole truth and nothing but the truth. But what if the truth looks like a lie? Or a lie looks like the truth? And how can people know the difference between them when the reality of those who are marginalised can be so different from that of the privileged? I ask these questions not to be pedantic about one of the fundamental purposes of our judicial system – to prove the truth and serve justice – but to draw attention to the fact that morality and credibility are sometimes ambivalent to the truth and are totally subjective, despite being heavily relied upon to establish truth or bring it into disrepute. We've already covered how likeability impacts how trustworthy you are, and now we're about to learn how difficult it is for a woman to be 'likeable' – a word synonymous with 'fuckable', in a court of law.

Without belief, the truth – that is, what *actually* happened – becomes obsolete. Moreover, we cannot believe in something unless it is credible. But credibility can be skewed by a number of things: first, there's the emotional victim effect, or EVE,[3] where the emotions displayed by the victim play a major role in how credible they are perceived to be. The way in which a victim presents themselves – through their posture, clothing and use of cosmetics – is also reported to impact the credibility of female expert witnesses.[4] Mental health status, or previous mental ill-health can render some being labelled as 'crazy' – a shorthand designed to discredit someone based on pre-existing prejudices, which are often compounded by identity factors like gender and race.[5] Trauma, as we've seen, is another thing that can impact a person's credibility – people who suffer high-impact trauma from domestic violence, sexual assault or emotional abuse are at significantly higher risk of developing substance misuse issues,[6] and although women are less likely than men to struggle with addiction,[7] both are likely to develop physical health problems as a result of trauma.

This all matters immensely, especially when we're talking about underreported crimes like rape, sexual assault and domestic violence, not only because trauma can impact case outcomes, but because the outcome of these criminal cases can open the door for defamation laws to become weaponised against survivors.

Libel falls under defamation, as does slander, but there are key differences between them – and, as you might expect, a sordid (and gender-discriminative) history. Broadly, defamation involves making derogatory and/or false statement regarding another individual or party, without any justification[8] – that is, saying or writing something untrue about someone, in a factual manner, that could result in a loss of earnings and damage to reputation. Put another way, defamation 'lowers a person in the estimation of right-thinking members of society generally'.[9] If the statement is written and then published via print or digital media (including social media), it is considered libel, and if it is spoken aloud or gestured – 'published' by something called 'transient publishing', which is legalese for speaking or saying aloud – it is slander.

When making a ruling on a defamation case, courts take into consideration a range of factors, such as the reach of the statement, the nature of the audience, the situation of the person making the alleged defamatory statement and the reaction to the statement by the people it was told to or who read it.[10] The crux of a defamation lawsuit, however, is built around being able to prove or disprove the truth of the statement in question, and, as we've already seen, the truth isn't always a representation of, well, the truth. In cases of sexual violence, in which there might only be two witnesses – the victim and the perpetrator – it is notoriously hard to prove what happened. This means that defamation can be and is being weaponised against free speech, impacting journalists and human-rights activists globally,[11] and it is particularly harmful for women who speak out about sexual assault and domestic violence.[12]

As discussed previously, in 2021, following the publication of Heard's op-ed on domestic abuse published in the *Washington Post*, Depp launched a defamation lawsuit against her.[13] Unlike the case between the *Sun* and Depp, however, which was tried in the UK, this trial was to be held in Fairfax Court, Virginia,[14] in the United States.

Depp wasn't mentioned by name in the op-ed, but he alleged that, because of its publication and the presence of facts in Heard's story that made him identifiable, he experienced substantial financial losses and found himself unable to secure film roles. According to an article published by the *Independent* in 2022, the op-ed detailed Heard's experiences with abuse from an early age, with her writing in the original op-ed, 'I knew certain things early on, without ever having to be told. I knew that men have the power – physically, socially and financially – and that a lot of institutions support that arrangement.'

Heard went on to detail her experiences of sexual assault by the time she was of college age, and how she felt that reporting these crimes would go unnoticed and that she 'didn't see herself as a victim'. She wrote that friends had warned her against taking a public stance against domestic violence, for fear that she might get blacklisted. Those fears then became her reality, as Heard alleges that she was recast in a blockbuster movie and lost out on fashion contracts with a global brand.

If you visit the original op-ed article by Heard, which is behind a paywall on the *Washington Post*'s website, you'll find an editor's note dated June 2022,[15] pinned beneath a photo of Heard looking over her shoulder. It details the case that followed the article's publication, reporting that a jury found Heard guilty of libel on three counts, though, again, it's worth noting that at no point does she reference Depp by name, instead detailing her experiences of domestic and sexual violence, and the wrath she experienced as a result of speaking out.

The editor's note also states that the jury separately found that Depp, through his lawyer Adam Waldman, defamed

Heard in one of three counts in her countersuit. Depp's lawsuit against Heard was filed in Virginia *after* Heard had aided English tabloid the *Sun* in its defence after it labelled Depp a 'wife beater'. Heard took the stand and recounted fourteen separate incidents of domestic violence, twelve of which corroborated the *Sun*'s statement, thus clearing them of defamation. Whatever you feel about the fairness of these highly televised proceedings in Virginia (a Netflix documentary was released in August 2023 in the UK), or their outcome, the case has sent a highly visible message about what happens when women speak out about their experiences of violence at the hands of men.

The weaponisation of defamation laws are known as Strategic Lawsuits Against Public Participation (or, SLAPPs). According to the Solicitors Regulation Authority, SLAPPs misuse the legal system 'through bringing or threatening claims that are unmeritorious or characterised by abusive tactics, in order to stifle lawful scrutiny and publication, including on matters of corruption or wrongdoing'.[16] Misusing the law like this leads to miscarriages of justice, but it also impacts public confidence in the judicial system.[17]

You would hope that gender discrimination and defamation in our post-#MeToo world would have improved. However, the opposite has happened.[18] Men's groups say that in the wake of #MeToo, their rights and liberties have been chipped away, though there is no tangible proof that men face prejudicial treatment that oppresses them or limits their access to opportunity. Research reported on by ABC News in 2018, which stated that 86 per cent of men had not changed their behaviour in romantic relationships post-MeToo, also proves that little has been learnt.[19]

Additionally, research published in 2022 by the *Australian Feminist Law Journal* has found that traditional legal processes achieve little in responding to gendered harm, and that 'victim-survivors encounter the same testimonial injustice typically experienced in the criminal jurisdiction, which harms them specifically in their capacity as knowers or givers of knowledge'.[20] This is because, in Australia, the United Kingdom and America, a claim of defamation assumes that the statement being made is false, and relies on the defence to prove its truth. What this means for survivors of gender-based violence and sexual abuse is that retraumatisation through testimony is an inescapable reality.

In July 2021, the stark increase in defamation cases towards alleged victims of sexual violence caught the attention of Bangladeshi British lawyer and human rights activist Irene Khan, who serves as the United Nations' special rapporteur for freedom of opinion and expression. She writes: 'In a perverse twist in the #MeToo age ... women who publicly denounce alleged perpetrators of sexual violence online are increasingly subject to defamation suits or charged with criminal libel or the false reporting of crimes.'[21]

The *Journal of Trauma & Dissociation* named this an 'opportunity to inflict DARVO through litigation'.[22] DARVO stands for 'deny, attack, and reverse victim & offender', and it is a tactic used by abusers to avoid accountability. DARVO through litigation is something that Alice Snape, a London-based journalist, witnessed first-hand when she found herself reporting on a defamation case in 2023. Snape has decades of experience in the tattoo scene, both through collecting her own tattoos and writing about the artwork and curating it for gallery showcases. Snape's journalistic work, which I have long been in admiration of, often covers themes of sexual violence against women and girls. When her two worlds collided, she found herself in the Royal Courts of Justice every day, watching someone she had once respected sue a woman who had named him as her abuser. The defamation case was brought by tattoo artist Billy Hays against Nina Cresswell, for speaking publicly about an assault by Hays (*Hays* vs *Cresswell*, 2023).[23] Like Heard, Cresswell had written about her abuse online, in a blog and in social media posts. Unlike Heard, however, Cresswell had explicitly named Hays as the perpetrator. As a result, Hays was able to bring a case against Cresswell, asking for £75,000 in damages. For Snape, this was a confrontational moment. 'I was scared,' Snape tells me over a video call one rainy mid-week afternoon. Snape knew Hays personally; she'd even invited him to participate in a gallery exhibition – an invite she later retracted.

'This is someone who knows who I am, who knows that I report on sexual assault. I report about boundaries in tattooing and consent in tattooing,' she adds. 'These were big names and, honestly, that first day that I walked into that courtroom, I was fucking terrified.' Snape watched on in shock from the gallery as Hays attacked Cresswell's character and credibility, calling her a liar in front of the judge. 'I just couldn't believe the arrogance,' says Snape. 'I found it astounding in the courtroom that Billy Hays just kept saying, "She's lying. This didn't happen."' Snape was equally shocked by the tactics employed by his lawyer, which she said made her skin crawl. 'He tried to use other evidence of her past relationships against her, which was completely unrelated.' I circle this in my notebook after I've written it down, not because it is new information, but rather because this is a pattern I have seen repeatedly, where a person's sex life becomes a measuring stick for their credibility. Not only does this echo all the previous points on purity culture, victim-blaming and the myth of the perfect victim – it also tells us that this way of thinking is rampant. I can't help but reflect that it's no wonder women have developed such a profound fear of formal reporting systems and that many prefer to self-censor instead of facing a prejudicial justice system.

I ask Snape what it was like to watch men band together to tear a woman down, and she sighs before answering, 'When you actually see it happening, playing out in real life in front of you …' She pauses. 'I think the scary part of it is that they felt very justified in how they dealt with the situation.' The fallibility of formal justice systems was further compounded by the fact that Cresswell had tried to report her assault at the time it occurred in 2010, only to have it dismissed by the police.

'In her initial police interviews, they really twisted what she said, because she said that it was like a nightmare, and then they wrote down in the police report that "she has dreams about being raped".' Snape is visibly upset as she tells me this, and a silence falls between us as we both digest the implications of this manipulation of the truth. This systematic failure is just one example of how women are let down by the people who are put in place to protect us.

Thankfully, Hays lost his case against Cresswell. The judge found Cresswell's account to be 'substantially true', which means that Cresswell is free to talk about what happened to her, and to publicly state that she was assaulted by Billy Hays.

I'm reminded of how much Amber Heard lost in her trial to Depp in Virginia – her reputation and her career were arguably damaged irreparably – and this is in part believed to be because, in America, defamation cases are heard in front of a jury, whereas in the UK, they are settled in front of a judge. This is something that journalist Lucia Osborne-Crowley muses over in the final chapters of her book, *The Lasting Harm*, an unflinching account of the trial against Ghislaine Maxwell, the former socialite and convicted sex trafficker who facilitated the abuse of many girls and women at the hands of Jeffrey Epstein. Osborne-Crowley's reporting on the trial is astute, compassionate and sympathetic towards all those who suffered at the hands of Maxwell and Epstein. She writes: 'Judges should have the authority to disallow lines of questioning about, for example, grooming, or traumatic memory, that are unscientific.' While Osborne-Crowley is in this instance referring to a line of questioning that was not sustained by the judge, she nevertheless raises a vital point that can be applied broadly to cross-examination tactics that seek to discredit and dismantle the prosecution's argument against sexual violence, or the defence of someone accused of defamation when speaking out against sexual violence.

Wanting to gain a greater understanding of this, I reach out to solicitor Adam Pavey, who is a partner at Beyond Corporate. Pavey has dealt with a fair amount of slander and defamation cases, in addition to appearing in a House of Commons parliamentary select committee on menopause and the workplace. Over a video call one afternoon, he tells me, 'As soon as credibility is lost it's almost impossible to come out of that.' The problem with widely held perceptions of credibility is that the actions of a traumatised person rarely conform to the picture-perfect set of behaviours that un-traumatised people believe to be reasonable. They might speculate on how they might behave in the same circumstances, and conclude that the traumatised person is untrustworthy because of this.

'I dealt with a case. It was a victim of child sexual abuse, and their lives as a result of what happened had been entirely chaotic in terms of substance misuse, relationships, criminal behaviour – you name it,' Pavey recalls. 'So then, when, at a later time, they're in a position to tell people about what happened when they were a kid – by that time they've become the type of person that isn't believed.'

According to the American Psychology Association, women who experience trauma are twice as likely as men to develop PTSD, reporting in 2024 that the lifetime prevalence for PTSD sits between 5–6 per cent of men, and 10–12 per cent of women.[24] This disparity in prevalence between genders is believed to be due to the fact that women are statistically more likely to experience trauma from a young age, which can therefore carry a greater impact, especially when these traumatic events accumulate and compound one another – which is known as complex PTSD, or C-PTSD.

Being trauma-informed is crucial to understanding the complexities of believability, because PTSD changes brain chemistry, impacting the way in which memories are stored and remembered in the body and mind.[25] That doesn't mean that the memories of people with PTSD are false or flawed, but rather that things that might be expected from someone without PTSD, like being able to recall the details of an attacker's face, or the ability to piece together a moment-by-moment timeline, aren't always possible, due to the fact that traumatic memories aren't stored or retrieved in a typical way. This means that when it comes to recounting traumatic events, there can be inconsistencies in the retelling, but hyper-specific details that may seem irrelevant – like what song was playing on the radio, the pattern on the duvet cover or the condensation on the windowsill – may be recalled vividly or come to the fore without warning. This is a result of the brain focusing on a specific detail in order to protect itself from the trauma that is occurring at the time, and the sudden resurgence of these memories is what's being referred to when someone talks about being 'triggered'.

I was diagnosed with C-PTSD in 2022, following historic domestic violence and consecutive sexual assaults in my teens and early twenties. I know, from personal experience, how world-ending and, frankly, reality-bending being triggered can feel. I've found myself curled in the foetal position more times than I have fingers and toes. I've collapsed in store cupboards at work, hyperventilating; found myself unable to wash, or brush my hair and teeth, all because a smell took me back to a moment when I was experiencing the abuse again, causing me to relive the trauma, stuck on repeat. Being triggered can feel like being forced to face a moment in your life where something inside you broke beyond repair. That isn't to say that people with PTSD can't recover, or have moments of recovery, but rather that the threads of our very make-up can become snagged on something intangible and permanent. Once the damage is done, it can be very difficult to undo; there is no apology big enough that could ever make up for the life sentence imposed by the trauma. There can never be erasure, or a return to the way you were before. This is why trauma unravels a person, continuously. Sometimes, it isn't possible to have the mental fortitude to be able to ground oneself in the present – a technique often taught to PTSD survivors to help interrupt the brain when it's jump-starting the sympathetic nervous system into overdrive. Sometimes, it's all you can do to make it through the day and hope that the next one is better.

In her book, Osborne-Crowley touches on the impact of trauma, and the need for trauma-informed juries, judges and other legal professionals, so that they have the knowledge to discern between questions designed to make the defendant of a defamation case, or the victim of a sexual violence case, appear untrustworthy because of their trauma, and questions designed to prove actual dishonesty. Osborne-Crowley also states that there should be procedures and support put in place that recognise the extent of the retraumatisation that takes place for someone being sued for defamation. She writes: 'If anything, defamation proceedings are more retraumatising, because victims are made the defendant, rather than the complainant; they are being sued in civil proceedings and required to get up on the stand and be cross-examined on their allegations. There are no support workers, no helplines, no legal aid or funding support to defend the case – or defend their truth.'

I think about how it must feel to stand up in court and relive some of the worst moments of your life, only to be besieged by hair-splitting details designed to discredit you and make your experiences unbelievable. I'm reminded, soberingly, of my own brushes with abuse and sexual violence, and why I never sought legal action. I can't imagine the bravery and courage it must take to put yourself in the firing line like Cresswell did. I simply cannot imagine the trauma of being sued by my rapist. On 3 June 2023, *Cosmopolitan* UK published an article that detailed the terrifying rise in abusers silencing their victims with threats of defamation and legal action for speaking out.[26] The article, authored by commissioning director Catriona Innes and features editor Jennifer Savin, reports the experiences of Verity Nevitt and her twin sister, Lucy, who claim to have been sexually assaulted by a man who, for legal reasons, can be referred to only as 'Thingy'. The two sisters went to the police to report the alleged assaults and rape, but, after hours of gruelling interviews and handing over their mobile devices, the police refused to investigate further due to a lack of evidence. Having been failed by the justice system, the women began sharing their experiences on social media, only to find themselves being sued for defamation by the man who had sexually assaulted them.

The fact that the police dismissed the Nevitt sisters' case should not surprise us. In 2022, Operation Soteria, a programme to deliver cross-system transformational change and improve support for victims of sexual violence by bringing more perpetrators to justice, found that, 'Police force investigators lack sufficient specialist knowledge about sexual offending,' and that 'disproportionate investigation effort was being put into testing the credibility of a victim's account' – something that was compounded by officer burnout and a 'detrimental' lack of capacity and specialist knowledge to train officers on the complexity of rape contexts.[27]

In 2023, one month after the *Cosmopolitan* article about the Nevitt sisters was released, the Operation Soteria programme was released across England and Wales.[28] A year later, Operation Soteria was heralded by Chief Constable Sarah Crew, the operation's senior responsible officer, as a 'true game-changer' that had resulted in an 18 per cent rise in charges for sexual offences and a further 38 per cent rise in charges for adult rape cases. In her statement, Crew does acknowledge that this is only the beginning: 'It is important to note that we were at an early stage of implementation at the time of the inspection and, while the signs are positive and strong, we still have much to do to transform.'[29]

Transformative change can't come too soon, with over 69,000 rapes recorded by police between 1 July 2023 and 30 June 2024, with just 2.7 per cent (fewer than 3 in 100 rapes) of these cases ending in a charge that same year – charges, that is, not convictions,[30] which are at an all-time low as of 2024.[31] This is partly because 70 per cent of rape victims drop out of legal proceedings. As Baroness Newlove, victims' commissioner, put it: 'Chronic delays, record backlogs, and high victim withdrawal rates paint a wider concerning picture. Rape cases are still taking far too long to progress through the courts.'[32]

Rape and sexual assault isn't an uncommon experience that only happens to a handful of women, either. As noted earlier, globally, one in three women (around 736 million) will experience sexual violence in their lifetime from an intimate partner or non-partner. This figure has remained largely unchanged for a decade. It's understandable, then, that towards the end of Innes and Savin's article on the Nevitt sisters, which includes a detailed analysis of the wider problems in popular culture that influence DARVO and weaponised legislature, the two journalists describe their feelings of hopelessness.

'I mean, just look at the statistics,' says Savin. It's the end of the working day and the nights have drawn in by the time I call her and Innes to discuss their article. My office is cold and lit solely by my laptop screen, a fitting environment for the chilling conversation the three of us settle in to have. 'Issues for violence against women [have] always been one of *Cosmo*'s cornerstones,' Innes explains. 'I'm always thinking, *What is the purpose of telling this story? What's the purpose of putting someone through telling this story? What's the purpose of the person reading this story?*'

For Innes and Savin, finding the balance between empowering someone's truth, staying within the law and not dissuading victims from reporting to the police is tricky. 'Defamation and DARVO [haven't] necessarily changed how we report or approach topics,' Savin says defiantly, 'but I would say the conversation has changed massively.' Savin is talking about the increases in sexual-assault charges and allegations made against male celebrities post-#MeToo. Particularly, those of Sean Combs, also known as P. Diddy, who was accused of racketeering, two counts of sex-trafficking and two counts of transportation for prostitution.[33] Combs was able to beat the RICO charges (violations of the Racketeer Influenced and Corrupt Organizations Act) and was found not guilty of two counts of sex trafficking, but found guilty of two federal counts of transporting people for prostitution and sentenced to fifty months in prison. People celebrated this 'win' by spraying bottles of baby oil on one another outside the court houses in a bizarre and grotesque display of solidarity. For those unfamiliar with the case, baby oil was often at the centre of testimonies throughout proceedings, after over 1,000 bottles were found in his home.[34]

Combs isn't the only celebrity who has been under the spotlight. Comedian Russell Brand has been charged with rape and sexual assault, though he has pleaded not guilty, and continues to deny all allegations made against him. Brand is accused of oral rape and sexual assault against one woman in July 2004, and accused of raping another woman in 1999.[35] One of the positives that Savin draws from reporting on these allegations and charges is that the preconception of what a violent rapist looks like is steadily being dismantled. 'They can be charismatic, they can be talented, they can be sociable. And it's this whole thing of a rapist doesn't just pop out of a dark alley.' Innes adds, 'They're more likely to be behind your front door than at the end of the alleyway.'

One thing Savin, Innes and I share as journalists is having to be meticulous with the evidence and depth of research in our reporting when speaking on statistics, allegations and charges against men accused of sexual violence before we can even think of publishing. 'I do wish that the general public had more of an idea of how restricted we've always been by courts on what we can and can't report on,' Innes says. 'I don't think people realise how beholden we are to the law and, in particular, to editorial standards.' Innes explains how vital it is to adhere to these protocols to retain the ability to write the stories of women experiencing such hardship. And yet, even then, adhering to these legal standards is not enough to shield Innes's, Savin's or my own reporting, nor that of our peers and colleagues, from disbelief and public scrutiny.

'Working for a women's title, you're always trying to push to be taken seriously,' Savin tells me. 'I suppose there is that extra layer of having to fight for your legitimacy, in that sense.' But both are resolute that – in view of the risks to their personal safety and the impact that telling these stories can have on their mental health – the victims who are coming forward and trusting them with some of the most traumatic moments of their lives must be listened to and supported throughout.

I'm reminded of another paragraph in Osborne-Crowley's book: 'Increasingly, what we are seeing is a war of opposing forces. There is a huge gulf between the cultural progress we have made in terms of having an open public debate about gender-based violence and the largely hidden but very effective legal backlash against cultural change. Legal mechanisms – like the threat of being sued for defamation – are imposing a chilling effect on the ability to speak openly about violence; a semblance of free speech that we finally arrived at, after centuries of silence, with the MeToo movement in 2017.'

This gulf that Crowley-Osborne describes is something

that anti-SLAPP legislation is trying to solve. The key aim of a SLAPP is to prevent information being published that is in the public's interest. But misusing the law to stifle and silence women isn't a new phenomenon. In fact, the story of how this law came into being in the first place shows us that stifling dissent has been part of its identity since conception.

To find out when, exactly, silence became the burden of women deemed untrustworthy and unbelievable, we need to turn the clock back to the moment gossiping became illegal. Defamation comes from the Roman law concept of *'iniuria'*, which, simply put, is the belief that verbal attacks have the capacity to carry the same weight as physical assault.[36] Before the sixteenth century, in the period spanning from the end of the Roman Empire to the beginning of the Renaissance, defamation was dealt with by the ecclesiastical courts (courts held within the church), and the punishments meted out were penance, rather than damages.[37]

While the transformative period of the European Renaissance is celebrated for art and culture, it was catastrophic for women's rights. Women were excluded from pursuing the arts or politics, and from education, with only noblewomen being granted access to literature and literacy in extremely rare instances. Regardless of social status, women belonged to their husbands like property and, as is still the case in some aspects of our modern world, the recurring theme of women's lives in the Renaissance was subjugation.[38]

This theme of subjugation would continue for women into the Victorian era, alongside the archaic development of the law of defamation. In 1903, Van Vechten Veeder, who was a lawyer in New York at the time and would later become a US federal judge, was so troubled by defamation's murky and difficult to trace origins that he determined to get to the bottom of things. He was able to trace defamation's roots back to medieval England, where many of the Commonwealth's legal systems still stem from today,[39] with defamation ultimately becoming 'a mass which has grown by aggregation'. Veeder declared that the resulting law is one that is 'open to criticism for doubts and difficulties', before surmising that defamation is 'absurd in theory, and very often mischievous in its practical operation'.

Meanwhile, during the Victorian era in Britain, extra protections to women's virtue and chastity were introduced that protected them from certain forms of defamation.[40] This type of defamation was known as sexual slander. In today's parlance, you could describe it as slut-shaming of epic proportions. The UK's Slander of Women Act 1891 protected women from sexual slander until it was repealed by the Defamation Act 2013.[41] Sexual slander centred around protecting a woman's reputation in instances where she had been accused of adultery and, unlike libel and slander, didn't necessitate 'special damage' (a loss of income or earnings) to be actionable. This made it easier for women to sue, because it removed the necessity of having to prove economic loss, which was a tricky barrier to overcome, as many middle and upper-class women were unlikely in any sort of paid employment and had no right to a bank account in their own name. Nevertheless, women brought actions in their thousands to try and clear their names of slanderous slurs of prostitution, unchastity, fornication or adultery.[42] What seems clear is that attitudes of the time were perversely focused on women's purity, and that attempts to defame a woman's character based on these sex-obsessed notions were rife enough for women to need protection from them.

In the US, the highly gendered nature of this specific kind of slander exacerbated racial and class tensions in the US, particularly in North Carolina, where rumours of 'illicit sex', or interracial relations, were circulated by European settlers, reinforcing burgeoning contempt for African Americans. Slander of this nature was often done with the intention of maligning wealthy neighbours, or to denigrate white women as 'whores'. These sorts of slurs in the context of North Carolina's growing slave economy entrenched the interconnected notions of class, gender and racial hierarchies. The Slander of Women Act was framed in the United States as a means of protecting 'innocent injured females', yet determining who would be deemed innocent enough to be injured by such slander and worthy of protection was based on deeply problematic and harmful prejudices.[43] The false accusations levelled against women were done with the intention of reminding them of what would happen if they stepped out of line. For white women, it would mean a reputation in tatters, ostracisation from the family, being unable to remain in work or find lodgings. For Black people, all these things were true too, along with other compounding factors, not least the prejudiced belief of Black women and men as being sexually lewd, which predated the Victorians and was a well-established stereotype.[44] With the courts of the time keenly in favour of eugenics, and, given the prevailing belief that interracial relationships were degenerative, many Black people found themselves institutionalised as punishment; sometimes for life.[45] All in all, the weaponisation of defamation during the nineteenth century was motivated by the need to control and punish.[46] Over a century later, has much changed? In short: no, not really.

In our modern world, our perceptions of gossip and women's speech haven't changed much from those in the past. Gossip is still thought of as belonging to women – and, more specifically, working-class women – and as a less intellectual form of communication. Today, women are often negatively associated with being overtalkative, or gossipy. In an article in *Psychology Today*, Dr Valerie Fridland writes, 'Literature and popular culture tell us to expect strong silent types to be named Tom, rather than Tiffany,'[47] and we see this play out from Heathcliff to Prince Charming – male protagonists say little and settle things by sword or fist, simultaneously communicating their feelings (usually jealousy, possessiveness or anger) and reinforcing machismo as the most powerful expression of masculinity.

Picture not being able to hear your best friend speak ever again. Your sister, your mother, your wife. Imagine the presence of their body, but not their voice, laugh or cry. And no, this isn't something fresh from a work of fiction. It is not *The Handmaid's Tale*. It is something happening now. In 2024, the Taliban, a militant group built on Islamic fundamentalist ideology, considered a terrorist organisation by the US Government,[48] and closely monitored by the UK Government for its associations with the Haqqani network (a known terrorist organisation),[49] announced a new law that would ban women from hearing other women's voices *anywhere*.⁵⁰ This new restriction follows the announcement that Afghan women could no longer speak in public.⁵¹ But this isn't a new form of gender-based violence we're witnessing. Aristotle wrote in *Politics* that 'silence is a woman's glory, but this is not equally the glory of man',⁵² which is broadly believed to be paraphrased from the Greek poet Sophocles' tragic play *Ajax*.

When women are coerced into silence, the threat of dismemberment, figuratively or otherwise, looms over their heads like a guillotine, ready to sever their bodies from their voices. I'm not being hyperbolic here. Women have often been the subjects of dismemberment throughout popular culture. There's the ancient Greek myth of Philomena, whose tongue was cut out after a sham marriage and brutal rape to ensure that she couldn't speak of what had befallen her. Her only recourse was to weave the story into a tapestry so that her sister could know her plight.⁵³ Then, there's Shakespeare's Lavinia in *Titus Andronicus*, who had her tongue and hands removed in attempts to prevent her from naming her attackers.⁵⁴ Even the Little Mermaid's voice is sacrificed to stop her singing and speaking.

Historically, women have long been prevented from vocalising, gesturing, signing and speaking in public, for being too loud and gregarious. Those who do not heed these cultural teachings are quick to be labelled as glib, frivolous or overfriendly. Take this extract from the Book of Deuteronomy, the fifth book of the Torah in Judaism: 'A loud-mouthed, talkative woman is like a trumpet sounding the signal for attack, and any man who has such a wife will spend his life at war.'⁵⁵ While talkative women are regarded with disdain by chauvinists, misogynists and sexists alike, this is compounded further by age and beauty. A young, pretty, chatty girl might be regarded as endearing, because of her naivety and youth, but an older woman, particularly one that doesn't align with youth-obsessed beauty standards, might be met with disgust for not sticking to her gender role.

As young girls, we are taught that to be tormented is to be wanted – that kicking, hair-pulling, bra-strap-twanging and all manner of physical assaults are demonstrations of desire. This is not only confusing but dehumanising. It signifies that a young girl's body is not her own. When she is subjected to unsolicited touching and attention, we blame her for having breasts and hips that are beginning to round out. Girls are congratulated on pertness, fullness, flushed cheeks and wide eyes. Then, all of a sudden, they wake up to find themselves being leered at by the men in their lives: teachers, friends, family members. Quickly, they learn that visibility comes with a price.

I'm reminded of a stat shared earlier in this book; that in 2021, 97 per cent of women aged eighteen to twenty-four reported that they had experienced sexual harassment in public spaces.⁵⁶ Furthermore, a 2020 report by the UK Government found that women, young people (ages fifteen to thirty-four), ethnic minorities (excluding white minorities), LGB individuals and those with disabilities were significantly more likely to experience forms of sexual harassment.⁵⁷

This means that from the get-go, there is an inherent understanding shared between women and other marginalised folks that setting clear personal boundaries or expecting adherence to laws is foolhardy when it comes to matters of the flesh. When, during a debate on domestic abuse, Baroness Jenny Jones made the internet-breaking statement that she 'might actually put in an amendment to create a curfew for men on the streets after 6 pm, which I feel will make women much safer'. This incited the hashtag 'CurfewForMen', which rapidly gained traction with women sharing stories of harassment and assaults across social media. The idea of a curfew for men was met with disdain and belittled by the likes of Nigel Farage, as well as the general public.[58]

The problem we are facing is that men's violent and sexually motivated behaviour is regarded as normal. It is an extension of masculinity and so must be expected and manoeuvred around. While young girls are seen as temptresses, or labelled as 'jailbait', men are seen as blameless for surrendering to imaginary seduction and lewd, often violent action. Then, as we metabolise these encounters with men as we grow up, we learn to live day to day with varying forms of sexual harassment and violence, while men continue to blame women for their criminal actions.

The trial of *Depp* vs *Heard* only reinforced these notions. It showed us why the interpretation of the law and its intersection with a person's character matters. It appears that, perhaps in America more acutely than in the UK, women's value hangs on race and purity; only so-called 'good women' are deserving of protection from the law, as it protects innocence. But what about women who aren't deemed by society to be innocent? What about 'bad women', 'nasty women', 'trouble-making women'? Are they less worthy of protection?

Fomenting distrust in women, particularly women with protected characteristics, is dangerous – even life-threatening. It makes us ignorant of the way our world works and desensitises us to the horrors that we can and do enact upon one another. This is why trusting in oral traditions, like whisper networks, gossip and girl code, and learning from them is crucial to the broadening of our empathy.[59] We often reflect on the horrors inflicted upon women of the past to remind ourselves that, in many ways, life as a woman isn't as bad now as it once was. But the violence we experienced historically has now evolved into something less detectable and even more difficult to hold to account, like image-based abuse and deepfakes (non-consensual pornography created with AI). Are these experiences any less violent or violating because they lack physical touch? Is having your nudes leaked to the internet any less reputation-destroying than being perceived as lacking the 'sexual honesty' required in the medieval age? Plus, these historical representations of violence that we shrink from in our modern world have far from disappeared in other parts of the globe.

Take the witch trials, for example. We speak of them mostly in historical terms, and yet witch hunts and the prosecution of women who hold wisdom, who are old, who have property and dispense community knowledge is still happening in countries across the world, such as India, where men have used witchcraft accusations to oust women from valuable land they want for themselves.[60] In other parts of the world, like Zambia, Papua New Guinea, the Congo and Tanzania, witchcraft is associated with the HIV/AIDS epidemic.[61] In

South Africa, fifty to sixty bodies of elderly women are brought to Umtata General Hospital mortuary every year who have been implicated in witchcraft.[62] The question remains, why does society distrust women? And why is that distrust met with punishment?

CHAPTER SEVEN

Rags to Reality TV

You can try and stop me or try and keep me quiet ... But the truth is the truth, and it always comes out.
— LISA RINNA, *The Real Housewives of Beverly Hills*

Bitching, backstabbing and sensationalist exposés: gossip's role in entertainment has created magazine after magazine dedicated to drawing attention to the tiniest 'flaw' on an unlucky celebrity. It has spawned entire channels and streaming platforms devoted to watching the rise and fall of affluent women, poverty-stricken teenage mothers, sassy pageant children and total strangers forced to live together under twenty-four-hour video surveillance. This gossip/entertainment ecosystem, where one feeds the other in an endless cycle, is flawed, poisonous and uncompromising. However, this cycle also holds a mirror up to society in a way that documents cultural discourse, spurs vital conversations and provides us with a lens through which to watch how other people navigate the most human aspects of life: love and friendship.

Gossip and scandal will always flourish where there are close-knit social networks and normative homogeneity, whether in a complex or small-scale society. Gossip helps us draw a social map of reputations and trust. It shows us where conflict is, gives information on who knows what about it, and empowers those seeking to navigate the politics of relationships.[1]

Reality TV and the gossip it generates has become a major money-spinner, both for the execs who come up with the concepts, and for some of the contestants, who can emerge to ready-made fame. Reality TV wouldn't be what it is today, however, without the humble scandal sheet, an early form of society journalism that grew in popularity – and reach – thanks to the distribution power of the printing press. These sheets would discuss high-society goings-on, reporting on affairs and scandals, not unlike Lady Whistledown in the Netflix series *Bridgerton*. For the Georgians, scandal sheets offered an opportunity for gossiping in plain sight, a highly titillating activity. As this form of media became more and more popular, gossip went through yet another metamorphosis. Notably, in 1864, an issue of *Bow Bells* magazine, which was considered to be 'family friendly', began describing gossip as becoming a 'more socially acceptable' device for men, and that gossip about art, literature and music was becoming a prominent feature for many magazines of the time.[2]

These scandal sheets were followed by society columns and books dedicated to understanding the relationship dynamics hidden behind moral panic and closed doors. Literary critic Phyllis Rose wrote in her book *Parallel Lives: Five Victorian Marriages* (1983) that 'we all desperately want information about how others live their lives, because we want to know how to live ours. However, we have been taught that this desire is nothing more than unjustified curiosity.'[3]

This insatiable desire to know a little something more about thy neighbour – or someone of higher stature – continued in society well past the turn of the century and into the 1930s. In the US, this time would be marked by journalist and broadcaster Walter Winchell, a notorious New Yorker with a penchant for peddling gossip. Winchell's career as a gossip columnist and radio host spanned three decades, during which time he cultivated a tremendous amount of influence and a massive audience. This was in part thanks to his, at times, polarising opinions, which attracted both admirers and detractors.[4]

This theme would continue into our more modern world, during the information and technology revolution of the West. In 1995, scholars were already predicting the impact of gossip's digitisation, and the subsequent shift of its 'verifiability from reliance on intimate social bonds and assurances of truthfulness to overt negotiations that emphasise honesty'.[5] They also observed how factors like status and hierarchies surrounding digital information shared on message boards are influenced by something called 'negotiated honesty'. This refers to the idea that information is subjective and, therefore, requires reflexive thought in order to determine the truthfulness of what is being shared. This process, which pulls on our emotional responses and personal experiences to decipher the truth of something, rather than the fact of it, leaves room for misinterpretation, disinformation, untruths and misinformation to leech into the way we choose to share information. It is the science behind 'a lie travels faster than the truth', if you like.

Because a lie travels faster – by being more shareable, clickable and potentially readable – scandalous headlines and storylines have become immensely profitable. Money is often synonymous with masculine identity signifiers, such as mass accumulation, wealth and the hoarding of resources. Given that we live in a patriarchal, capitalist world, it's easy to see how we transitioned from the humble gossip sheet to the celebrity blog.

The infamous, eponymous blog by Perez Hilton (real name Mario Lavendeira) is a prime example of someone being able to cash in on this formula because of the immediate access the internet afforded them.[6] Hilton has made a career of lampooning A-listers, drumming up speculation surrounding up-and-comers in the entertainment industry, and trading in rumour and, on occasion, misogynistic language to come for people in the public eye, earning his blog a reputation as the most hated website in Hollywood – a description Hilton embraced.

Hilton first gained traction by posting prolifically throughout the day on the goings-on in Hollywood and beyond. He was the first to break the news of Angelina Jolie and Brad Pitt's relationship, he outed gay celebrities – though he has since stated that this is no longer something he believes in – and his cutting takedowns gathered infamy. His readiness to say the unsayable, to report on the most scandalous stories and to speculate wildly would eventually earn him a reported 10 million hits a day by 2011.[7] Years on from this peak, the hit count is far lower, but in 2021, the *Press Gazette* reported that Perez Hilton's blog was still receiving around 2 million hits a day.[8]

Such was the power of Hilton's opinion that he could turn the public against celebrities, even if they hadn't done anything to warrant falling out of favour. When Christina Aguilera released her album *Bionic* in 2010, he repeatedly referred to her as 'Floptina', a name he has admitted to coining with the sole intention of damaging her sales and boosting those of his then friend Lady Gaga. It's difficult to imagine that someone who began a blog in a coffee shop around the corner from their apartment on the free Wi-Fi could wield such clout, but, at the time, when Hilton shared a rumour it became truth.[9] In his memoir, Hilton describes himself as being 'super petty' towards Ariana Grande for years, after the then eighteen-year-old refused his offer of representation to be her manager in 2011.[10] In 2018, Mila Kunis blamed Hilton for the rise of 'ugly news', stating that she believed him responsible for creating internet trolling.[11] In his 2020 memoir *TMI: My Life in Scandal*, Hilton showed some remorse for his maliciousness, saying, 'I have a ton of regrets, particularly because I now see that I never needed to be so mean or cruel … One of the many things I regret is that I hurt so many people by giving them nasty nicknames, and above all that, I was unkind to the children of celebrities.'

Regardless of your opinion of Hilton's behaviour and his arguably somewhat limp attempts at apology, he was able to capitalise on something that had only been seen as a frivolous distraction from more serious content surrounding the news of the day.[12] Celebrity tittle-tattle is entertainment, and who *doesn't* have an opinion on something a celebrity has or hasn't done? Still, it is how Hilton went about things – in a manner that, in my opinion, could only be described as ghoulish – that has set the tone for subsequent celebrity media.

That said, Hilton was far from the only person using this 'build them up and then tear them down' formula to gain eyeballs and ad revenue. Gossip sheets, tabloids, columns and blogs have always been enormously popular because they all employ the same blueprint. As such, our eagerness to consume the rise and fall of Hollywood starlets like Lindsay Lohan, Britney Spears, Mischa Barton, Paris Hilton and other socialites, actors and celebrities has made the distribution of such gossip all too easy to monetise. We yearn to observe their downfall and pick apart what's left of the carcass. In this way, we torture them – perhaps because they have the things capitalism tells us we should want: talent, success, fame, money, beauty, thinness and adoration. It's all too easy to gaze upon the privilege and opportunity afforded them with envy and to disregard the millions of eyes watching their every move; the endless sea of notifications; the hounding by the paparazzi; the death threats and the stalking, to name only some of the dangers and limitations that come with losing one's anonymity. But our appetite for the proverbial social guillotine has always been insatiable, especially when there is a royal head to cut off – just ask Marie Antoinette, or, indeed, Meghan Markle, metaphorically speaking. Perhaps we should also question whether the temptation to get swept up in the content vortex stems from a desire for juicy gossip or from a longing for the opportunity to speculate on the truth of a thing.

Reality TV, or the bones of it, began with *Candid Camera*, an American reality show that first aired in 1960, though it began life as a radio show called *The Candid Microphone* in 1947. The show's premise was based on putting people in strange situations or pranking them and filming their reactions through hidden cameras. It is widely regarded as the starting block for reality TV, and it ran until 2014, but in its lifetime, TV would give rise to more extreme versions of this programme that placed contestants in a fishbowl – most notably, of course, *Big Brother*, which first aired in the Netherlands in 1999.[13]

Following its Dutch debut, the show was adapted for UK and US audiences in 2000 and was immediately a huge hit in terms of ratings. The show's formula is Orwellian in both name and nature. For anyone unfamiliar with the format, it involves putting several strangers or B-list celebrities in a house together, under twenty-four-hour surveillance. Totally cut off from the outside world, unable to leave the confines of the house and subjected to numerous – and sometimes bizarre – tasks, the contestants, or 'housemates', are all competing to be the last person left, earning themselves a vast cash prize. Contestants are voted out by the viewers at home, based on their observations and perceptions of them.

During the height of its popularity, when it was amassing 10 million viewers, housemates would develop large and loyal followings, thanks to the parasocial relationships the show encouraged, finding themselves catapulted into the limelight upon their emergence from the house. People like Nikki Grahame, Jade Goody, Aisleyne Horgan-Wallace, Alison Hammond and Imogen Thomas gained enormous traction for their highly quotable antics and viral soundbites.

One of the standout features that had audiences tuning in to *Big Brother* in their droves was the diary room, a place where contestants would come to bitch, scheme and emotionally offload about the goings-on in the house and the interpersonal dynamics of their fellow housemates. This space in which housemates could vent also offered viewers the chance to be in on the gossip, watching the drama and scandal play out in real time. The authenticity and intimacy of these moments helped viewers bond with contestants at their most vulnerable, when their guard was down, and to empathise with them, for better or worse.

With the public voting for and developing parasocial relationships with the cast members they felt were most relatable, the production line to transform someone from a normal person to an overnight celebrity was created, and with it, more fodder for culture commentators to gossip about. More often than not, these ordinary people, who had no media training and received none of the wraparound care we might expect today, would inevitably slip up, implode, lash out and create scandal, both inside and outside of the *Big Brother* house, with the public oscillating wildly between incensed uproar and unshakeably fierce support.

From Nikki Grahame's explosive meltdowns, Makosi Musambasi's claims of being 90 per cent sure she was pregnant minutes after a steamy encounter in the hot tub, or Kinga Karolczak's apparent dalliance with a wine bottle,[14] the tabloids and gossip columnists had plenty to write about. Everything that took place in the house was recorded, and viewers could even watch a twenty-four-hour live stream. It was pure chaos, and the cameras meant that very little was deniable, but winning the hearts of the public offered the chance to also win big money and instant fame upon leaving.

Alongside *Big Brother*, other TV shows like *Pop Idol*, *The X Factor*, *Britain's Got Talent*, *Love Island*, *Ex on the Beach*, *Teen Mom*, *Jersey Shore* and *Geordie Shore* all exploded in popularity in the UK and US in the noughties, as members of the public clamoured for the chance to get on TV and turn their ordinary lives into extraordinary ones.

Those who tuned in to watch this sometimes debauched, often heartwarming and wildly unpredictable TV were also fuelled by the endless content it offered up for discussion. But the 2000s and 2010s were a dire time for women in the public eye, and despite the body positivity movement becoming the zeitgeist of 2012, things haven't improved much when it comes to the way women's bodies are talked about or how their actions are scrutinised.

Today, it seems to be perfectly acceptable for individuals to take to social media to discuss, argue, stand up for, denounce and harass people's public profiles, and women's bodies, diets and sex lives have remained some of the most discussed aspects of tabloid media. In the noughties, unflattering images of relaxed stomachs, cellulite and double chins were front-page news, while bone-thin celebs were praised for their skeletal bodies. News website Vox has dubbed the period between 2000 and 2010 the 'bubblegum misogyny' era of pop culture.[15] As someone whose formative years, from teenager to young adult, took place during the period, I can think of no better way to describe the long-term impact that the media's dissection of weight and appearance has had on a generation of women.

This was the era of 'girl power' feminism, followed by 'girl boss' feminism, which capitalised on the hard-won political and social progress made by activists for women's rights in previous decades. We were told that women were supposed to have it all, but more than that, they were supposed to want it all – the kids, the job, the marriage, the home – at all costs. This is where the expectation of women as both housemaid and top-earning career gal clashed with inadequate childcare provision and a property boom and economic collapse that has made achieving these things nigh on impossible a decade later. Systematically, this was the lie we were sold. Even if we were able to scramble together homes near our social and care networks, where we could work but still manage to spend a day folding laundry and doing the school run, we were expected to do it all while looking incredible. And by incredible, I mean thin. After all, even if you had the kids, the job, the marriage, the home, you hadn't really succeeded unless you still looked young and fuckable. How else could you expect your marriage to last or for your boss to respect you? The focus on weight loss during this period cannot be overemphasised. I watched as my mother, who has always been petite, drank cabbage soup for days on cleanses. My friends' mothers would attend weekly WeightWatchers meetings. I vividly recall the conversations among my school friends and me as we shared one school dinner between four of us, terrified of what it would mean to be considered unattractive by the boys in our year. All this was not only a colossal waste of time, but also dangerous.

I remember coming to school in September 2007, to be faced with one of my dearest friends weighing no more than 6 stone. I watched girls in my year throw up their lunches time and time again. In my late teens and early twenties, I battled privately with bulimia and anorexia, keeping photos of thin people in my diaries, swallowing handfuls of laxatives every night, until one of my friends, who could no longer look the other way, intervened. All this was set against a backdrop of empowerment and the expectation that we would win at being a woman by doing this, and yet the goal posts were always shifting. Even the most beautiful people were criticised and chastised. So, when I hear the phrase 'bubblegum misogyny', it brings to mind a sickly-sweet 'you-go-girl' package containing nothing but unattainable beauty standards and rebranded gender roles with unreasonable and damaging expectations. It encapsulates the millennial experience of coming of age and into womanhood, only to realise that the agency sold to you was nothing more than a means of shrinking you down, distracting you and making you compliant.

Even now that I am old enough and wise enough to be able to choose the full-fat option – and indeed do – there's still the little voice in the back of my head that counts the calories, or bargains with a step-counter to assuage the guilt of eating. That feeling has only intensified now that 'thinspo's' dangerous cousin #SkinnyTok has entered the public consciousness and weight-loss drugs are easily acquired with a few clicks. Add to that the use of AI models in *Vogue* reinforcing unrealistic beauty standards that centre whiteness and thinness, and the age of body positivity and acceptance feels truly over.

You may be wondering why these messages creep through in the media we consume, be that on social media platforms or in the press. The truth is, our attention and our data equal money, and nothing seems to capture our attention more than a scandal. There always has been serious money to be made from gossip columns condemning anything other than the highest beauty standards and chaste – though not frigid – dating practices. Men were portrayed as playboys, while women were heralded as beacons of morality until their inevitable demise as sluts, bad mothers, drunks and addicts, with cellulite to boot. There is no greater casualty I can think of from this era than Britney Spears. While many Gen-Zers may only recognise her from her dance videos, millennials will remember her rise to fame as the girl next door whose virginity was always debated, her body and weight frequently commented on, her parenting scrutinised, her relationships torn apart. This decades-long fixation with her produced countless repugnant upskirting pictures – in some cases to 'prove she wasn't pregnant'[16] – and shots of her crying with her children after being relentlessly followed by paparazzi. Nick Stern, a photographer who 'worked on team Britney' and quit after just a week due to the severity of what he witnessed, said in an interview with *Glamour* in 2021, 'It was a culture of male toxicity and bravado amongst the photographers, and doing the craziest things was almost worn as a badge of honour.'[17] Eventually, Spears's 'breakdown' was caught on film in 2007 and her conservatorship began soon after in 2008, with her father placed in charge of her finances, fertility and work schedule. 'The conservatorship stripped me of my womanhood [and] made me into a child,' Spears would later reveal in her memoir,[18] which made scathing accusations of abuse at the hands of her father and conservator, Jamie Spears.

Watching all this play out in real time didn't prevent people from wanting a shot at fame, though. There was so much blame against women for the harms that befell them that there was almost a delusional mindset that if you were to become famous, you would somehow be more perfect. Nevertheless, this new dawn of reality star now also meant that the pool of people who could find themselves becoming front-page news was wider and far less privileged than traditional celebrities. Reality TV has led to people fighting for the opportunity to be recognised and to waive their anonymity in favour of public scrutiny, fortune and fame.

Today, shows like *Jersey Shore* and *Geordie Shore* can feel like a hard rewatch. From the level of alcohol consumed by the predominantly working-class cast, to the sexual harassment, gaslighting, hair-ripping, body-shaming and sex on screen – it all feels like a fishbowl that makes clear the attitudes held towards women at that time. Image was everything, and not fitting into a prescribed beauty ideal was punishable by humiliation.

It will perhaps come as no surprise that the people behind the creation of these shows are predominantly male,[19] which may go some way towards accounting for the gender stereotyping that plays out time and time again. However, reality television also provides a lens through which to view problematic behaviour from female and male cast members, as well as an opportunity to call it out online, write about it on a blog, read about the reactions to it in the press and discuss it peer to peer. In 2018, *Love Island* contestant Adam Collard was called out publicly for his gaslighting behaviour on the show, prompting UK charity Women's Aid to intervene and call out the emotional abuse.[20] This led to a somewhat lacklustre apology from Collard upon leaving the villa, and to much-needed conversations about emotional abuse that extended beyond the incident. Over and over again in these shows, we observe women getting hurt in the romantic relationships they form on screen, while the men involved appear not to care and repeatedly reoffend, and the other women in the group attempt to either support them or tear them down behind their backs. It's brutal, bear-baiting television. The level of public-shame-based discourse has been devastating to some, with Sophie Gradon, from series two, and Mike Thalassitis, from series three, taking their own lives. It was only after Thalassitis's death that *Love Island* committed to providing 'bespoke training'[21] to future contestants to cope with fame after the show. It's my opinion that compassion for contestants during this time, especially the women, was at an all-time low for two reasons. The first is because they had chosen to go on the show, signing contracts that had clauses around embarrassment, which extended to not being liable for 'public humiliation' and being permitted to 'portray them in a false light'.[22] Second is the existing misogyny that was pervasive in the discourse surrounding celebrity women, who were treated as entertainment commodities, and cautionary tales for girls who aimed a little too high. I imagine this left many contestants of reality shows feeling powerless to confront the gossip about them being published and discussed online – and it's no wonder to me that we saw such tragedies as a result, as we witnessed downfall after downfall in the public eye and didn't ever consider the part we as an audience might be playing in their mental health decline.

As time has gone on, reality TV has evolved, taking on other forms for us to watch and become obsessed with. In the beginning, there was *The Osbournes*, credited with setting the stage for shows like *Keeping Up with the Kardashians* and the *Real Housewives* franchise. These shows were targeted at adults, but *Laguna Beach*, a reality TV show about wealthy kids in California during their final two years at high school, was aimed specifically at younger teen audiences. Unlike other reality TV shows that centred around ordinary working- or middle-class people having their shot at fame, love or a mix of both, these shows sprinkled aspiration over everything. From having brand-new cars bought for them by their parents, to getting their hair and nails done in high-end salons, carrying expensive designer bags and wearing the latest fashions, the subjects of these reality shows were 'worthy' of the fame and notoriety. These were not ordinary people; they had the kind of privilege people like me could only dream of.

The success of *Laguna Beach* carried through to *The Hills*, following the same cast members and continuing their scripted storylines as they took on LA, fashion and PR. As a teenager like me, growing up in a disused quarry village in North Wales, watching the show felt like being included in a lifestyle I could never hope to truly be part of. I couldn't have been further removed from the glitz and glamour, and yet it still imprinted on me in a way that's hard to articulate. I knew I wasn't an upper-class, heterosexual American girl from Laguna Beach, and yet, I felt a connection to these people. The parasocial relationships the show created meant that I felt as if I knew Lauren Conrad personally, and if we were ever lucky enough to meet, I could slot right into her world, bitch about Heidi Montag and tell her how much of an a-hole I thought (and think) Brody Jenner was (and is). Of course, I also knew that this daydream was ludicrous, but the escapism was important to me. It also enabled me to contextualise the things happening in my own friendship circles – the bitching, the backstabbing, the parties, the boys (and the girls). I could live vicariously through the on-screen cast, observe the bad behaviour and witness the fallout. I could learn about female friendships and metabolise them without the risk of a misstep. That's not to say that *The Hills* was an example of perfection. It wasn't diverse, it had problematic storylines, it glorified overspending and made it look easy to get the dream job or internship at *Teen Vogue*. But buying into the escapism was part of why it charmed so many of us.

Indeed, I wasn't the only person to become completely transfixed by the LA socialites. In fact, 2007 was a boom year for bloggers ready to share their commentary on everything relating to *The Hills*.[23] This area of cyberspace was trendsetting, creating a dialogue outside of reality TV *about* reality TV and everything it touched on, from relationships and bodies to fashion and even feminism. The noughties marked a new kind of era where women could organise and discuss aspects of their worlds like never before.

Throughout history, we've held a fascination with socialites and celebrities, and social media has put us one step closer to the people we admire and fawn over, giving us 24/7 access to their lives. There are now entire streaming platforms dedicated to reality television, enabling viewers to consume the content on demand. Take Hulu or Hayu, where episode after episode of the *Real Housewives* franchise – a show almost entirely built on the relationships between affluent women – is available to tap into. Reality TV has become our modern-day equivalent of high-society papers, except now, we can tune in and listen to the gossip and scandal any time, first-hand. In a weird sort of way, our attention and subscription pay for the most intimate aspects of their lives to be laid bare. In that regard, perhaps not much has changed since the heyday of the printing press. Our fascination with relationships is an inherent and undeniable part of our human make-up. We long to see ourselves contextualised in the reactions of others. While we enjoy suspending our disbelief for a good storyline, above all we crave authenticity and emotion. We want to connect. We want to be part of the private conversation taking place between friends, because this inclusion is something we all desire in our own lives.

Moreover, the larger-than-life characters and their emotional outbursts allow us to observe the interconnected nature of female friendships in their most extreme, heightened states. We watch girl code in action; we witness the manipulation of and adherence to the politics of niceness. We're led by the editing, camera angles, music and more to read into the unspoken subtext. We're encouraged to speculate, to take sides and create belief systems around semi-scripted storylines of people we'll likely never meet or know. What's more, we can talk about it to each other all the time, on social media, at work, with friends in WhatsApp groups or in person.

I have watched *The Real Housewives of Beverly Hills* countless times. I am endlessly enthralled, fascinated, disgusted and astonished by the pettiness, nastiness, camaraderie, closeness, frivolity, and deep- and surface-level connections shared between the various cast members over the seasons. Where else are you invited to watch the complete self-destruction of a middle-aged child star, or a woman rebuild her life after her husband's been found guilty of embezzlement and fraud? Or someone wearing their fur coat upside down while appearing to be completely off their trolley, or survive an at-gunpoint robbery in a mansion? Where else can you watch someone spin outrageous rumours about Munchausen syndrome? It's the kind of fodder soap operas and telenovelas can only dream of.

Despite all this television gold, though, *The Real Housewives of Beverly Hills* and all the spin-offs within the franchise perpetuate gender expectations of femininity, power and social roles, which can also be harmful. The show normalises some of the more difficult things the women deal with in their interpersonal relationships, like cliques, competing for dominance and navigating gossip,[24] often as teenagers might. Nevertheless, I don't think we should entirely dismiss the behaviour we witness on screen as infantile or brattish – or at least, not wholly. When gossip is shared in dynamics like those of *The Real Housewives*, it is done in an effort to exert social control, or to control the narrative and influence people's perceptions. Why might we want to control narratives in our own, very real lives? Think about it. Years ago, what people said about us held currency – we could be brought into the fold or banished from it. While a bad reputation might have ended in us being ostracised, publicly shamed or accused of witchcraft at some point in our history, today it might mean moving schools, cities or even countries to start afresh. Being in a position where you can steer the gossip away from your own indiscretions can mean safety from judgement, shame and, in some cases, accountability. Controlling the narrative is about maintaining our reputations.

This is why reality TV show's 'characters', or 'personalities', try desperately in reunion shows to claw back their right to reply, and how shows like *Keeping up with the Kardashians* are such important brand marketing tools, not just for the people they showcase, but for those wishing to be a part of the action. That's why the curation of a reality TV show's 'characters' blends popularity, beauty, relationships, and the lifestyles of the rich and the famous. The glamour and debauchery of reality TV presents another fantasy the public have desperately wanted in on: that of progressing from a complete unknown to an influencer and celebrity. While observing gossip is one of reality TV's delights, there's a price to pay for being a consumer of it, especially as a woman. As it's often seen as unimportant, unproductive, pointless TV, women who watch it are assumed to be the same. There's a supposition that they are unable to engage with 'proper' entertainment; that they lack critical-thinking skills. I would argue that this is far from the truth. People who enjoy watching reality TV do so for a multitude of reasons – for the escapism it provides, for example: the opportunity to tap out of everyday monotony and stress.

A study in 2004 found that, by applying psychologist Steven Reiss's sensitivity theory – which suggests that human behaviour is motivated by a range of fundamental needs, offering a rationale for why people behave as they do – they could surmise that people preferred to watch television shows that arouse the joys that are most important to them.[25] Reiss's sensitivity theory argues that people are motivated by sixteen fundamental desires or needs that influence how we think, feel and act. The theory suggests that these are personal to each individual, and that everyone has different levels of sensitivity regarding their needs, which can be uniquely combined and categorised into the following basic principles: power (the need to influence others); independence (the need for autonomy); curiosity (the need for understanding); acceptance (the need for approval from others); status (the need for social standing or recognition) and romantic relationships (the need for love and companionship). The study found that there were three main motivations for enjoying reality TV. The most significant was 'status', with researchers suggesting that the more status-oriented a person was, the more likely they were to watch TV with high-profile characters (even though these 'characters' are supposed to be unscripted, representing real people). The second motivation was 'vengeance'. 'People with a strong need for vengeance have the potential to enjoy watching people being humiliated,' Reiss says.[26]

This demonstrates that there is a strong desire from people who watch reality TV to witness and maybe even participate in the cast's humiliation in order to feel better about themselves. This phenomenon is termed 'humilitainment', which relies on a sense of *Schadenfreude*.[27] Other motivations for engaging with reality TV included social contact, honour, order and romance.

What these researchers suggest is that most people who watch reality television have an 'above average need to feel self-important'. The argument is that the focus on ordinary people portrayed on reality TV gives 'psychological significance to the viewer's perceptions of superiority'.[28] The message of reality television – that millions of people are interested in watching real-life experiences of ordinary people – implies that ordinary people are important. Ordinary people can watch the shows, see people like themselves and fantasise that they too could gain celebrity status by being on television.

However, the study by Reiss and Wiltz could not find any relationship between laziness or a lack of intellectualism and reality TV watchers, which disproves the commonly held belief that people who enjoy reality TV can't think for themselves, or otherwise lack critical-thinking skills. While it's refreshing to see these results, which disprove the prejudices at play regarding people who enjoy reality TV, I'd argue that there are additional factors to consider surrounding why 'status' ranks so highly, particularly when there is a long history of portraying women who want to elevate their status in a negative light. The notion that, to find a level of security, women must marry someone wealthy to raise them from their class has become a stereotype in and of itself. The term 'gold digger' originated in the US in the early twentieth century as slang among sex workers and chorus girls, and has been part of sexist language since the term was popularised by an

Avery Hopwood play in 1919.[29] The phrase denigrates this capitalist-enforced desire for socioeconomic status. Despite this, though, little girls have long been fed the message that their purpose in life is to enter society, marry well and procreate in order to succeed.

Their imposed destiny as socioeconomic climbers is an example of yet another double-edged sword that women must face: marry a man of higher status and risk being labelled a gold digger, or, failing that, be perceived as lacking the class or substance to attract a man of higher status. There's no winning, because women are never worthy of the standards they're told to strive for. Should we blame women for wanting to elevate themselves? Definitely not. But do we? Yes. It's easy to see how negative opinions about women watching reality TV, as well as those who put themselves forward for the shows, can arise unchallenged.

In 2022, journalist Lindsey Spencer wrote an article about whether or not you could be a feminist and a reality-TV fan. In it, she dissects the way in which these shows give us an unflinching insight into people's lives and interactions. While a lot of Spencer's rationale aligns with Reiss and Wiltz's 2004 study, she makes another observation worthy of note: 'We, as viewers, need to analyse reality television as a space where women can be authentic, while criticising problematic portrayals when disapproval is necessary.' Spencer adds that reality TV provides a lens through which we can dissect gender-based blame and shame, as well as inspire mass conversations online and in real life about behaviours that are harmful or worrisome.[30]

The problem with the consumption of reality TV by women, who form the majority of the audience,[31] is the negative perception of the influence it has on their daily lives. However, the gossip-reliant structures of reality TV present an opportunity to examine problems from another perspective. Speaking to *Vogue* journalist Darshita Goyal in 2024, a woman anonymised as 'Natalie' explained that, after finding her boyfriend had been cheating on her, watching a similar story arc play out in *Vanderpump Rules* helped her to make sense of her emotions: 'There were times when I couldn't articulate my anger, and [Ariana Madix's] arc helped me make sense of my feelings,' she explained to Goyal. 'I personalised the show so much that it made my reaction feel proportionate ... [but] while Ariana was being propelled to fame, landing Broadway gigs and Duracell ads, I was seething with hatred all alone in my bedroom.'[32]

This personalisation is something that Dr Danielle J. Lindemann, professor of sociology at Lehigh University, has found to be normal. Research for her book *True Story: What Reality TV Says About Us* found that 'heavy watchers were more likely to think females in the real world engage in inappropriate behaviours (e.g. arguing, gossip) more than males. These viewers were also more likely to overestimate the extent to which real-life romantic relationships involve conflict.'[33]

It is vital when consuming reality TV that we remain attuned to the fact that we are watching a piece of entertainment that has been edited to elicit an emotional response, and that the drama that unfolds on screen draws on some of our most basic human instincts. Research conducted by Professor Robin Dunbar into grooming, gossip and the evolution of language,[34] and our inclination to gossip and form social bonds, is part of what makes *Homo sapiens* emotionally intelligent above other species. Our human ability and need to keep track of the lives of those around us and beyond has enabled us to survive dangerous circumstances. It's why we have politics and social games that test allegiances. It's why we tend and befriend as a stress response.

Reality TV is the concentrated exaggeration of many women's lived experiences, while also encapsulating the hopes and dreams of so many others: searching for love and navigating the ups and downs of relationships; getting over ex-partners; building and developing friendships; seeking adventure and affluence; the experience of parenthood, and so on – all vital components of what makes us human. Seeing these experiences writ large on screen can help us feel less alone as we navigate our own lives. The joy of reality TV is the opportunity it provides to see our actions mirrored in other people. As humans, we are hard-wired to seek connection, and this much-maligned media form ultimately offers us the chance to learn more about what it means to be human. Much like gossip itself, reality television isn't inherently good or bad. It contains multitudes.

CHAPTER EIGHT

Biddies, Codswallop and Witches

That old women are repulsive is one of the most profound aesthetic and erotic feelings in our culture.
— SUSAN SONTAG, 'THE DOUBLE STANDARD OF AGING', 1972

Distrust is such a fascinating topic. You could argue that it pulls on the very threads of our deepest, most primordial fears; our instincts and our innermost insecurities. It also underpins the very fabric of our relationships, dictating their depth and duration. Distrust – like trust – can be inherent, as well as earned. It is both brittle and strong, depending on the circumstances of its pressures. However, for women, distrust is an everyday struggle, which only becomes more complex as we tread the path of ageing, progressing from maiden to mother to crone.

As maidens, our burgeoning puberty means that, while we are regarded as virginal and 'pure', we are also fetishised, likened to ripening fruit or blooming flowers – ripe for picking and consuming, and then discarding. Men and boys are taught to clamber over one another to be the first to have a young woman's nectar running down their chins and thighs, because from that moment on, the belief is that a woman's body is spoilt, soiled and sullied, just like a flower wilting in a vase, or apple flesh browning once bitten. Our youth and intertwining fertility are coveted and sexualised alongside our naivety about sex and our fragile, unassertive autonomy. We are mouldable and breakable because society teaches us to be. Young girls are trained to respect authority and trust in patriarchal norms, which are often reinforced by our female peers. Fear of the consequences that might befall us should we break those rules acts as a powerful motivator to comply.

Motherhood transforms us into the 'Madonna', and as a result we lose our sex appeal. We take on the role of caregiver, one that is taught to us in our maidenhood and that we carry with us thereafter. In this archetype, sex is expected, though not lusted after. It is transactional, for the purposes of childbearing, with the woman maintaining some level of chaste sexlessness through her dutifulness and subservience. Even if we aren't rearing children, this archetype is still applied to those who enter marriage or relationships with men, as it becomes our responsibility to keep them fed, cleaned and dressed. Historically, married women have been the caregivers of the home too. Here, we are productive in our labour, supporting the industrious nature of the traditional provider – the husband or other man of the house, who could be a father or a brother – by supplying unpaid, thankless domestic labour such as cooking, cleaning and home economics.

In 2020, 'tradwives' began trending on social media,[1] with videos and posts that harked back to 'simpler times', the emphasis placed on female domesticity. As *Teen Vogue* rightly pointed out in 2024,[2] tradwives, particularly on TikTok, sell biblical gender roles, but to an increasingly disenfranchised youth, the simplicity of these roles is seductive. Who wouldn't love the time and energy to make some bread or grow some tomatoes? The sell is into more than just a lifetime of prosperous subservience to a doting partner, however – it's an alt-right pipeline that re-domesticates the female population.

When we grow out of the wife-and-mother role, we eventually reach cronehood, our final season – a time when we're no longer seen as productive in the same way we once were, as maidens and mothers, who always have sex and the promise of new life and legacy between their legs. Our perimenopause and menopause strike fertility off the list of goods and services, leaving us withered, dry and without sex. Interestingly, it is also traditionally this period of our lives that is associated with the witch.

As we grow older and unable to participate in the same physical labour of the home, the crone's role becomes one of a different sort of care, that of looking after grandchildren – schooling them and telling them stories, passing along oral traditions and family histories. As with the domestic labour of the mother, this work is not perceived as truly 'valuable', when compared to bringing in a salary, but rather a means to an end when it comes to child-rearing. Despite the gathered wisdom and lived experience of older women, we are seen as undesirable and without purpose. We are forgotten, ignored and left behind.

It might seem as though we're far removed from these archetypes in our modern world, not least because they provide a limited, cisgendered, predominantly white and heterosexual view of patriarchal womanhood. But it is within this limitation that we can begin to understand why, when women step outside of these roles, they are seen as pariahs and duly treated as such. Unmarried, but engaging in casual sex? You must be a 'whore'. A young woman seeking arrangements with wealthier older men? You're a 'sugar baby'. An older woman engaging in sex with younger men? A 'cougar'. None of these labels are culturally acceptable to the broad population, and despite their recurrence and normality, they are not normalised. They all fall under the umbrella idea of the mad, bad, money-hungry woman. These issues are compounded by racially motivated archetypes attributed to Black women and women of colour. From 'Mammie', a racist name given to a matronly or maternal Black woman, to 'Dragon Lady', a term reserved for Asian women, particularly mothers, the racial components of womanhood make for further marginalisation and more complex experiences of oppression. Much of the folklore surrounding these caricatures of womanhood is entrenched in patriarchal and religious tropes. When we move away from seeing these figures as cautionary tales for women, and instead towards seeing them as culture's curation of what women ought not to be – assertive, autonomous, comfortable in her own skin – we can begin to find compassion for who these women represent. The disruptors, the outcasts, the women who most needed us to stand by them. By adopting this approach, we can begin to dismantle the shame attached to stepping outside the norm and point the finger at the culture that is driven by oppressive systems and processes designed to subjugate and 'other'. We can create an equilibrium in a world unbalanced by gender-based expectation and exploitation.[3]

This is perhaps why Butler points out in *Gender Trouble*[4] that there have been 'plenty of debates' about whether or not women have a commonality that 'pre-exists their oppression', or whether this bond that they share is by 'virtue' alone; that is to say, do we rely on our social bonds with one another because patriarchy is our fundamental experience, or because we share an identity as people who are socialised to become women. I would argue that both these explanations are fitting, but there is more to the picture than this. The way in which our youth- and beauty-obsessed society handles older women is to make them disappear if they can't shapeshift into Eurocentric beauty standards. This erasure is a slow erosion, over time, whereby post-menopausal and sometimes pre-menopausal women's identities are suddenly flattened to one single signifier: their age.

While women are certainly made up of more than just how old they are, age itself carries with it numerous nuanced omens and implications. As we age past infanthood, youth and into our adulthood, we continue to learn and grow, and in turn, so does our wisdom. Despite this hard-won knowledge, our authority diminishes in an odd exchange with time. Suddenly, our identity is synonymous with impotence and sterility – perhaps because we mirror men's slow decline into uselessness, we remind them of their own mortality, their lessening sex appeal. Maybe this is why older men often kick back so hard against ageing by 'trading up' to keep their wives young. For the sake of my editor and my word count, I won't unpack here why this problematic phrase is emblematic of the way we treat women. I trust if you've read this far, you'll understand it for yourself.

Women, and particularly old women in the West, are no longer able to perform the womanly role as the maker and carer of children, and for that, we are perceived as unproductive, silly and time-wasting. Older women are often regarded as a waste of resources too, despite the fact that, in old age, women and grandmothers have always shouldered the burden of familial care,[5] carrying tales of interpersonal relationships between family members throughout their generations, and keeping historical documents of marriages, photographs, letters and legal papers.[6] Soon, though we know plenty, our words are more likely to be dismissed and discredited as we age, chalked up to nothing more than a load of old codswallop.

The etymology of the word 'codswallop' is based on dismissive and gender-specific language. According to the Oxford English Dictionary, it comes from the East End of London, meaning a 'woman who cannot keep her mouth shut',[7] and is often used to describe gossip or an overly talkative woman, or as a 'mildly depreciative' term for a person. It's synonymous with 'biddy', thought to originate from the Irish for maidservant, usually denoting someone who is interfering and gossiping without discretion.[8] The broadly understood notion that old women have nothing important to say speaks to what is referred to as the 'authority gap', a term coined by Mary Ann Sieghart in her 2021 book *The Authority Gap*. It disproportionately affects older women in the workplace and across society, and I'd argue that it also impacts the credibility gap, which is gendered in much the same way.

Conversely, as men age, they gain more authoritative power than women.[9] Older women have to contend not only with ageism, but also with the gendered expectations that they must still appear youthful and attractive to be taken seriously, resulting in their expertise becoming overshadowed by a forensic societal focus on their appearance. However, should they overstep the mark in their quest to appear youthful, they'll be attributed other derogatory names: 'mutton dressed as lamb' or 'cougar'. Men, on the other hand, often enjoy greater freedom to age without their authority being undermined, unless by another, younger man – the trope of the 'silver fox' is one only attributed to men, after all.

The perpetuation of the authority gap by these gendered expectations devalues older women and casts them as less capable, while reinforcing the idea that older men are more capable of holding positions of power and influence. We've seen this play out first-hand in America, on both republican and democratic sides. Joe Biden, who was seventy-eight at the time of his presidency, and Donald Trump, who was aged seventy and seventy-nine, were both deemed fit to take office. In contrast, the women who opposed Trump, Hillary Clinton and Kamala Harris, faced lashings of gender- and age-based debasement. Clinton was repeatedly labelled a 'witch', 'shrill' and a 'bitch', in addition to being labelled as too old and out of touch – too much like the 'old guard' of Washington. Comments were made about her 'grandmotherly' figure, as though a person's physical shape could determine their ability to preside over one of the world's biggest super-powers. Harris's experiences of ageism were of a different ilk. Her younger age was portrayed as inexperience, and her ambition was seen as hasty and 'too much'. That's not to say that Biden and Trump didn't get called too old for the job, but their age and gender didn't result in the same discriminatory prejudice – they both won the presidency, after all.

In the UK, female candidates from the Conservative Party, the Scottish National Party (SNP), Labour, Plaid Cymru and the Liberal Democrats have all faced the same sexist stereotyping – notably, the occasion when the legs of then SNP-leader Nicola Sturgeon and then Prime Minister Theresa May made front-page news. The *Daily Mail* ran with the headline: 'Never Mind Brexit, Who Won Legs-it?'[10] after the two leaders met to discuss Brexit and the second Scottish referendum in 2017. Though there was plenty of outrage at the time for the overt undermining sexism displayed by the journalist, who had totted it up as a 'light sidebar', the *Daily Mail* told people to 'get a life', dismissing the attempts to hold them to account for their sexist remarks.

It goes to show that, whatever side of the political divide you sit on, women are not safe from ageist and sexist scrutiny. Women, regardless of age, qualifications, experience, appearance, capacity and ability, are doomed to face these double standards.

In 1972, American writer and critic Susan Sontag wrote in her seminal essay titled 'The Double Standard of Aging': 'That old women are repulsive is one of the most profound aesthetic and erotic feelings in our culture.' In the essay, she details the gender-based struggle women face as they move from child to adult, and the panic-inducing social process of becoming invisible sexually, and the impact that it has on our perceived value. Sontag writes that 'Growing old is mainly an ordeal of the imagination – a moral disease, a social pathology – intrinsic to which is the fact that it afflicts women much more than men.' She does this after observing her friend's fixation on landmark birthdays signifying the end of her youth at each interval, and the sense of grief, shame and distaste she experiences as she passes through twenty-one, thirty, forty and then fifty. At each juncture, a little more of her is lost, Sontag observes, though with each passing birthday the sense of loss is lessened.

Even though this essay was produced over half a century ago, the same sentiment rings true for me as a thirty-three-year-old woman. I went grey at eighteen, and now my temples are white if I let the hair dye grow out. I've watched my collagen production wain, allowing for the permanency of laughter lines, marionette lines, bunny lines and all manner of wrinkles, which have reshaped my face into a sterner, less rounded and youthful image. I've pulled at my skin in dismay. I've had Botox and fillers. I've covered any signs of ageing that might make me look prematurely older or, indeed, the age I really am. We are all conditioned to be captivated by the process of becoming older, for better or worse. No matter our feminist principles, there are always things to push back against, even though the inevitability of getting – and looking – older waits for all of us, if we are lucky.

Sontag suggests we do this because women's value in heterosexual society is dominated by remaining youthful, but I'd go one step further and argue that retaining an appearance of youth, or at least a willing adherence to beauty standards, positively impacts our credibility. It shows that we are still willing to play the game; to disguise our steps towards death and participate in the West's fanatical obsession with living forever. 'For most women, aging means a humiliating process of gradual sexual disqualification,' writes Sontag. Once we are sexually disqualified, what we have to say is regarded under the patriarchy as less important, or 'unproductive'. All of this is tremendously humiliating and demeaning. It's no wonder that the threat of sexual disqualification conjures the fear of social ostracisation so greatly that the only thing left to do is to wage an impossible battle with time itself. Instead, we must choose to shift the shame or eradicate it. Only then can we stop being distracted by the most natural thing to happen to us – to grow old and die.

This erasure of older women happens culturally too, with fewer nuanced representations of fully rounded, mature characters in the media, and restrictive policies in workplaces that push women out of jobs before retirement. Visibility is diminished further by a social policy that ignores the existence of older women and makes equitable treatment impossible.[11] We see fewer older women in popular media, and when we do, it's likely they'll be stereotyped – cast as a grandmother, a lonely spinster or a widow. This creates a conversation that only discusses older women in relation to their age and caregiving potential. It's a soft sort of dehumanisation that reduces our identities down to age and the end of our productivity, be that in the workforce or the home.

Some have called ageism the last socially acceptable prejudice,[12] but it hasn't always been this way. Once upon a time, we listened to what old women had to say and placed extraordinary value on old wives' tales, so it's ironic that it has now become a catch-all term for nonsense. In pre-capitalist society, the social, emotional and physical labour of women was still relied upon in the production of artisan goods and agriculture. However, this way of being was rejected by the capitalism of surplus value, production lines and the Industrial Revolution, which removed power from women and children and forced them into silent domesticity beneath the patriarchal figure, though this was only prevalent in middle- and upper-class households, as working-class and poverty-line women and children were expected to earn money to support their families, often doing dangerous work. The men would take on the role of the breadwinner, and the capitalist construction of the housewife began with the domestication of women.[13]

In the period before the gender roles of today were established, the wisdom of older women was often relied upon to navigate the very real, very likely eventuality of maternal death. For centuries, across cultures and continents, women have relied on the oral traditions of their elders, sisters and friends to help them navigate childbirth. In the first chapter, we explored how the belief in monsters and demons helped women understand the unimaginable grief and fear they must have felt when faced with the prospect of pregnancy, and to contextualise the potential horrors that could befall them. In the early Byzantine period, women would be discredited and looked down upon by the elites of their religion for maintaining the use of amulets and spells as a means of protection. The Graeco-Roman scholar Strabo claimed that belief in these monsters was a way to control the uneducated, while Plato would imagine his utopian Republic with a distinct absence of stories about monsters.

Whatever importance we have placed on these philosophies and opinions, Plato, Strabo and men like them failed to recognise the need women had for a system of care that could protect them from the high-risk process of childbearing and childbirth. While most institutions, scholars and theologians mocked both women and impoverished people for believing in rituals, spells and tinctures, they did nothing to assuage the very real, very valid fears they had, or to mitigate the dangers they were facing. There was no attempt to replace the existing care system with one that could genuinely, proactively care for women. The Catholic Church refused to give credence to anything that could challenge the omnipotence of the Christian God, and therefore ridiculed the notion of monsters coming after women in the night. For the scholarly elites of Byzantium, the beliefs of women and the practices that centuries of women had nurtured for generations became nothing more than embarrassing fairytales to believe in.

While the dismissal of monsters seems like a logical conclusion – and, OK, it is fair to assume that there weren't big snake-women flying around with femicide in mind – scholars and thinkers of the Roman–Byzantine eras were happy to suspend disbelief in female monsters that paid attention to men, such as the seductresses and temptresses, or those that could 'possess' corporeal forms. On the other hand, belief in monsters that harmed women remained ever present in Byzantine cultures and were continually scoffed at as old wives tales. As Sarah Clegg writes, with some passion, in her book *Woman's Lore*: 'In defiance of all the mockery and derision of the church scholarship, our demons were present throughout Byzantine society. If foolish old women were passing on the belief in her, they had a cultural and societal reach that is undeniable.'[14]

Clegg suggests that the spread of these stories was likely thanks to the oral traditions women would take with them to new homes when they married. Men would have generally stayed with their land and inheritance, whereas women would set up in new places, carrying their stories, traditions and care systems with them, sharing them with other women. These stories were often the only knowledge available to women about healthcare, with church scholars able to provide nothing but penance and prayer for sickness, infertility or infant death. However, the women who carried these stories don't show up as named thinkers in our history books, as scholars, botanists or alchemists. In fact, Clegg refers to them as vague groups of so-called 'foolish women', as they would have been regarded. But it was these 'foolish women' who were responsible for our understanding of incantation, spell-weaving and magic, and whose practices can be linked back to the cradle of civilisation in Mesopotamia and the beginnings of medicine in ancient Egypt's Alexandria.

As the strengthening Catholic grip in Europe clawed at power, wealth and status following the fall of Rome, a schism between the old world and the new was stoking a distrust in women's knowledge and the influential power it wielded in the community. The kind of sacred knowledge that had protected women for centuries from the absence of any formal structures of care was soon to be rebranded as evil-adjacent. It took centuries, and many civilisations, to slowly transform the idea of women caring for themselves, and their communities, into a suspicious action – one that would eventually become egregious enough to sentence them to a torturous death. For the idea to become popularised, specific social and political conditions needed to be present for the mass slaughter of women to feel like a rational and proportionate response. Author and professor of history at the University of Bristol Ronald Hutton states in his essential book *The Witch: A History of Fear, from Ancient Times to the Present*: 'It seems that cultures which had defined magic as an illicit, disreputable and impious activity, and in which women were excluded from most political and social power, such as the Greek and Roman (and Hebrew and Mesopotamian), were inclined to bring two together into a single stereotype of the menacing Other.'[15]

After reading his book, I knew I had to sit with Dr Hutton. A few days after fool's spring in 2025, I was in Dr Hutton's office, where I was surprised to find myself somewhat starstruck. His eyes were fixed and curious as he offered me a seat, while I fumbled for my phone and notepad. I explained that I was keen to understand how the witch figure is caught up in female oppression, and to find out more about the role gossip had played in the witch trials. I was also curious to understand more broadly how gossip fuels social disruption, which could cause a moral panic of any sort to swell out of control. How is it that society repeatedly arrives at a point where witch trials and witch hunts are a normal occurrence?

'Because it's normal for most human[s], and always has been, and still is for most of them,' Dr Hutton answers. His tone is considered and affirmative as he explains: 'Basically, human beings have traditionally had a real problem with the idea of genuinely uncanny misfortune, i.e., that if bad things happen to people and not to other people, that's just the way it is. They always seem to want, traditionally, to find somebody to blame.'

Dr Hutton outlines the three categories of blame that are found across the globe in the face of that which seems inexplicable and incomprehensible: first, to blame spirits of the land, fairies and gremlins; second, to focus instead on dead humans, ghosts and ancestors who have been wronged, dishonoured or disrespected; third, to lay blame at the feet of evil human beings working magic, which is where the figure of the witch comes from. Dr Hutton's next point is a stark reminder that there is something far more threatening and sobering to consider in the way gossip, witches and women are interwoven: 'Witches weren't first attacked by men, but by women,' he says. 'Not because the other women thought they were powerful, but because the other women truly believed that they would and could bewitch their children and husbands or disrupt their homes.'

The idea that other women were responsible for the downfall of their peers is an uncomfortable pill to swallow. It has been a long-held belief that witch hunts were started by men in the upper echelons of society – those in power within the church and state. The stark truth is that it was the people, en masse, who went after women. The power of ordinary people's words – rumours and gossip and accusations – were enough to sentence women to death. The idea of women being to blame for misfortune was nothing new, though – before the witch hunts of Europe could make their bloody mark on history, women were already being killed by their communities. The blame for social disruption had long been laid at women's feet, due to a majority-held belief across Europe that women were the more magical sex. Because of this association, they could be blamed for the woes that often befell households due to factors beyond human control, such as pestilence, bad weather, disease and crop failure.

'Even a split butter churn – these things could ruin you, and especially in the Early Modern period, because a prolonged period of bad weather, coupled with a rising population, meant that people were pushed to the margin of subsistence in a way that they hadn't been since the Middle Ages,' Dr Hutton explains.

In his book, Dr Hutton explains that this menacing 'othering' of women was easily ascribed to in the Middle Ages because the idea was 'planted in soil made fertile for it'. The Romans had put 200 women to death in their city only centuries before after they were believed to be guilty of producing a major epidemic that claimed a 'huge number of lives' through the use of *'veneficium'*, a Latin word that translates to poisoning, but also carries with it allusions to witchcraft and magic. As Dr Hutton points out, though: 'According to medical realities, all of them would have been innocent of this offence, and so their society would already have needed to believe in the capacity and will of women to commit it.'

I'm reminded of this when Dr Hutton explains to me that, while men were believed to be able to do magic, they would have to learn it from books or teachers, whereas women were thought to possess the knowledge inherently. 'That's why, when the idea of the witch is disinterred when Christianity fractures [during the Reformation], having damped it down for a thousand years, and [the Church] now begins to encourage it, it's the really ancient beliefs that come welling up again like water from a burst pipe,' he says.

'It can't help but surface,' I add.

He smiles. 'Exactly.'

This knowledge makes clear that women's very identities were underpinned by a sense of suspicion and distrust, and a belief that they had a proclivity and capacity to cause godlike devastation. They were guilty by association, regarded as the fairer sex; the weaker sex; the frailer sex; the evil sex; the sex of Eve, and now, inherently the magical sex. It is in these incoherent tapestries of shame and blame, enforced by centuries of heteronormative stereotyping and rigorous religious interventions, that end with repeated atrocities being committed against women.

Take Rome in 180 BCE – a city, if you'll remember, mythically built on the rape of Rhea Silva by the war god Mars and the subsequent birth of her two sons, Romulus and Remus – and where an unknown number of women (Professor Hutton estimates a likely majority, in their thousands) were murdered in mass trials for witchcraft. Romans 'knew' that women were agents of social disruption who used hidden means to enact their evil deeds. And so, the notion that women were wicked is embedded in the very foundations of Western civilisation. This is why, even today, the idea of beguiling, enchanting, spell-casting, poisoning and cursing still all feel woman-adjacent and micro-aggressive.

There is a link between incantation, spell-weaving and the ritualistic nature of speech we attribute to women and the subsequent weaponisation of these forms of speech against women. It's a violent prejudice that spans centuries and civilisations, which is well documented across Europe, before the witch hunts of the Early Modern period. The witch and women's speech have been interwoven from the first utterings of prayer and incantation.

For those women keeping oral traditions on health and social care alive in Europe during the fourteenth century, a new fear of being branded a witch began to emerge, though the witch trials wouldn't reach their peak until the sixteenth and seventeenth centuries. Disabled women, or women experiencing mental health problems were becoming increasingly likely to be accused of witchcraft. Being shunned by your community could also lead to an accusation of witchcraft, as well as the risk of death. Village bonds were key to survival, but it also made mob mentality an ever-present threat.

Thanks to the mass spread of Catholicism across Europe from the Roman–Byzantine period and throughout the Middle Ages,[16] being accused of heresy would further cement being branded a witch as a spiritual transgression, something Catholics felt aligned with the general malaise felt towards women because of the sins of Eve, and therefore less so a precondition of man. Deriving from the Greek *hairesis*, 'heresy' was originally a neutral word, much as the word 'gossip' once was, and could be translated as 'a choice' or 'something chosen', often in reference to a particular set of philosophical opinions or beliefs. When this word was negatively co-opted by Christianity, however, it quickly became a signifier of someone going against prescribed Christian teachings, and therefore against God, and was an act punishable by death. The term has also been used by Jewish people, but its concept is much less present in religions like Islam, Buddhism and Hinduism.[17] Being considered heretical during this period was deadly. Witches were deemed inherently heretic because of the widely held belief that they used black magic, or *maleficence*, to harm animals, crops and innocent children.[18] As such, those most likely to be accused of witchcraft would be women who worked in the home, with livestock, or as caretakers, governesses and wet nurses[19] – essentially, anyone responsible for health and care work; roles that would traditionally be held by women.

The general belief was that these women accused of witchcraft had formed sexual pacts with the devil,[20] who they supposedly worshipped, thus making them heretics, and adding a particular brand of fetishised slut-shaming to the long list of ways to persecute women, who were expected to uphold impossibly conflicting standards. Given that the Church denied the existence of the monsters that women feared, under the teaching that everything was by God's design and nothing could interfere with His will, it seems deeply hypocritical that it supported a belief in witches. Yet, despite this, their existence was never in question, suggesting that the ideology behind witch-hunting was borne out of a misogynistic desire to enact harm on women.

Of the 40,000 to 60,000 executions that took place during the European witch hunts, the region we now know as Germany was responsible for almost half the deaths recorded.[21] Other countries with high death tolls included Lutheran North Norway and Calvinist Scotland (which executed five times as many people for witchcraft as England, despite having a population that was one-fifth of the size). Dr Hutton explains that those countries with such high death tolls share a commonality in their judicial systems, whereby immense power was placed in the hands of communities to put the accused on trial.

'In places where the body counts are high, populations go into hysteria and sweep the judges with them, or alternatively justice is decentralised. So you have quite a big country and you have a central government, but the central government doesn't spend time on criminal trials. Instead, if you accuse somebody in your neighbourhood, you send up the paperwork to the centre, and if the centre thinks it looks OK, they give you, the accuser, the power to put the person on trial, in which case they have zero chance of escaping – which is the case for Scotland, Norway and Germany,' he explains.

While some data suggests that the number of people accused of witchcraft decreased during the Protestant Reformation, which questioned the established teachings of the Catholic Church, the rise of the printing press brought with it two books in particular that would incite the deaths of hundreds of women in the Early Modern period:[22] Heinrich Kramer's

Malleus Maleficarum (1486), and King James VI of Scotland's *Daemonologie* (1597). The widespread dissemination of these texts, coupled with their authoritative authors' wholehearted – and, some might argue, obsessive – belief in witches, enabled the seeds of hatred to be sown further. The 'fairytales' that spoke of the harms done to women that the Church had scoffed at soon became the ammunition used against women. And while the majority of men in power weren't spearheading witch hunts, they were nevertheless doing little to stop them. Under their watch, patriarchal influences continued to push the narrative of the evil woman. The pattern of 180 BCE Rome was being repeated.

The European witch trials had begun in the fourteenth century and ended in the eighteenth, with the last known execution taking place in Switzerland in 1782,[23] though Dr Hutton tells me that in his research he has found evidence of hunts and trials in the UK up until the 1940s. This might sound astonishingly recent, yet there are numerous countries where a belief in witches, witch trials, and executions for 'witchcraft' are still common practice.

It's worth pausing here to take in the magnitude of what this means. For 400 years, women, predominantly, were hunted, persecuted, tortured and killed – for nothing. Before that, the historical precedent for dealing with disease, famine, dead livestock, drought, infant death, maternal death, any number of natural disasters or poor fortune was to blame women and kill them. Still more uncomfortable to consider is the notion that gossip, the very tool that can be used to bring communities together and empower the disenfranchised, was inextricably linked to these moral panics and the mass spread of misinformation they spawned.

When the witch trials did eventually come to an end in Europe, it was thanks to a concoction of scientific advancements and the end of a period of political uncertainty and war.[24] 'Initially, science inspired witch-hunting,' Dr Hutton tells me, adjusting his glasses, 'because you have this theory of a demonic conspiracy, and people do confess to it, admittedly – though usually when tortured.' Increasingly, however, courts became sceptical of the inhumane methods used for proving a witch's guilt[25] (though it did take them four centuries to care). Even then, as Dr Hutton reminds me, the real reason for the end of witch hunts in Europe wasn't because they were suddenly deemed inhumane – it was because they didn't work.

'Witch-hunting is a way of testing a [conspiracy] theory. You find that it doesn't work. It doesn't produce a better society, a better world. It just seems to do damage, traumatise everything, and the lagging question of the evidence just gets bigger and bigger.' Hutton goes on to explain how it was lawyers who first raised questions about the efficacy of the process. 'There's just no way securely of proving that somebody is a witch unless they confess. And if they are confessing, how do you show that they're not terrified, mad, or that they're not simply confessing to get other people into worse trouble; for instance, children and adolescents – who are responsible for a lot of the stories across Europe, and got the adults killed?'

Towards the end of my conversation with Dr Hutton, we turn back to gossip, and the role it played in perpetuating the misogyny of the witch trials in Europe, as well as witch hunts that had gone before and those that are still happening in the world today.

'Gossip is integral to witchcraft, suspicion and accusation. We as a species are good at getting swept up in moral panics. We're also good at conspiracy theories, and witch-hunting is the ultimate conspiracy theory and the ultimate moral panic.'

Between 1644 and 1647, self-proclaimed witch-hunter Matthew Hopkins, who was a lawyer, and his assistant John Stearne, were successful in turning gossip into witchcraft accusations, killing over 100 people.[26]

As much as gossip has proved itself an immensely destructive social force, responsible for many needless, violent deaths – as Dr Hutton explained, we should see the witch hunts as a form of 'power of the people gone wrong' – we can choose not to repeat these mistakes.

And yet, around the world, particularly in Commonwealth countries, or those that have been invaded by European powers, witch trials remain endemic and are still perpetuated by community gossip. It takes a village to hunt a witch. India is one such place, with a long history of witch-hunting that still plagues it to this day.[27] In June 2023, a middle-aged woman named Salo Devi was allegedly beaten to death by villagers in Jharkhand for practising witchcraft.[28] When her husband, sister and sister-in-law came to her rescue, they were beaten too. This is far from an isolated incident, with India's National Crime Records Bureau reporting that 2,500 people were chased, tortured and killed in witch hunts between 2000 and 2016.[29]

In other places across the globe, like Papua New Guinea, which is experiencing worsening socioeconomic conditions, including a complete collapse of the healthcare system, accusations of witchcraft still threaten lives and are becoming ever more prevalent.

Similarly, in rural areas of sub-Saharan Africa, a misunderstanding of disabilities and albinism can be enough to sentence someone to death. The problem is so rife that the Human Rights Council released a 'special resolution' in 2021 that called for the elimination of harmful practices related to accusations of witchcraft and ritual attacks.[30]

As much as we might like to think we've moved on from witch hunts in the West, we still run to grab our torch and pitchforks when looking for someone to blame. The Southport attacks in Lancashire in 2024 are a prime example of this. Axel Rudakubana targeted a dance class and stabbed and murdered three young girls, a depraved crime that is unforgivable. Seventeen years old at the time of the crime, Rudakubana wasn't named by police until criminal proceedings took place. This was a legal requirement to uphold the integrity of the case. In the absence of information, a vacuum of misinformation and malinformation (a term that describes a type of information dissemination with the intent to mislead and harm) quickly misnamed him as 'Ali al-Shakati', without an official source. Across social media, predominantly on X, 'influencers' like Andrew Tate, who is facing numerous charges for human trafficking and rape, posted that Rudakubana was an 'immigrant' who had 'come over on a boat'. 'The soul of the Western man is so broken that when the invaders slaughter your daughters, you do absolutely f****** nothing,' said Tate. This led people to take to the streets of Stockport, in a surge of Islamophobia that saw bricks thrown at mosques, people attacked and nationalistic, xenophobic rhetoric being screamed at anyone who 'didn't look British' (read: white).

The truth was that while Rudakubana was Black, he was a Cardiff-born British citizen with Ghanaian heritage. He was also not Muslim. However, the rage-bait that had been perpetuated online was enough to ignite a powder keg of hate aimed at innocent people. And once the misinformation-driven witch hunt had begun, it became hard to rein it in.

In contrast, on 26 May 2025, Paul Doyle, a white man in his fifties, drove into a crowd of people in Liverpool, injuring hundreds, including two young girls.[31] Merseyside Police were able to reveal Doyle's personal details because of his age. While some have argued that more could have been done to disseminate the information more quickly, the transparent approach to who the suspect was and the status of his citizenship led to any misinformation online being soon dismissed. No one took to the streets, and his crime was not considered an act of terrorism. Just a white man having a bad day.

Predictably, headlines surrounding Rudakubana were inflammatory, calling him a 'coward'[32] and 'evil',[33] while Doyle was quickly humanised as a 'father of three' and an 'ex-Royal Marine'.[34] I'm not suggesting that Rudakubana deserved to get off as lightly as Doyle did in the press. His actions were heinous, but so too were Doyle's. So why did we quickly ask the public to cut him some slack? Why did we need to know he was a father? The lack of fairness in the reporting is worthy of further investigation.

We must ask the question, why do we need to know a person's race to prevent racially motivated hysteria en masse? Why does someone's citizenship matter when it comes to male violence? While misinformation and community gossip certainly help to stoke the flames, the prejudicial embers of hatred are already there. White men thrown on the pyre seem to act more like damp wood than men of colour, who are like tinder. One fizzles and sputters, while the other catches and spreads like wildfire.

We must remember that racially motivated attacks on civilian populations as a result of someone else's crime are not reasonable responses. More innocent people are harmed; more lives are ruined. And nobody will feel that more keenly than Muslim women, who experience some of the worst misogyny in the UK.[35]

What we must take from this is the knowledge that gossip can drive people either towards atrocities or towards community. It can divide us, leading us to turn on one another and drive out or scapegoat those we perceive to be outsiders. If we employ rational, critical thinking to moments when we get swept away in moral panics that are baseless and unfathomably destructive, we can avoid future witch hunts from happening to more marginalised communities.

CHAPTER NINE

Tea

An archaeology of gossip can liberate the ways we understand history, opening up new horizons of queer possibility.

— EDWARD SIDDONS, *The Common Ear*

Throughout the process of writing this book, I've been savouring the thought of writing a chapter on gossip in relation to the queer community, but I've been nervous about it too. Each piece of research I've done into gossip and the LGBTQ+ community – *my* community – brings with it pangs of sadness and anger, as well as moments of joy, familiarity and, of course, immense, unshakeable pride.

Gossip, in its most simplistic form, is an oral history; an evolving language that carries with it culture, news and, at times, a sense of knowing what it means to be on the fringes of society. The LGBTQ+ community's relationship with gossip is about necessity and urgency in equal measure. Gossip embodies the need to whisper, to warn, to teach, just as it can be intended to titillate, manipulate and cause harm. All this has made it a formidable and necessary tool for those of us who do not fit the cookie-cutter shape of hetero hegemony.

Journalist Edward Siddons's seminal essay 'A Common Ear', published in *Tank* magazine in spring 2017,[1] helped my research about gossip within LGBTQ+ communities fall into place in a delightfully stirring fashion.

Siddons's essay recognises that so much of history is written by the victors – who just so happen to comprise predominantly white, heterosexual men. As a result, there is very little contained in the history books about who LGBTQ+ folks truly were – how they lived, loved, survived and, in some cases, thrived, in spite of the times they lived in.

Siddons writes:

> Gossip is camp communication par excellence. Anarchic but not revolutionary, disrespectful but not damning, parody but not pastiche, it sublimates information into gaseous data that expands into any space available. Its modus operandi is a carnivalesque disrespect for boundary, and its mercurial refusal to ever stay put has lent it power as both intimate whisper and political weapon throughout queer history.

Siddons captures the joyous duality of gossip; its ability to convey both joy and action, purpose and frivolity; the way in which it can act as both a device for social mobility and a source of raucous entertainment mirrors the complex existence of LGBTQ+ folks in contemporary society, historically or otherwise. More specifically, Siddons touches upon the untouchable and untameable nature of gossip. It can't be stopped or reined in – people will always seek to talk about, or to, other people. It's as natural as any other human quality.

However, for LGBTQ+ people, gossip has an additional dimension that serves to record histories that cannot – or could not – be written. Gossip is a keepsake in these instances, telling the truth about lives from within the community, and how they lived during a time that criminalised their existence. The leftover artefacts, like letters and diaries, give us glimpses into the true lives of historical LGBTQ+ people passing under the radar with their friends and companions. It is the gossip shared in these documents that lends these artefacts such historical significance, as work is done to queer the past and remove the shame from those who could have been persecuted for living brazenly in the open – a privilege shared only by a small handful of the bourgeois class.

For queer people, living openly in the West is still a relatively new privilege – and one that is not wholly recognised by the legal system, including law enforcement, where there already exists a deficit in trust from centuries of brutality. Existing outside of heterosexuality – especially white heterosexuality – still carries with it dangers and prejudices, particularly for transgender women of colour, who are most at risk of all forms of minority-motivated violence. Rights for LGBTQ+ folks in the UK and most other developed nations have been hard won, and only recently, with many monumental changes to the law happening in the last twenty or so years.

In the UK, the Civil Partnership Act was passed in 2004, which granted similar rights to marriage for same-sex couples. The year before, the offence of 'gross indecency', which referred to the criminalisation of sexual relationships between men, even in private, was repealed, having been illegal since the Criminal Law Amendment Act 1885. Then, in 2013, legislation was passed to allow same-sex marriage.

These new rights were widely condemned by those who opposed same-sex marriage, who, in the same breath, insisted that this opposition wasn't – or shouldn't be considered – homophobic.[2] It's clear that progressive action for marginalised people in the queer community is often met with an aggressive and immediate backlash, which refuses to take accountability for its vitriolic nature.

Homophobic behaviour and a refusal to acknowledge the harm it inflicts is something we see time and time again among anti-LGBTQ+ activists and some right-wingers. This denial chips away at progressive education and critical cultural analysis like intersectional feminism and critical race theory. Such views invariably seem to link back to feelings of censorship, and the idea that free speech is being prevented by 'woke' nonsense. The real-world impact of these increasingly vocalised beliefs is that we've seen huge U-turns by formerly inclusive, pro-LGBTQ+ corporations like Meta, who, in 2025 decided to put women and LGBTQ+ people at greater risk on their platforms by removing fact-checkers who had become too 'politically biased', according to founder Mark Zuckerberg.[3] These fact-checkers were replaced with 'Community Notes' functions, which purport to empower users by enabling them to 'add context to potentially misleading posts' – a decidedly desperate attempt to capitalise on engagement. This has resulted in widespread misinformation and disinformation about LGBTQ+ identities. Old, grotesque tropes likening gayness and transness to paedophilia and zoophilia have re-emerged, along with notions that sexuality and gender identity set a precondition of predation against women and girls. We've seen these ideas gain traction and detract from the very real problems faced by many women, girls and LGBTQ+ people, like the endemic nature of violence against them enacted by cisgendered men, the radicalisation and escalation of this violence perpetrated by young boys, particularly in the digital sphere, and the systematic dissembling of LGBTQ+ rights in the UK.

The algorithmic push for this kind of content, and the subsequent engagement it creates, increases ad revenue for brands and platforms alike, while the direct payments from platforms to creators make hate speech lucrative – especially in developing countries – as well as consequence-free. Using AI tools, this spam-like content, known as AI 'slop', can be made quickly. Hundreds of pieces of content can be produced, bootlegging other people's work and stoking the fires of hatred against marginalised communities, radicalising their audience by exacerbating their existing prejudices through confirmation biases and a lack of digital literacy.

According to a study by researchers at the University of Southern California, hate speech has increased tremendously across social media. Between January 2022 and June 2023, there was a 50 per cent rise in hate speech, while homophobic tweets specifically rose by 30 per cent, and transphobic slurs increased by 260 per cent. Overall, the study found that hate speech's likes grew by 70 per cent, compared to random English-language posts, whose likes grew by 22 per cent.[4]

Zuckerberg has now also removed Pride and LGBTQ+ themes from the Facebook Messenger app,[5] in a sprint to create a Meta that President Trump can throw his weight behind, despite the fact that Zuckerberg appeared at the Pride parade in San Francisco in 2013,[6] flags and all. While social media is one thing, we might think it's harder for rights to be stripped from law and government policy. Unfortunately, we're increasingly seeing that this isn't the case.

In 2024, Wes Streeting, Labour's secretary of state for health and social care, passed a bill banning the prescription of puberty blockers for under-eighteens experiencing gender dysphoria or gender incongruence. The bill came about following an investigation into gender-identity services for children and young people by paediatrician Dr Hilary Cass. Dr Cass's subsequent report, the Cass Review, has been described by journalist Serena Smith in *Dazed* as 'hazardous' and 'traumatizing',[7] and has been criticised for its methodology. I'd guess that the bill being passed in 2024 had something to do with the moral panic that has been whipped up about trans people – and particularly trans youth – a panic that has been made possible by the same free speech that is apparently under such censorship.

Perhaps we should have seen this coming, though. History is a cruel prophet. We only need glance over our shoulder to see that the hurts of the past are easily and often repeated; that rights can be stripped instantly and the freedoms we've come to accept as part of normal life can be eroded by a tormenting and tumultuous ocean of hate. All it takes is a carefully orchestrated storm to stir up the frenzied moral panic and give permission for homophobic rhetoric to proliferate. What is perhaps most upsetting is the knowledge that nothing is likely to change as long as power remains in the hands of those without the empathy to truly understand the magnitude of the harm such decisions inflict on those whose freedoms they limit. To put it plainly, and to paraphrase Pastor Martin Niemöller's famous poem, 'First They Came': if the powers that be unapologetically come for the rights of the most marginalised, concealing their hatred and need for control under concern, then your rights and freedoms are undoubtedly next in line.

On a more joyous note, though, it is this level of impermanency when it comes to the rights of marginalised groups that means the power of gossip can never diminish. The connections and codices are all key to preserving proof of existence and experience – they are affirming and powerful, like hands held beneath a table, or stolen glances in plain sight. The stories we tell one another echo the lives of marginalised people from century to century. Even today, it is unlikely that you'll be taught why so many gay men didn't make it to old age while at school. In fact, you're probably more likely to learn this important piece of cultural history from community teachings about the hardships of those forgotten by our heteronormative society. After all, LGBTQ+ experiences are not considered curriculum-friendly, thanks to the lingering notion that homosexuality is some kind of perversion of nature; that failing to embody heterosexuality and the biological purpose of reproduction is some sort of pathological mental illness, a deviance akin to paedophilia.

This is why gossip has transcended time for the LGBTQ+ community. Whether it takes the form of hushed voices filled with concern, nasty words, reputation-ruining rhetoric, vitriolic warning shots, scandalous news or genuine outreach and community care, there is a shared knowledge that to speak plainly out in the open may come back to bite you.

Edward Siddons writes in his essay, *A Common Ear*, that the history of LGBTQ+ people often resembles 'elegy, rather than eulogy' – looking back opens wounds, and witnessing the lack of progress rubs salt in them. As a result, extrapolating from LGBTQ+ history to find the perspectives of those who lived it is almost impossible. As Siddons says: 'Our histories are hidden beneath centuries of censorship.'

Language plays a vital role in deciphering how people lived under such oppressive censorship, making it crucial that we preserve elements of gossip from the past so that we can retrospectively analyse the lives of those forgotten: the poor, the downtrodden, the gay. By doing so, we might learn a thing or two about how to survive the onslaught of online hate speech and the whipped-up public fury at LGBTQ+ people who are merely existing within a system that proactively harms them. Perhaps one of the most notable ways in which people within the gay community used language to protect themselves and others was Polari, an 'anti-language' born and mutated from a type of Italian that was adopted by gay men, sex workers, carnival workers and seamen. Polari is estimated to have existed between the 1930s and the gay liberation movement of the seventies, and while there would certainly have been lesbian and bisexual women and men who spoke it, there's an argument that even straight women in proximity to the gay community would have known a word or two.[8]

Polari is described as an 'anti-language' by Paul Baker, a professor of English language at Lancaster University and author of *Fabulosa! The Story of Polari, Britain's Secret Gay Language*, because, unlike a conventional language, which offers transactional translations, it is encoded with something additional. He describes this in his book as 'a kind of "us-against-them" worldview within the meanings of words'. This shows us how language can be used to capture the alternative lived reality of LGBTQ+ people, in the values of 'anti-society', instead of reinforcing mainstream norms. Indeed, anti-language is a disguise of sorts, but it also 'mocks' mainstream society. Polari, for example, had numerous mocking words for 'police', such as 'Lilly' or 'Lilly law', 'Hilda Handcuffs', 'Betty Bracelets', 'Jennifer Justice' and, my personal favourite, 'orderly daughters'. This shows us that Polari was more than a disguise; it was a subcultural attitude that subverted institutional harms with absurdity and very good humour. 'We might ask whether or not this feminization [of the police] was properly intended as an insult, especially as Polari speakers "christened" one another with female names and often used them with real affection,' writes Baker, although he suspects that, when all is said and done, the feminisation –or 'femme-inisation' – of the police officers *was* meant to insult. 'They knew that the police would have hated them,' he concludes. This subversion was common in Polari. Take the pronunciation of 'homosexual', for instance. In Polari, it would be pronounced as *'homma-sex-yul'*, in a drawling, posh voice to express the contempt queer people felt when being referred to as such by the law or in medical textbooks. Baker describes 'homosexual' as a 'sneery kind of word' that was 'used in contexts where such people were often categorized as criminals or mentally ill, at best objects of pity'.[9] It is this kind of sentiment that Siddons shares in his *Tank* essay. I'm reminded of a particular segment where he writes, 'Gossip murmurs through time, and in tracing it we might draw up a list of prospective ancestors by piecing together snatched fragments, parlour tales and bar talk, and as a result, we might begin to people the queer nation.'[10] This is what I believe Professor Baker has achieved through his research into Polari – a bringing to life of those who might otherwise have disappeared from memory, or we might not have fully known depending on how they presented themselves to the public. Through his work, Baker not only documents the ways in which the anti-language was spoken from a linguistics point of view – which in and of itself is an immensely interesting piece of the LGBTQ+ history puzzle – but he also unearthed the rich humanity behind the people who used it.

One such person was the actor Kenneth Williams. Williams, who was born in 1926 and died in 1988, was best known for his camp, nasally delivered double entendres in the *Carry On* films. Williams was often portrayed as a solitary, sad figure, but his letters and diaries show us that he was actually warm and generous.[11] Baker's research into Williams's diary entries in 1949 tells us a lot about the secrecy that was necessary at the time, even when writing to oneself. Baker points out that his choice of spelling out 'q' (to mean queer) as 'queue' was a means of codifying his most personal entries in case they were to fall into the wrong hands. It also shows us that the word 'queer' was already being reclaimed as early as the forties and becoming part of the Polari lexicon. These diarised archives are immensely valuable to us today. Polari was, and remains, a predominantly spoken form of language, not written, which means there is very little by way of text-based archives to dig into, with few people still speaking it today. It also has regional variations, meaning each person's version of Polari has dialectal considerations. 'There is a good chance that there are other sources of Polari out there, perhaps in letters and birthday cards, home videos or as part of messages recorded on old telephone answering machines,' Baker writes.[12]

The secrecy of Polari is completely understandable when you consider the state of Britain, and indeed Europe, after the First and Second World Wars. Baker notes how, in Britain, any indiscretions and homosexual behaviour of the past were no longer tolerated as the nation, in grief, set about asserting family values and rebuilding Britain. Amid the rising number of arrests for 'homosexual offences' during this moral panic, which leapt from 178 in 1921 to 2,437 in 1963, the casualties included Alan Turing, the man who broke Germany's Enigma code, who was arrested by police after reporting a burglary at his home in 1952. When the police arrived at the property, they were greeted by nineteen-year-old Arnold Murray, who was Turing's partner. Instead of investigating the burglary, they arrested Turing, revoked his security clearance and banned him from working with GCHQ and entering the USA. Later, upon his conviction for 'gross indecency', he was chemically castrated by injected synthetic oestrogen, which caused him to grow breasts and become impotent. Two years later, the man who had saved countless lives by helping to bring about the end of the Second World War was found dead from cyanide poisoning. Turing was not given a formal apology for his despicable treatment by the British authorities until 2009. It was a further four years before he was posthumously pardoned for 'gross indecency'.

However, it was during the postwar period that Polari 'came into its own'. Speaking in secret meant being under the radar, while still having the freedom to express yourself during a time of tremendous oppression and repression. 'There was no such thing as a "safe space" in 1950s Britain, but Polari helped to create a kind of symbolic safe space for gay people of the time by allowing them to talk in ways which otherwise would have revealed their sexuality to anyone who was listening,' Baker explains. He describes it as a 'secret handshake', and a means of 'opening the closet door a crack'.[13] In short, thanks to Baker's research, we now know where this anti-language came from and why it was so sorely needed.

The few remnants of Polari that we have, which we can view through Baker's research, give us an uncensored and intimate insight into the way LGBTQ+ people would relate to one another in the mid-twentieth century, as well as an unbridled look at character, sentiment, humour and personality. Despite that, though, Polari has its limitations: it provides us with mere glimpses into a majority-male world for a period of less than a century. Before Polari emerged on the scene, however, there was cant, another form of anti-language created by marginalised communities to preserve secrecy and 'protect group dynamics in order to survive'.[14]

There was thieves' cant, of which many words have made it into our common language, such as 'slang', 'shoplifter', 'swag', 'rascal' and 'birds of a feather'. Then, there's Cockney rhyming slang, associated with working-class Londoners,[15] *Verlan* from France, *Rotwelsch* in German and *furbesco* in Italian.[16] Still, the problem remains that this examination of gossip through the mouths of men misses a broadly undocumented side of the queer population's experience. So, what can gossip tell us about the lives and language of women who loved women?

It has long been the predilection of biographers and historians to deny the existence of lesbians or same-sex couplings between women, with the assumption that such relationships 'didn't exist at the time' or that women 'wouldn't have known what to do in bed with each other'[17]. This would be laughable if it wasn't such a damaging position to take. Historically, lesbians would have had to keep their love lives strictly secret, because while there were no laws that specifically prevented lesbian relationships from happening, that didn't mean that sapphic couples didn't face litigation and oppressive persecution, or shame-based ostracisation from their families.

There is a pervasive myth that women who loved other women weren't recognised by Queen Victoria, and as a result, they weren't taken to be a serious threat and could get away with living their lives however they wanted. The truth is that women in relationships with other women were at risk of being persecuted for fraud, particularly if those women had married under the guise of their partner presenting as masculine. We might understand this type of coupling as a trans man and cis woman today; however, the courts would see this as an impersonation of a man, and so could (and did) prosecute for fraud. They were able to do this because of the state of women's rights at the time. Women couldn't own property, or have a bank account in their own name, so two women marrying each other with one 'disguised' as a man was seen as an attempt to take something from men that rightfully belonged to them. This was a very specific kind of weaponisation of the legal system that achieved two things: punishing same-sex couples and delegitimising the notion that lesbianism was happening for any other reason than to prevent men from owning property that might have belonged to them. But given that the majority of these cases involved working-class women, who likely owned very little, it shows us that this was a way of demarcating what was culturally and socially acceptable without drawing too much attention to the fact that women could, and indeed did, love other women. They didn't want to be seen as advertising or validating lesbianism with specific punishments and social sanctions.

These types of fraud cases died out in the latter half of the nineteenth century as emphasis was put on women's sexual knowledge being pretty much non-existent in order to be considered marriage material. That didn't result in a culture of tolerance, though. Neither did it mean that lesbians ceased to exist, of course. As late as 1929, 'Colonel Barker', an officer of the National Fascisti, was found to be 'Valerie Arkell-Smith', who was subsequently convicted for perjury for using a male name to marry a woman. The presiding judge said Barker had 'profaned the house of God' and 'outraged the decencies of nature'.[18]

The truth is that love, yearning, kinship, friendship, sex, passion and eroticism doesn't belong exclusively to heterosexuality, but to all romantic relationships. Martha Vicinus, in her book *Intimate Friends*, references the influential work of William Rounseville Alger, primarily *The Friendships of Women*, which was published in 1867. Vicinus notes that, over the ten chapters, Alger fails to acknowledge, or as Vicinus puts it 'evades', the reality of erotic friendships. Alger's writing makes clear how heterosexually focused historians have missed these relationships between women, despite the evidence of overt proclamations of love and a clear sense of erotic yearning.

You only need read a letter from Virginia Woolf – author of one of my favourite books, *Orlando* (1928) and the famed feminist extended essay *A Room of One's Own* – to fellow poet and writer Vita Sackville-West to know that these two were devoted to one another. Woolf writes to Vita:

> Dearest Honey,
> No letter since you were careering through the snow in Westphalia – that is nothing since Monday. I hope this doesn't mean you have been eaten by brigands, wrecked, torn to pieces. It makes me rather dismal. It gets worse steadily – your being away. All the sleeping draughts and irritants have worn off, and I'm settling down to wanting you, doggedly, dismally, faithfully – I hope that pleases you. It's damned unpleasant for me. I can assure you.[19]

Clearly, just a letter between two *very good friends*.

This erasure continues to happen even today. You can find

entire subreddits dedicated to correcting the 'just really good friends' tropes placed on historical sapphic relationships. Take r/SapphoAndHerFriend,[20] which has 394,000 members pointing out news articles, social media posts and 'hot takes' that show us the trope is still very much alive and that there is still cultural discomfort around labelling women as lesbians. Such relationships would have been underpinned by the threat of discovery in Victorian Britain and in much of Western Europe, where such an action could be enough to earn you a one-way ticket to a convent – though it has been speculated that such a punishment might at least have provided some reprieve from the patriarchal society at large.[21] Women who devoted their lives to God would have had access to an education that might not have been available to those women living more secular lives. That's not to say that a life lived surrounded by women, as a woman who loved other women, would be in any way easy, as demonstrated by the life of Mother Superior Benedetta Carlini, an Italian nun, born in 1590. For many years, Carlini was remembered as a 'woman of ill repute'.[22] The plot of Carlini's apparent fraudulency thickened when it was discovered that she had been involved with another nun. The medieval period isn't exactly known for its toleration of female sexuality, particularly within the Church, so this clandestine transgression was met with a specific kind of fury.

Carlini, who experienced intense visions of God, would eventually find herself branded a heretic following the confession of Bartolomea Crivelli, a nun assigned to watch over Carlini during her visions. The two women shared a bedroom, their beds separated by a curtain. Crivelli told an investigation into Carlini that she had kissed her 'as if she were a man' and that 'she would speak words of love to her'. The nail in the coffin, so to speak, for Carlini was that Crivelli said that 'she would stir on top of her so much that both of them corrupted themselves'.[23] Carlini was removed from her post as abbess and spent decades imprisoned in the convent, with her peers forbidden to speak to her.

If sapphic women didn't find themselves devoting their lives to God, whether willingly or not, the options available to them were limited and bleak: primarily, they might be forced into an arranged marriage so that familial reputations remained unsullied by the taint of debauchery, or they could become a spinster and carry the risk of not being able to financially support themselves if the patriarch of the family couldn't – or wouldn't – pay for their upkeep. That's not to say that some queer women didn't or weren't able to carve out some sort of life for themselves without the Church, marriage or familial support, but it was rare and not without incredible hardship, and those women usually (though not exclusively) came from advantageous backgrounds in the nobility or aristocracy.

The act of sweeping queer lives under the rug in favour of an adherence to virtuous ideals has meant that, within historical documents, there is little evidence of them to find, given the heterosexual lens through which these lived experiences have been documented and examined. Even today, some historians are still unwilling to say 'dirty words', or to label the sexuality of historic figures for fear of besmirching a posthumous reputation. Some historians believe that, due to the time period when the term 'lesbian' was popularised in the late nineteenth century, anything before the nineteenth century that could be read as sapphic-coded or 'lesbian-like' is deemed anachronistic and not applicable to the types of relationships women had with one another.[24] This does the queer community a great disservice, because this sort of historical acknowledgement of the LGBTQ+ experience gives us a fuller truth to work with that helps us understand the existence of queer people living in an enforced heterosexual society over the centuries. Within the Suffragist movement, for instance, many relationships between women were often downplayed as a 'Boston marriage', a term that describes a particularly sexless but fond romantic relationship between women. They did this to prevent intimidation brought on from the notion of autonomous sex and pleasure without men present.[25] It's worth remembering that, at the time, women's sexual desires were more likely to send them to an asylum than to be respected and fulfilled. The powers that be swapped the convent for institutionalisation, branding lesbianism as a mental health disorder.[26] This has led to the systematic erasure of the lesbian experience throughout history. It is a distortion and a dismissal that not only plays into the way queer women are being failed by legal systems and services when it comes to domestic and sexual abuse perpetrated by same-sex partners,[27] but also adds to and enforces a false nostalgia for an imagined past in which LGBTQ+ people didn't exist,[28] when in fact we always have and *always will*.

Much as we do today, queer women in the eighteenth and nineteenth centuries found themselves gossiping to help define the parameters of their culture. This meant learning about other queer people like themselves and uncovering the stories of those who had gone before them through the stories they were told. As a result, gossip has played a vital role in the community of queer women throughout history, but just as we see today, it could also be used as a tool of shame and ostracisation. Queer couples would have to know how to evade gossip and innuendo, although interestingly, before the eighteenth century, it was broadly accepted that women were sometimes born more masculine in 'appearance and aptitude' (it's worth noting here, however, that masculine – or feminine – traits do not automatically denote queerness). Nevertheless, it is well documented that Lady Eleanor Butler (1739–1829) and Sarah Ponsonby (1755–1831), more commonly known as the 'Ladies of Llangollen', ran away together in 1780 to escape Ponsonby being sent to a convent because of the shame of public gossip. Rosa Bonheur, a successful painter of animals, spent her life with Nathalie Micas defending their love from family shame and public gossip. In fact, the five women detailed in Vicinus's book, *Intimate Friends* – Lady Eleanor Butler, Rosa Bonheur, Anne Lister, Harriet Hosmer and Charlotte Cushman – all felt that their attraction to women was as natural as their appearance. With our modern eyes, of course, we can see that they were absolutely right.

One of the only reasons why we know so much about these women, however, is because of their adoption of masculine traits. In doing so, they shunned heteronormative edicts and the enforced heterosexual hegemony in favour of their authentic selves and relationships. Here we must take a moment to reflect on the fact that their partners, who were perceived as being softer and more effeminate because they chose to adopt a more feminine way of dressing and presenting, as well as those couples throughout history where both parties were more feminine (or femme), are not documented nearly as much as their more masc-presenting counterparts, let alone celebrated or even necessarily recognised. Gender and the way we express it has long impacted the way we are received in society. In the same way that effeminate gay men are often overlooked for not adhering to the stereotypes of masculinity, so too are femme gay women. The only reason we know that femmes 'existed', other than through common sense, is because of their romantic relationships with masculine women who defied societal norms in a way that was more palatable for the patriarchy. It made sense that women would want to be masculine, but it was impossible to comprehend the idea that men might want to be effeminate – a duality that we still contend with today. Masculine-presenting gay women were also a challenge to male dominance, drawing greater interest due to the perceived threat they presented in a patriarchal society.

Communication between lesbian couples had to be discreet, or at least had to resemble the fondness of friendship to avoid arousing too much suspicion. Woolf and Sackville-West would joke about oysters and draw little illustrations to represent the busyness of Sackville-West's bed.[29] This meant that literature shared between lovers, or aspiring lovers, in the form of poetry, fiction and prayer books became a way to express the complexities, nuances and deep emotionality of sapphic love and desire. Much like the mixtapes of my own teenage years, these words offered a way of expressing their feelings through someone else's voice. Incredibly romantic, I think, if not also heartbreakingly tragic, to have to conceal oneself behind the words of fictitious characters.

Gifts that concealed the depths of affection between two women weren't the only expressions of sapphic intention that have been left behind. While history has insisted that many of these women were nothing more than *very* good friends, letters were often sent with burning desires and proclamations that suggest something far deeper. The gossip shared in these letters and the subsequent gossip they've caused has sent something of a shockwave through society, undermining the commonly held notion that LGBTQ+ people didn't exist before a certain point in history. These artefacts of gossip have helped prove that queer people have always existed, and their discovery and interpretation as objects of intent and desire have created something of a lifeline for LGBTQ+ historians looking to challenge the rhetoric that LGBTQ+ people simply didn't exist in the past. It means that they are able to correct historical ambiguity around sexuality and present an inclusive, queer and feminist history.[30] As such, historically preserved gossip is transformational to our understanding of the past.

Non-normative forms of communication, like gossip, have the power to resist the dominant, linear and formal ways of knowing and being.[31] For those women who were not lucky enough to have their relationships accepted by society, gossip's double-edged sword could be both a gateway to community and acceptance, or a dangerous conspirator. Falling foul of community gossip and being outed could mean being shipped off, ostracised, or having to live in disrepute; it could mean anything from convents to lobotomies and even conversion camps. Living in secret was the only way to exist with a glimmer of authenticity. Gossip could threaten people's safety, and it did, frequently.

Today, not much has changed. We still rely on those bonds and signals to navigate society. Gossip tells us who to trust, who we can rely on, and can equally act as a signal to other queer people that we are trustworthy and reliable. If your belief system is based on dehumanising a marginalised group, the likelihood is you'll harm them. Look at the declining rate of acceptance for trans people as a case in point. The merest speculation that you could be a trans man, or woman, can end in a torch-and-pitchfork moment in any public bathroom – something we've seen increasingly since TERF-ism has proliferated, unchecked by social media platforms or by governments.

And yet we still need gossip as a mode of speech within marginalised community groups. As for women in the Victorian era, or any era of the past, gossip has been our conduit for closeness and community, as well as an outstretched hand to the future, waiting to be clasped by someone who can read between the lines. Marginalised groups, including queer people, need alternative methods of communication like gossip to subvert mainstream historical norms. These information exchanges are a means to pass on hidden histories that are overlooked by traditional archives.

This is why the phrase 'tea' has become synonymous with the queer community, although its roots lie in the Black community. To ask for tea is to ask for news; for gossip about someone or something that has happened; to be filled in and to learn the state of interpersonal relationships within a community where people are likely to know one another.

In Dr Kwame Holmes's research, published in the *Radical History Review* in 2015, he explores how gossip acts as a means of maintaining tight-knit cultural bonds, particularly those in the Black queer community. For Holmes, gossip and the idea of asking for 'tea' is a way to retain cultural memory, which is frequently overlooked by mainstream historical institutions, mirroring the significant deficit of diverse and inclusive record-keeping by majority white, heterosexually focused historiographers.[32]

But gossip in minority communities goes even further by acting as a tool to carve out and understand identity, be that Black, LGBTQ+ or any kind of marginalised group. It has the power to validate and affirm aspects of personhood that are unique to an individual's marginalisation, be that familial ostracisation because of their sexual identity, or the criminalisation and inequalities they might face in education, healthcare, employment and housing – something that LGBTQ+ people know a lot about given the extensive history of prejudice towards them by health, legal and employment institutions.[33] Gossip can be an empathetic conduit of intersectionality, offering a way to understand similar lived experiences in a broader relatable context; it helps us to find friends, build trust, and share stories and cultural knowledge.

For Black queer people and LGBTQ+ people of colour, gossip plays an integral role in mobilisation and the sharing of information. As with all marginalised groups, in this community gossip becomes a social lifeline and a means of bonding, facilitating support networks and organising political activism, as well as acting as a cultural oral history in the absence of more formal methodologies. Much like whisper networks can empower, warn and relay information to reduce harm to others, gossip throughout history has been the greatest connector and preserver of humanity – particularly for women.

Talking to the *Guardian* in 2025, Frank McAndrew, a professor of psychology at Knox College, Illinois, says we simply can't stop people from gossiping. 'It's a part of who we are, like eating or breathing … It's not whether you do it or not – it's whether you do it well, or not.' Later in the article, McAndrew explains that gossip has been a vital lifeline for women, and (less so) for men, but also that it has been a means of exploiting power and using it to defend, warn, ostracise and shame.[34]

Thanks to gossip, marginalised people who face systemic oppression have been able to survive, connect with each other and control who stays within their community groups. Those of us who are marginalised know that, without gossip, the nuances of simple eye contact, or the inflection we add to a specific word to denote meaning, can become abstract and lost. There is joy in sharing the secret; in trusting another whose life is marred by the same oppressive forces as your own. Gossip can overcome and overthrow; it is something to indulge in and a way to record histories. There is a sense of safety in the knowledge that the gossip shared between people now will echo further down the line, and that lives now regarded as marginal will be brought to the fore by our humanity and our desire to be known by one another.

CHAPTER TEN

Unbelievable

As psychologists have told us, the more you mistreat people, the more pressing your need to explain why your victims deserve their fate.
— MARGARET ATWOOD, *Burning Questions* (2022)

Spring has finally arrived in Bristol. The sunlight pours into the room and prickles my arm. I can't help but feel more hopeful when the sun shines, yet there is arguably precious little hope to be found when surveying the state of the world.

I had hoped, perhaps naively, that by now, the global situation might have shown some sign of positive change. Progression suggests a forward momentum, working in tandem with time, and I had believed that, the more time that passed, the better things would be; that the voices of women and marginalised folk might be given greater space to be heard; that our reliance on whisper networks and alternative means of care might have been lessened by the provision of tangible, meaningful change. I was hopeful that, following the end of fourteen years of Tory governance in the UK, we might enjoy a political swing to the left, an adoption of socialist ideals like feminism into the heart of things, to help women and many others oppressed under patriarchy to navigate the world. I was optimistic that I could end this book on the positive note I had envisaged when I first mapped out the chapters three years ago, but I'm sorry to report that this will not be entirely possible. Instead, what I have learnt is that progression can soon turn into regression if we become complacent.

Nothing has shown this more than the first quarter of 2025, which, I am not ashamed to admit, I have spent feeling somewhat helpless, watching the horrifying descent of the world into what I can only describe as right-wing fascism. I found myself weeping at the news, watching a Labour government supply arms to Israeli forces committing genocide against the Palestinian people in Gaza; gawking in disbelief as another cut was made to welfare from a government that is supposed to champion the working classes, knowing full well that it is primarily women – particularly disabled women – who bear the brunt of poverty the hardest; horrified as one lonely, insecure man stood on a global stage and performed a Nazi salute in front of the world's media; and sitting dumbfounded while felon and president of the United States Donald Trump continued to withhold the Epstein files from the public. I can't help but feel like the world has taken a brazen step in the wrong direction, away from justice and towards totalitarianism.

You only need scroll social media to see that it is awash with growing anti-feminist, anti-trans, misogynistic, racist and homophobic sentiments, posted by people waving the martyred flag of free speech as justification and in defence of hate speech, while sex educators and sex workers are silenced and censored by the Online Safety Act 2023, which ironically has done little to prevent harm to those most in need of protection: women and children. It feels like the dark underbelly of our world is exposed like never before. I've watched the hate ooze from the Dark Web into public social media platforms and forums, like a dog that has rolled in faeces and dead fox, and then runs around flaunting its stench and putrid ideologies. There isn't so much as a slap on the wrist for this form of bigoted posturing, which is blatant and belligerent in its use of misogynistic language, and yet there is a mass deplatforming happening of sex educators, sex workers and fem-tech companies who dare to use the word vagina without butchering its spelling beyond recognition. The double standard is undeniable. But these largely unregulated, privately owned tech companies aren't held to account as they colonise access to information on health, sex and so much more. As Julianne Schultz wrote in the *Guardian* in 2024, 'The perverse principles of the 1970s that powered the tech titans have left us with a world where the richest 1% own nearly two-thirds of its wealth.'[1] The right is rising, and Big Tech is facilitating it in a quid pro quo,[2] so much so that the School of Oriental and African Studies has warned that Big Tech is having a catastrophic impact on human rights.[3]

'From the censorship of pro-Palestinian voices seeking to call out the Israeli military's atrocities in Gaza on social media, to the algorithmic facilitation of mass violence in Myanmar, Ethiopia, and beyond, social media platforms and their parent companies have become central players in practically all struggles for justice and human rights,' said Pat de Brún, the head of Big Tech accountability for Amnesty International, while giving a talk at SOAS University of London in 2024.

Additionally, as Silicon Valley – the epicentre of our global technology – makes a conscious lurch to the right in an effort to retain its 'move fast and break things' mentality, it is clear that its 'red-pilling' is nothing more than an obvious business move that allows these companies to cosy up to the political elite, whose business interests are just as at odds with the public as Big Tech's are.[4]

What a terrible and terrifying thought. The times, like the title of this book, are truly *beyond belief*. While this closing chapter might not feel like a rallying cry, or a tremendously positive air punch, it will tell you why there is an urgency to vindicate gossip and the women who do it. Things will get worse before they get better. We are going to need gossip and the social bonds that it reinforces now more than ever if we are to dismantle the system we are faced with. As the old proverb goes, it's always darkest before the dawn, and I fear that the sun is only just setting – there is a whole night to live through yet.

Gossip is, fundamentally, a form of social grooming; a tool that is driven by human evolution, biology and the stress response system. Gossip can be used for good and for bad, and that's why it is vital that all of us remain aware of its powerful impact on our communities. It is a potent force that connects ideas, forges social bonds and fortifies solidarity. We must not forget, though, that gossip wields a parallel and far more dangerous power in the hands of the irresponsible and reckless. Gossip is not aligned with a single ideology and, however much it is lamented as a predominantly female activity that carries little importance, intelligence or value, it is nonetheless used unflinchingly by those across the political spectrum, regardless of gender. The truth is that everybody gossips. But we face a new threat and gender-based discrimination thanks to the policies of social media companies and their moderators, and the subsequent digitisation of gossip, whereby male voices are exalted while others are censored and weaponised against the people they try to protect. Our legal system is limping behind too, meaning that our words posted permanently online can come back to bite us if we aren't careful, or if we put our trust in the wrong technology. This gender-based hypocrisy, or the 'sexual double standard', is something that feminist philosophers and anthropologists have been commenting on for decades. American radical feminist activist and writer Andrea Dworkin makes clear the disparity in how our words are treated in the opening to her seminal 1983 book *Right-Wing Women*:

> There is a rumour, circulated for centuries by scientists, artists and philosophers, both secular and religious, a piece of gossip as it were, to the effect that women are 'biologically conservative'. While gossip among women is universally ridiculed as low and trivial, gossip among men, especially if it is about women, is called theory, or idea, or fact. This particular rumour became dignified as high thought because it was Whispered-Down-The-Lane in formidable academies, libraries, and meeting halls from which women, until very recently, have been formally and forcibly excluded.[5]

Even though this was first penned over forty years ago – and even if we take what she says with a pinch of salt, as Dworkin is what we might consider today a SWERF (sex-worker-exclusionary radical feminist) and TERF (ideologies I certainly don't give credence to) – this critical analysis of the state of expectation in which women are condemned to live is as pertinent and poignant today as it was then. Growing anti-feminist sentiment is propelled by gossip, both online and offline, invigorating misogynistic beliefs towards women that threaten – and, in some cases, manage – to break down access to vital, necessary resources and rights, from equal pay and maternity leave to abortion, childcare, healthcare and more. In 2025 alone we watched in horror as the president of the United States, Donald Trump, decided to spend $10,000,000 on burning 900,000 birth control implants, 2 million doses of injectable long-acting birth control, 2 million packs of contraceptive pills and 50,000 IUDs, instead of redistributing them to Planned Parenthood.[6] We are living in a world that has normalised the perpetration of male violence against women and girls. They have been allowed to do this because of continued passive attitudes to the warnings women and feminist groups have been screaming for years. The patriarchal world doesn't want healthy women with agency and access to fair, due process. They seek to dismantle our dignity by continuing to police femininity, confusing 'sex' and 'gender', limiting our access to reproductive services and subsequent rights, and restricting the broader conversation on who gets to call themselves 'woman', despite second-wave feminism fighting relentlessly not to be defined by our sex organs.

Meanwhile, on WhatsApp groups and closed networks, men have spoken brazenly about the harms they have enacted, even those who have sworn to uphold our rights and to protect us. The police officer Wayne Couzens, known by his colleagues as 'the rapist',[7] abducted, raped and murdered Sarah Everard in 2021. When police gained access to his phone, they unearthed a WhatsApp group between Couzens and six other Metropolitan Police officers, in which the group repeatedly discussed sexually assaulting women, including victims of domestic abuse. It's worth repeating here that this WhatsApp group was comprised of seven men, all of whom were serving police officers. Seven.

One of the messages shared by PC Matthew Forster stated: 'They've only got to say yes once,' when discussing sex. Other messages are just as distressing. Officer Joel Borders asks his peers how long it takes for a body to decompose, while discussing being asked out on a date by an Asian woman. Officer Cobban suggests to Borders, who is being reprimanded by his governor, that he 'slap her arse and give her a tickle' as it is *'probably what she wants'*. When PC Neville chimes in with, 'There's a question about sexual offences, halfway through intercourse the woman says no, that is rape / supposedly', Borders, who sent 1,983 messages in this WhatsApp group, replied with: 'Even if you pretend you didn't hear it?' This locker-room talk – that uniquely male brand of gossip – was published by the Independent Office for Police Conduct (IOPC) in 2023. All members of the group were found guilty of sending grossly offensive messages on a public communications network contrary to section 127 of the Communications Act 2003 and were barred from the police force.[8]

This sort of behaviour – the kind that churns stomachs – is emboldened by right-wing ideologies, because of the fundamental belief underpinning so many of their views that women should be 'back in the kitchen'. Those who promote these ideologies want total, unfettered access to women's bodies; they want the legacy of children without any of the emotional and physical outlay that goes with them and with running a home. These ideals are reliant on the unpaid and unacknowledged labour of women. Nothing under capitalism works without the exploitation of women. This means shrinking women down again, demonising their peer-to-peer care strategies and questioning the integrity of their words more than ever before.

The rise of the far right is perhaps an inevitable backlash to the rise of fourth- and fifth-wave feminism. Progress towards gender equality has always faced some form of counterattack. Even after the Second World War, women were forcibly corralled back into the domestic sphere after experiencing a fleeting taste of social and economic freedom at work, and in service to their country. Rosie the Riveter was forced back into her singular identity as Rosie the housewife, and plied with Quaaludes to keep her docile.

Even today, we have seen this entitlement to exert control over women play out with deadly consequences, as evidenced by the US Supreme Court's decision to overturn *Roe* vs *Wade* abortion ruling in June 2022. This law granted women an absolute right to an abortion in the first trimester, the right to access it under certain government regulations in the second trimester, and a state restriction or ban on abortions in the last trimester. Since its overturning, Josseli Barnica has become one of a number of women who has suffered a preventable death. Barnica died in 2024, days after the state of Texas's ban on abortions past six weeks of pregnancy took effect. She presented at hospital at just over seventeen weeks' pregnant, suffering from cramps, and shortly afterwards was informed by doctors that a miscarriage 'was in progress'. Despite this, the new ruling meant that medical staff were unable to speed up the delivery or empty her uterus while the foetus still had a heartbeat, leaving Barnica dangerously vulnerable to infection for a period spanning forty hours. Three days after delivering, Barnica died of an infection caused by the delays.[9] The preventable deaths of Amber Nicole Thurman and Candi Miller in Georgia have also been tied to the six-week abortion ban.[10] While it's easy to assume that these issues are predominantly impacting women in the US, there is great cause for concern here in the UK too, as populist leader of the Reform Party Nigel Farage has been linked to an extremist anti-abortion group and has called for a debate in Parliament on restricting abortion rights in the UK.[11]

This drive to control women's bodies, this proliferation of hate – all of it comes from somewhere, and it has a name. This is the work of anti-feminism. This concerted effort to re-domesticate and subjugate women to strengthen patriarchy is a sign of the times. What is disconcerting is how well anti-feminist ideologies are sticking. In 2024, *ArtReview* published the essay 'Is Feminism in Its Flop Era?' Reporting on the research in Alice Cappelle's book *Collapse Feminism: The Online Battle for Feminism's Future*, journalist Amelia

Abraham opines that, among young people, feminism has become somewhat 'cringe'. Thanks to the churn of trends seen online, and the immediacy with which things hit peak virality and then inevitably become passé, feminism doesn't seem able to stick as a movement in the minds of young people. Speaking with Abraham, Cappelle observed that during the writing of her book, she struggled to say the word feminism, 'because of its negative connotations'.[12]

If you are questioning the truth of that sentiment, we can see it play out in the data: in the impact it's having on heterosexual relationships, for instance. A 2025 study by dating app Flirtini revealed that 44 per cent of women reported being dumped because of their feminist beliefs,[13] with a further 62 per cent of women finding it difficult to date as a feminist. While I would argue that if being outspoken about your feminist beliefs is an 'ick' for someone, that person probably isn't worth getting to know romantically, it isn't the only arena where this aversion to feminism is being seen, copied and repeated. Take Hannah Neeleman, the woman behind Ballerina Farm, for example – the idyllically framed tradwife whose kids flit around her apron skirts while she throws together a sourdough loaf and makes mozzarella from scratch. As we've already discussed, this yearning for an apparently simpler life and fewer 'masculine' responsibilities is nothing more than propaganda. There is no world where motherhood and domestic labour isn't productive work, but there is a world where financial compensation for that role is non-existent. While the choice to enter into a 'stay-at-home' role might seem like quitting the rat race in favour of being provided for, we must remember what is expected of us in exchange, at least, in the traditional sense: access to our bodies and sex as a service (not as consensual participation), unpaid domestic labour and childrearing, and an obliging and non-confrontational personality. I'm not suggesting that this choice is wrong if it is freely made. I can certainly see the attraction in not being responsible for earning the lion's share of the household income, or even half the rent money – especially when the system is rigged to make sure you earn less than men throughout your lifetime, no matter how good you are at your job. I can see the appeal of domesticity – I hear the calling to step into my divine feminine just like everyone else who feels exhausted by having their hand slapped away every time they reach for parity in employment, wealth and education. However, the likelihood of being in a relationship where you can manage on a single income is low, and is still an aspiration that doesn't account for class and the gender-based prejudices associated with marrying above one's station. I hate to tell you that, no matter where you end up, there's no winning while we're playing at patriarchy. The only way to win is to change the system, not 'cheat' at it.

Feminism promises to change the system. And yet, feminism is falling out of fashion spectacularly with young people. Of course, it's counterintuitive, given that feminism has given so many young people the rights they now take for granted. Perhaps it isn't such a surprising eventuality, particularly when we return to Dworkin's work on women and right-wing ideologies, and the way in which women's speech becomes discredited and disempowered. 'Feminism is hated because women are hated,' she writes. 'Antifeminism is a direct expression of misogyny; it is the political defence of woman hating.'[14] Throughout her book, as she explores abortion, sex work, sexuality, racism and anti-feminism, Dworkin explains that the right is adept at both exploiting and quelling women's justified fears of male violence. Knowing what we know about stress responses, Dworkin theorises that right-wing women are acquiescent to male authority for protection and power because their survival depends on it – an idea that sits in perfect parallel with the concept of fawning. Characterised by people-pleasing, over-dependence, emotional suppression and a difficulty in asserting boundaries, fawning is a trauma response just as fight, flight and freeze are – one that tries to sidestep conflict and aggression in search of safety and protection. This is one way in which we are disempowered and made meek in our own fight for equality.

'So, the woman hangs on, not with the delicacy of a clinging vine, but with a tenacity incredible in its intensity, to the very persons, institutions, and values that demean her, degrade her, glorify her powerlessness, insist upon constraining and paralyzing the most honest expression of her will and being,' writes Dworkin.[15]

Women who fawn under the stress of misogyny are likely to do so because it fits in with the rules and world view perpetuated by those on the right: a perverse amalgamation of traditional family values, morality, and the subjugation and domestication of women. Dworkin explained that the right wing of America in 1978 made 'certain metaphysical and material promises to women that both quiet[ed] and exploit[ed] their deepest fears'. The same is undoubtedly true today. All this poses a significant gender-based double standard for the use of gossip and the perception of gossip, despite the undeniable value it holds for those failed by systemic misogyny and sexism.

Feminism, then, is a collective cry that recentres women's voices. It listens to them. It builds upon the theory. It organises. It speaks to power. This is why anti-feminism seeks to discredit feminism by deploying these right-wing tactics that rely on systemic patriarchal social grooming to be effective. Think peer-to-peer pressure to conform to heteronormative ideas of the nuclear family, religious teaching of female inferiority, and post-feminism beliefs that any further rights given to women strip away men's. This is all 'fake news', but it is effective in preventing strides towards equality because it creates a 'fear of the unknown' – a world where women can talk, congregate, care for each other and be on an equal footing with men[16] – rather than asking you to play the impossible game of womanhood well enough to make it to the end as unscathed as possible. But, oh! The shrinking you must do to yourself to get there! While you may not be bloody and bruised from life, you'll no doubt be bleeding internally from the pressure.

The rise of the far right, be it Trumpian, Musk-ian (vom) or Farage-shaped, in addition to the societal trend of doubling down on hetero-centrism, misogyny and post-feminism, has perpetuated the myth that intelligent women aren't sexually valuable and so cannot be 'protected' under the rules the far right has laid out for them. We know from Sontag that sexual disqualification can be a humiliating experience. This creates a dilemma in which women are forced to either fall in line or be cast out from the perceived protection of more 'traditional' frameworks. Using Sontag's theory on ageism here, parallels can be drawn between the 'un-fuckability' of 'outspoken' women and the 'humiliation' of being sexually disqualified. If you are outspoken; if you are not pliable; if you do not adhere to a standard that prizes youthfulness, virginity and modest sensibilities, then it doesn't matter whether you hold feminist or anti-feminist beliefs – you still won't be 'chosen' by the far right; at best, you might be tolerated. Just ask any male right-wing mouthpiece why they won't date fellow right-wing influencer and commentator Hannah Pearl Davis, a woman who aligns with all the same anti-feminist beliefs as them. These men demand that women be silent and compliant. They demand power over them. And intelligent, sexually liberated, autonomous, healthy, wealthy women are the antithesis of what they want women to believe they can be, because these are 'masculine' aspirations, which are not focused on subservience and care.

'Intelligence is full of excess,' writes Dworkin, and as a result women are pressured to be apologetic about their cleverness, and experience a subsequent shrinking of mind and autonomy. As Dworkin puts it, 'Rigorous intelligence abhors sentimentality, and women must be sentimental to value the dreadful silliness of the men around them.'[17] Indeed. My great-grandmother once told me, 'Never suffer fools gladly.' Maybe this is why I have built an immunity to this kind of sentimentality, and I would impose that same advice on anyone reading this book. But it's more than just a notion of sentimentality that keeps us locked in an endless cycle of progression and regression. It is the frankly biblical fear of what happens to women who reach for 'forbidden knowledge' and who, by doing so, are cast out into a world of pain and suffering. This fear runs deep and has been compounded by centuries of propaganda likening curiosity to sin.

To reinforce this exploitation of women's fears, the far right abounds with anti-intellectualism. Time and time again, we've seen the confident denial of expert testimony, statistics, facts or science, thus rendering them useless in the face of misinformation and prejudicial disinformation. And this only strengthens the belief in the conspiratorial tales that position women time and time again as the over-emotional, illogical sex.

Despite this anti-intellectualism, though, men like Jordan Peterson can spew all sorts of clever-sounding verbiage while communicating very little, while Russell Brand delivers speeches on what he dubs 'common-sense issues'. Both are praised and revered as clever thinkers for the everyman (and woman). It's an effective magic trick, one that I've seen beguile and entrance smart men. I've watched their rhetoric infect the minds of women I have known too. The world is set up for these sorts of men to gain notoriety. Meanwhile, women who dare to assert themselves as autonomous human beings face the very real threat of sexual disqualification, which carries with it a motivation to resist potential social ostracisation through infantilisation and obsessive preoccupations with remaining sexually viable in order to maintain some semblance of authority.

Being an outspoken feminist doesn't fit the shape of morality that patriarchy has defined. How can it when women's bodies have powered capitalism with their silent subservience? The good woman is seen but not heard; she is available, obliging and acts solely in service to her home and husband.

The morality of gossip, and by extension, the perceived goodness of women, has been a central theme of this book, as has the shame attributed to women and other marginalised persons acting with self-determination. It is as Ash Sarkar states in the introduction to her brilliant book *Minority Rule*: 'The message of who is good, moral and decent is conveyed through repeated propagandising about who is deviant, dangerous and illegitimate.'[18]

There is both a lesson and a warning inherent in these words: do not become embroiled in notions of goodness and purity, because they won't save you. They still won't pick you. No matter how well we adhere to the rules, regardless of how stringently we police one another and perpetuate the myths that excuse male violence towards women, we will never experience legal, economic, political or social equality. The system and the game are both rigged against us.

If we want to close equality gaps for women and other marginalised people, we must critically examine why our knee-jerk reaction is to disbelieve women and undermine their credibility. As it stands, this credibility gap is preventing women from receiving vital care and support for their basic needs. And just as women are suffering under this enforced patriarchal existence, so too are men.

When Mark Zuckerburg, the CEO of Meta, announced on the infamous podcast *The Joe Rogan Experience* on 10 January 2025 that corporate companies needed more masculine energy, he presented us with a perfect case study of how weak the current state of masculine expectation is. Zuckerberg made this statement despite the fact that two-thirds of Facebook employees are men.[19] He went on to say, 'I think having a culture that celebrates the aggression a bit more has its own merits that are really positive.'[20]

This was a calculated way of repositioning Meta, especially given that on 7 January that same year, Zuckerberg had announced that he was removing third-party fact checkers from his sites in favour of free speech – something the far right are eager to uphold. But they do not truly mean freedom of speech. They mean freedom from consequence.

If we want to keep the rise of the far right from gaining more traction, we must maintain equilibrium and we must continue to talk. Now, more than ever we must rely on vocalising, organising, petitioning, rallying, protesting – raising our voices, loudly – if we are to have any hope of combating this bubbling pot of hate. Words have long been the sole weapon afforded to women in their exigent demands for equality. Silencing our voices by diktat, or by branding talk as sinful, stifles these cries for humane treatment, leading to unconscionable solitude, pain and suffering. And, frankly, women have been through enough.

Throughout this book, I've tried to prove the myriad ways in which women's voices are disregarded as dishonest by showing the knee-jerk tendency to question their integrity rather than to believe them. We've seen how our 'quality' and 'value' are the measuring sticks for how worthy we are of belief whenever our voices put money, power and stature at risk. Repeatedly, we've seen a pattern where credibility plays a key role in justice, where slut-shaming and misogyny have run rampant, sowing seeds of doubt in the minds of those who don't understand the powerful effects of trauma responses. We've seen how, in the absence of belief, women congregate to believe one another, instinctively lowering their cortisol,[21] and developing whisper networks with subtle language cues to vent to one another. These bonds are what help us survive and thrive. Without them, we are at the whim of an ever-threatening force hell-bent on revoking the rights we've fought so long and so hard for.

The far right needs us to believe that we aren't strong enough to overcome the obstacles they put in our way, but as Professor Ronald Hutton told us of witch hunts, the power of the people is a strong and binding force, so we must use it for good, or risk becoming collateral damage to the moral panics of our times. We must continue to care for one another and be aware of the words we use to talk about others, even the famous ones who feel out of reach.

The more we invest in these social bonds, the harder it will be for patriarchal and misogynistic institutions to silence us. We must continue to work to preserve the rights we have, while striving for better treatment in the legal system, in the workplace and in the home. Whether we are born women or become women or both, we need to recognise that our fate as women is what connects us. For us to know one another better, to care what happens to our sisters, we must continue to talk. We must place value in gossip.

Acknowledgements

Writing this book brought many things to the fore, including an introspection of my own interpersonal relationships with the women and gender-nonconforming people I am fortunate enough to call my family and friends. The process of burying my head into the research, putting pen to paper and analysing reams and reams of evidence showed me, above all else, how incredibly rich I am to have such brilliant women and gender non-conforming friends by my side. Aside from my own deep sense of gratitude to each and every one of these people for choosing me to be in their lives and supporting me more broadly, I must also take a second to thank my partner, friends, family, peers, and, of course, my editor and agent, who have been instrumental in the development of this book. Without this community of people around me, giving me the space, time and reassurances I needed, as well as the nerve and audacity to try, this book would have no doubt remained on the great shelf of ideas. And, what a shame that would be. It's only right that there is space to thank each and every one of them for their unwavering camaraderie while I fell off the face of the Earth in search of answers.

It is good and right that I begin with the two women to whom this book is dedicated. Doris Millicent Gray and Menai Vaughan, though the rest are arranged in no particular order of importance.

Doris, my grandma, was a Lancashire-born woman. She was tough. Doris worked and lived through the Second World War and demonstrated great strength in leaving her marriage to my grandfather, who was a brute. She never let her trauma take away from her power and raised my mother, aunties and uncles in poverty and hardship – but found solace in her love of music and dancing. I wish, beyond all else, that I could sit with her as I had done as a child to show her what her tenacity and resilience paved the way for. She never gave up, and I will always be in awe of who she was and what she was able to accomplish with so little.

To Menai, my Nain, I promise all those years of putting up with me telling you I was allowed to do whatever I wanted have come to a happy fruition. Your memory of our family history has shaped my thirst for gossip and ensured that we have kept track and record of the Pant family characters, scandals and all. Thank you for putting our lives in technicolour, with good humour, even though seeing the funny side hasn't always been easy or without personal sacrifice. You are everything I aspire to be.

To my mother, Dr Doris May Gray, who has instilled in me a sense of justice and who has never told me I couldn't do anything. Thank you. For introducing me to feminism, for believing in me when I wasn't able to, for being my patron and for helping me make sure I could put food on my table during this process. You will never know how grateful I am to you and all that you have given to me so freely, with no expectations. I love you.

A thank you to my father, David Ian Jones, who has always encouraged me to ask *why?* Who ensured that, when I chose a career in the arts, I was armed with knowledge and curiosity and enough nous to wonder. Such a gift you have given to me in being able to think critically and scrutinise, but also to appreciate a slower pace of life, to stop and look to the stars from time to time. Thank you for being there to put the lids back on my felt tips and for giving me the confidence to climb trees with my brothers.

To James West, my stepfather, and Janet Ruth Davies, my stepmother, for showing me that change can be good and even in the most impossible of situations, is possible. I also thank both my brothers, Osian David Linton and Cai Thomas, for supporting my big ideas and ambitious projects from the get-go. I hope you're as proud of me as I am of both of you.

My fiancé, and by the time you're reading this, husband, Peter David Hills, whose support has never faltered. In those moments of crippling self-doubt, you have built yourself around me and have been the shelter from myself I have sorely needed. You are the break wall to my stormy weather, the shore to my tide – ever patient, forgiving and protecting. Without you, this book would not have been possible, and the sacrifices you have made so that I can make something so urgent are why you will always be my person. Know that when your time comes (and it will), that I will build myself around you, too. I love you. Same team.

To Claire Morris, my childhood friend, who has been by my side since we were just six years old. Your enthusiasm for my 'I'm just gonna give it a go' attitude has bolstered my nerves and self-confidence (or lack of it) more times than you know. I will always remember sitting on the couch with you, in our matching pyjamas, of course, and telling you my ideas and ambitions for this book. You told me I could do it, so I believed it, and now I have done it. Thank you.

To Kate Cox, who was there the moment I formed the idea and said, *Wait a minute, I think you're onto something?* You were right, and I can't wait to be able to tell people who ever dismiss gossip again that they're wrong and that they should read my book about it.

To Beth Ashley and Charlotte Moore, who held my hand through the initial stages of this process and have reminded me time and time again that working-class people deserve to be in the publishing world. You kept the door ajar for me, thank you.

To my editor, Marleigh Price, I am eternally grateful for your patience and sensitivity as I pulled this work together. Your guidance chiselled this book into what it is. Thank you for helping me navigate this industry and process with my dyslexia, and for seeing through the spelling mistakes.

Abi Fellows, my agent and, I think, guardian angel. Thank you for seeing this book the way I did. For encouraging me to find the right home for it and not to settle for the wrong vibe. You continue to shine a light on me in a way I didn't know was possible. The future is going to be very exciting for us.

There are many contributors to this book who gave up their precious time and energy to spend hours with me on the phone, over video calls and in confidence. Those of you who were happy to be named in this book and those who rightfully chose anonymity, I again thank you.

Lastly, but by no means least, my dog, Lula. Who sat by my side, on my lap and sometimes, on my computer. You faithfully kept me company and gave me great comfort in what has been the most isolatory yet rewarding experience. You are a very good girl.

Endnotes

Introduction

1. Maryanne L. Fisher (ed.), *The Oxford Handbook of Women and Competition* (Oxford University Press, 2014), 191-206.
2. Francesca Giardini and Rafael Wittek (eds), *The Oxford Handbook of Gossip and Reputation* (Oxford University Press, 2019), 47–68.
3. Aria Bendix and Phil Helsel, 'Indiana board reprimands Dr. Caitlin Bernard over 10-year-old's abortion case', NBC News (25 May 2023): https://www.nbcnews.com/health/health-news/indiana-doctor-gave-10-year-old-girl-abortion-disciplinary-hearing-rcna86214
4. PoliticsJOE, 'Judith Butler: How the far-right wants to control your body', YouTube (21 March 2024): https://www.youtube.com/watch?v=8Aul0vWIfTg&feature=youtu.be
5. Rafia Zakaria, *Against White Feminism* (Penguin, 2022), 28-46: https://www.penguin.co.uk/books/317241/against-white-feminism-by-zakaria-rafia/9780241989319
6. Francesca Giardini and Rafael Wittek (eds), *The Oxford Handbook of Gossip and Reputation* (Oxford University Press, 2019).
7. Ariel L. Beccia et al., 'Methods for structural sexism and population health research: Introducing a novel analytic framework to capture life-course and intersectional effects', *Social*

Science & Medicine, 351: 1 (2024), 116804. DOI: https://doi.org/10.1016/j.socscimed.2024.116804

8 Mikki Kendall, *Hood Feminism: Notes from the Women White Feminists Forgot* (Bloomsbury, 2020), 6–7.

Chapter One: A History of Gossip

1 'Gossip', Oxford English Dictionary: https://www.oed.com/dictionary/gossip_n?tab=etymology

2 R. Podd, 'Reconsidering maternal mortality in mediaeval England: aristocratic Englishwomen, c. 1236–1503', *Community and Change*, 35: 2 (2020), 115–37. DOI: 10.1017/S0268416020000156

3 Ben Widdicombe, 'Poparazzi: A History of Gossip', *New York Times Style Magazine* (7 December 2010): https://archive.nytimes.com/tmagazine.blogs.nytimes.com/2010/12/07/poparazzi-a-history-of-gossip/

4 'Women in Medieval Literature', British Literature Wiki: https://sites.udel.edu/britlitwiki/women-in-medieval-literature-and-society

5 Eleanor Janega, *The Once and Future Sex: Going Medieval on Women's Roles in Society* (W.W. Norton & Co., 2023), 2.

6 Ned Schantz, *Gossip, Letters, Phones: The Scandal of Female Networks in Film and Literature* (Oxford University Press, USA, 2008), 3-9.

7 'Results of the "Women's Health – Let's talk about it" survey', Department of Health & Social Care (13 April 2022): https://www.gov.uk/government/calls-for-evidence/womens-health-strategy-call-for-evidence/outcome/results-of-the-womens-health-lets-talk-about-it-survey

8 Arienne King, 'Family Planning in the Ancient Near East', World History Encyclopedia (2 August 2022). https://www.worldhistory.org/article/2054/family-planning-in-the-ancient-near-east/

9 Sarah Clegg, *Woman's Lore: 4,000 Years of Sirens, Serpents and Succubi* (Head of Zeus, 2023), 1-35.

10 Ulrike Steinert (ed.), *Systems of Classification in Premodern Medical Cultures: Sickness, Health, and Local Epistemologies* (Routledge, 2020). DOI: https://doi.org/10.4324/9780203703045
11 Rowan Hulitt, 'Lamashtu amulets and motherhood in Ancient Mesopotamia', The Bristorian (16 February 2024): https://www.thebristorian.co.uk/the-forum/https/wwwthebristoriancouk/lamashtu-amulets-and-motherhood
12 Rosan A. Jordan and Susan J. Kalcik (eds), *Women's Folklore, Women's Culture* (University of Pennsylvania Press, 1985), 1-26.
13 Andrea Falcon, 'Aristotle on Sexual Difference', *Analysis*, 84: 4 (2024), 916–23. DOI: https://doi.org/10.1093/analys/anae006
14 Sumru Nur Elden, 'Aristotle's Account of the Place of Women within the Polis', *LSE Undergraduate Political Review* (28 January 2022): https://blogs.lse.ac.uk/lseupr/2022/01/28/aristotles-account-of-the-place-of-women-within-the-polis
15 Richard Cresswell (translator), *Aristotle's History of Animals* (Project Gutenberg, 2019): https://www.gutenberg.org/files/59058/59058-h/59058-h.htm
16 M. Masango, 'Aristotle's philosophical influence on Western civilization, history and theology placed women in inferior positions', University of Praetoria: https://repository.up.ac.za/bitstream/handle/2263/10121/Masango_Aristotle%27s%282003%29.pdf?sequence=1&isAllowed=y
17 Catherine Rider, 'Medical Magic and the Church in Thirteenth-Century England', *Social History of Medicine*, 24: 1 (2015): 92–107. DOI: https://doi.org/10.1093/shm/hkq110
18 Mohammad Taher et al., 'Superstition in health beliefs: Concept exploration and development', *Journal of Family Medicine and Primary Care*, 9: 3 (2020): 1325–30. DOI: 10.4103/jfmpc.jfmpc_871_19

19 D.M. Kieser, 'The Female Body in Catholic Theology: Menstruation, Reproduction, and Autonomy', *Horizons*, 44: 1 (2017), 1–27. DOI: 10.1017/hor.2017.51

20 'Medieval washer woman notes', Reading Museum: https://www.readingmuseum.org.uk/sites/default/files/downloads/Waasher%20woman%20character-notes.pdf

21 'Black Death: Effects and Significance', Britannica: https://www.britannica.com/event/Black-Death/Effects-and-significance

22 Kim M. Phillips, 'Review: *The Invention of the Scold*', *History Workshop Journal*, 66 (2008), 253–8. DOI: http://www.jstor.org/stable/25473020

23 Hetta Howes, *Poet, Mystic, Widow, Wife: The Extraordinary Lives of Medieval Women* (Bloomsbury, 2024), 149.

24 Law Commission: Proposals to Abolish Certain Ancient Criminal Offences (Report), (1966) EWLC 3: https://www.bailii.org/ew/other/EWLC/1966/3.html

25 Barbara Hanawalt and David Wallace (eds), *Bodies and Disciplines: Intersections of Literature and History in Fifteenth-century England* (University of Minnesota Press, 1996), 7.

26 Criminal Law Act 1967, GOV.UK: https://www.legislation.gov.uk/ukpga/1967/58/section/13?view=plain

27 Melissa Vise, *The Unruly Tongue: Speech and Violence in Medieval Italy* (University of Pennsylvania Press, 2021), 61-85: https://www.pennpress.org/9781512824872/the-unruly-tongue

28 Roberta Magnani, 'Powerful men have tried to silence abused women since Medieval times', *Independent* (2 November 2017): https://www.independent.co.uk/news/long_reads/powerful-men-have-tried-to-silence-abused-women-since-medieval-times-a8028571.html

29 Vanessa Corcoran, 'Silencing Medieval Women's Voices – Nevertheless, She Persisted', The Public Medievalist (8 November 2018). https://publicmedievalist.com/she-persisted/

30 David Crowther, 'Medieval Prices and Wages', The History of England (2016): https://thehistoryofengland.co.uk/resource/medieval-prices-and-wages/
31 'Medieval Sourcebook: *The Golden Legend* (*Aurea Legenda*), Compiled by Jacobus de Voragine, 1275, Englished by William Caxton, 1483', Fordham University: https://sourcebooks.fordham.edu/basis/goldenlegend/
32 'St. Agatha, Sicilian martyr', Britannica: https://www.britannica.com/biography/Saint-Agatha
33 Howes, *Poet, Mystic, Widow, Wife* (2024), 149.
34 Corcoran, 'Silencing Medieval Women's Voices' (2018): https://publicmedievalist.com/she-persisted/
35 Magnani, 'Powerful men have tried to silence abused women since Medieval times', *Independent* (2017): https://www.independent.co.uk/news/long_reads/powerful-men-have-tried-to-silence-abused-women-since-medieval-times-a8028571.html
36 Beth Allison Barr, *The Making of Biblical Womanhood: How the Subjugation of Women Became Gospel Truth* (Brazos Press, 2021), 40.
37 Ibid., 39.
38 A. Falcon and D. Lefebvre (eds), *Aristotle's Generation of Animals: A Critical Guide* (Cambridge University Press, 2018), 171-187.
39 Howes, *Poet, Mystic, Widow, Wife* (2024), 118.
40 Karen Jones, *Gender and Petty Crime in Late Medieval England: The Local Courts in Kent, 1460–1560* (Boydell & Brewer, 2006), 94-128. DOI: https://www.jstor.org/stable/10.7722/j.ctt14brth4
41 'About History: the Scold's Bridle', Tastes of History (7 November 2022): https://www.tastesofhistory.co.uk/post/about-history-the-scold-s-bridle
42 Geoffrey Abbott, 'Cucking and ducking stools', Britannica (2024): https://www.britannica.com/topic/cucking-stool

43 Mark J. Joshua, 'Women in the Middle Ages', World History Encyclopedia (18 March 2019): https://www.worldhistory.org/article/1345/women-in-the-middle-ages/#google_vignette
44 Clare Crowston, 'Women, Gender, and Guilds in Early Modern Europe: An Overview of Recent Research', *International Review of Social History*, 53: S16 (2008), 19–44. DOI: 10.1017/S0020859008003593
45 Ibid.
46 Chris Briggs, 'Top of the Campops: 60 things you didn't know about family, marriage, work, and death since the middle ages', Cambridge Group for the History of Population and Social Structure: https://www.campop.geog.cam.ac.uk/blog/2025/04/10/law-in-medieval-england
47 Crowston, 'Women, Gender, and Guilds in Early Modern Europe' (2008), 19–44. DOI: 10.1017/S0020859008003593
48 Jeanne de Montbaston, 'Codpieces and Demons: The Dangers of Female Gossip', Reading Medieval Books (22 October 2013): https://readingmedievalbooks.wordpress.com/2013/10/22/codpieces-and-demons-the-dangers-of-female-gossip/
49 Crowston, 'Women, Gender, and Guilds in Early Modern Europe' (2008), 19–44. DOI: 10.1017/S0020859008003593
50 'Medieval Religion', English Heritage: https://www.english-heritage.org.uk/learn/story-of-england/medieval/religion/
51 Diane Purkiss, 'Witchcraft: Eight Myths and Misconceptions', English Heritage: https://www.english-heritage.org.uk/learn/histories/eight-witchcraft-myths/
52 'Witchcraft', UK Parliament: https://www.parliament.uk/about/living-heritage/transformingsociety/private-lives/religion/overview/witchcraft/
53 Fred Lewsey, 'Witchcraft accusations were an "occupational hazard" for female workers in early modern England', University

of Cambridge (19 September 2023): https://www.cam.ac.uk/stories/witchcraft-work-women
54 'Topical Bible: Slander', Bible Hub: https://biblehub.com/topical/s/slander.htm
55 'Lashon Hara (Evil Speech)', My Jewish Learning: https://www.myjewishlearning.com/article/gossip-rumors-and-lashon-hara-evil-speech/
56 'Gossip (Ghibah) And Tale-Bearing (Namimah)', Association of Islamic Charitable Projects: https://www.aicp.org/index.php/islamic-isip-ghibah-and-tale-bearing-namimah
57 Jotsimran Singh Dua, 'Gossip/Ninda', SikhNet (12 May 2009): https://www.sikhnet.com/news/gossip-ninda
58 'The Five Precepts – Buddhist beliefs', BBC Bitesize: https://www.bbc.co.uk/bitesize/guides/zf8g4qt/revision/9
59 'Sadhana 14 – No Gossiping', Chinmaya Mission Mumbai: https://www.chinmayamissionmumbai.com/chinmaya/42chinmayasadhanas/sadhana_14_no_gossiping
60 Judith Butler, *Who's Afraid of Gender?* (Allen Lane, 2024), 3.
61 Simone de Beauvoir, *The Second Sex* [1949], (Vintage, 1997), 632.
62 '11. JOURNALISM', *Communication Booknotes Quarterly*, 40: 2 (2009), 92–8. DOI: https://doi.org/10.1080/10948000902847585
63 Erin Blakemore, 'What Gloves Meant to the Victorians', JSTOR Daily (24 February 2018): https://daily.jstor.org/what-gloves-meant-to-the-victorians/
64 Alexandra Starp, 'The Secret Language of Fans', Sotheby's (14 July 2025). https://www.sothebys.com/en/articles/the-secret-language-of-fans
65 Martin Fone, 'Curious Questions: Did English ladies really have a secret "language of fans"?', *Country Life* (23 September 2023): https://www.countrylife.co.uk/luxury/curious-questions-did-english-ladies-really-have-a-secret-language-of-fans-260053

66   Kate Millet, 'The Debate over Women: Ruskin Versus Mill', *The Victorian Woman*, 14: 1 (1970), 63–82: http://www.jstor.org/stable/3826407

67   Stephen Garton, Chapter 6: 'Victorianism', *Histories of Sexuality: Antiquity to Sexual Revolution. Critical Histories of Subjectivity and Culture* (Acumen Publishing, 2004), 101–23. https://www.cambridge.org/core/books/abs/histories-of-sexuality/victorianism/4ADD4EB1729128604FC22E75AE75C8B2

68   Cherish Watton, 'Gossip, men, and Victorian politics', Doing History in Public (2018): https://doinghistoryinpublic.org/2018/04/17/gossip-men-and-victorian-politics/

69   Amy Milne-Smith, 'Club Talk: Gossip, Masculinity and Oral Communities in Late Nineteenth-Century London', History Faculty Publications, Wilfrid Laurier University (2009): https://scholars.wlu.ca/cgi/viewcontent.cgi?article=1020&context=hist_faculty

70   Susie Steinbach, 'Victorian era', Britannica: https://www.britannica.com/event/Victorian-era

71   Linton Weeks, '18 Rules Of Behavior For Young Ladies In 1831', NPR History Dept. (20 November 2015): https://www.npr.org/sections/npr-history-dept/2015/11/20/456224571/18-rules-of-behavior-for-young-ladies-in-1831

72   Cecilia Tasca et al., 'Women and hysteria in the history of mental health', *Clinical Practice and Epidemiology in Mental Health*, 8 (2012), 110–119. DOI: 10.2174/1745017901208010110

73   Eliot Slater, 'Diagnosis of "Hysteria"', *British Medical Journal*, 1: 5447 (1965): 395–1399. DOI: https://www.jstor.org/stable/25402452

74   Ada McVean, 'The History of Hysteria', Office for Science and Society, McGill University (31 July 2017): https://www.mcgill.ca/oss/article/history-quackery/history-hysteria

75 Maria Cohut, 'The controversy of "female hysteria"', Medical News Today (13 October 2020): https://www.medicalnewstoday.com/articles/the-controversy-of-female-hysteria
76 Joyce Carol Oates (ed.), *A Darker Shade: New Stories of Body Horror by Women Writers* (Footnote Press Ltd, 2024), 7.
77 Rachel V. Cote, 'Oh, Do Tone It Down, Ladies', *Paris Review* (3 March 2020): https://www.theparisreview.org/blog/2020/03/03/oh-do-tone-it-down-ladies/
78 Diane P. Herndl, 'The Writing Cure: Charlotte Perkins Gilman, Anna O., and "Hysterical" Writing', *NWSA Journal* 1: 1 (1988), 52–74. DOI: https://www.jstor.org/stable/4315866
79 Kendra Cherry, 'Hysteria: Over-the-top Emotions or Psychological Condition?' Very Well Mind (7 July 2024): https://www.verywellmind.com/what-is-hysteria-2795232
80 Julianna Little, '"Frailty thy name is woman": Depictions of Female Madness', Virginia Commonwealth University (2015): https://scholarscompass.vcu.edu/cgi/viewcontent.cgi?article=4744&context=etd
81 Kiera Boyle, 'Hysterical Victorian Women', Historic UK: https://www.historic-uk.com/CultureUK/Hysterical-Victorian-Women/
82 'Victorian Era Lunatic Asylums', VL McBeath: https://www.valmcbeath.com/victorian-era-england-1837-1901/victorian-era-lunatic-asylums/
83 Dubravka Ugrešić, 'The Scold's Bridle', *World Literature Today*, 90: 5 (2016), 36–42. DOI: 10.1353/wlt.2016.0093
84 Lynsey T. Cullen, 'The First Lady Almoner: The Appointment, Position, and Findings of Miss Mary Stewart at the Royal Free Hospital, 1895–99', *Journal of the History of Medicine and Allied Sciences*, 68: 4 (2012): 551–582. DOI: 10.1093/jhmas/jrs020
85 Martha Vicinus, *Suffer and Be Still: Women in the Victorian Age* (Routledge, 2013), 10.

86 Richard Samuel Deese, 'GOSPEL OF EVE', *Journal for the Study of Religion Nature and Culture*, 11: 4 (2018), 435. DOI: https://www.researchgate.net/publication/340038034_Deese_GOSPEL_OF_EVE

87 Aleksander Bednarski, 'Hybrid Made of Flowers: Blodeuwedd in Gwyneth Lewis's "The Meat Tree"', *Borderlands: Art, Literature, Culture* (2016), 235–52. DOI: https://www.academia.edu/34499715/Hybrid_made_of_Flowers_Blodeuwedd_in_Gwyneth_Lewis_s_The_Meat_Tree_

88 'Gossip Wolf and the Fox – Fairy Tale by the Brothers Grimm', Childstories: https://www.childstories.org/en/gossip-wolf-and-the-fox-1733.html

89 Eitan Elaad and Ye'ela Gonen-Gal, 'Face-to-Face Lying: Gender and Motivation to Deceive', *Frontiers in Psychology*, 13 (2022). DOI: 10.3389/fpsyg.2022.820923

90 Jessica A. Kennedy and Laura J. Kray, 'Gender similarities and differences in dishonesty', *Current Opinion in Psychology*, 48 (2022), 101461. DOI: https://doi.org/10.1016/j.copsyc.2022.101461

91 Koa Beck, *White Feminism: From the Suffragettes to Influencers and Who They Leave Behind* (Simon & Schuster UK, 2021), 3-8.

92 Francesca Giardini and Rafael Wittek (eds), *The Oxford Handbook of Gossip and Reputation* (Oxford University Press, 2019), 33.

Chapter Two: Friend or Foe

1 S.E. Taylor et al., 'Biobehavioral responses to stress in females: tend-and-befriend, not fight-or-flight', *Psychological Review*, 107: 3 (2000), 411–29. DOI: 10.1037/0033-295x.107.3.411

2 Bassem Khalil et al., 'Physiology, Catecholamines', StatPearls (11 December 2024): https://www.ncbi.nlm.nih.gov/books/NBK507716/

3   Shelley E. Taylor et al., 'Behavioral Responses to Stress in Females: Tend-and-Befriend, Not Fight-or-Flight', *Psychological Review*, 107: 3 (2000), 411–29. DOI: 10.1037//0033-295X.107.3.411

4   T. M. Brown and E. Fee, 'Walter Bradford Cannon: Pioneer Physiologist of Human Emotions', *American Journal of Public Health*, 92: 10 (2002), 1594–5. DOI: https://pmc.ncbi.nlm.nih.gov/articles/PMC1447286/

5   'History of Women in Clinical Trials', MediData (8 March 2025): https://www.medidata.com/en/life-science-resources/medidata-blog/women-in-clinical-trials-history

6   Quinn Grey, 'Period products tested with blood for the first time', Socialist Party (4 October 2023): https://www.socialistparty.org.uk/articles/116193/04-10-2023/period-products-tested-with-blood-for-the-first-time/

7   Katie Baskerville, 'Should you be hormone mapping?', *Women's Health* (30 October 2022): https://www.womenshealthmag.com/uk/collective/healthy-habits/a41712079/should-you-be-hormone-mapping/

8   Constantine Tsigos et al., 'Stress: Endocrine Physiology and Pathophysiology', Endotext (17 October 2017): https://www.ncbi.nlm.nih.gov/books/NBK278995/

9   'Minority Stress Model', ScienceDirect: https://www.sciencedirect.com/topics/psychology/minority-stress-model

10 A. Flentje et el., 'The relationship between minority stress and biological outcomes: A systematic review', *Journal of Behavioral Medicine*, 43: 5 (2020), 673–94. DOI: 10.1007/s10865-019-00120-6

11 F. Angum et al., 'The Prevalence of Autoimmune Disorders in Women: A Narrative Review', *Cureus*, 12: 5 (2020) e8094. DOI: 10.7759/cureus.8094

12 S.E. Taylor et al., 'Biobehavioral responses to stress in females: tend-and-befriend, not fight-or-flight', *Psychological Review*, 107: 3 (2000), 411–29. DOI: 10.1037/0033-295x.107.3.411

13 'Oxytocin: the love hormone', Harvard Health Publishing: https://www.health.harvard.edu/mind-and-mood/oxytocin-the-love-hormone

14 J.K. Hlay et al., 'A Psychometric Evaluation of the Tend-and-Befriend Questionnaire', *Journal of Personality Assessment*, 107: 3 (2024), 346–60. DOI: https://doi.org/10.1080/00223891.2024.2413148

15 Ibid.

16 Robin Dunbar, *Grooming, Gossip and the Evolution of Language* (Faber & Faber, 1996), 30.

17 'Neocortex', ScienceDirect: https://www.sciencedirect.com/topics/psychology/neocortex#definition

18 Chad J. Donahue et al., 'Quantitative assessment of prefrontal cortex in humans relative to nonhuman primates', *Proceedings of the National Academy of Sciences of the United States of America*, 115: 22 (2018), E5183–E5192. DOI: 10.1073/pnas.1721653115

19 Christine Ro, 'The dangers of women's speech', Wellcome Collection (7 April 2020): https://wellcomecollection.org/stories/the-dangers-of-women-s-speech

20 Gabriella Swerling, 'Women's equality has gone too far, say half of Britons', *Telegraph* (1 March 20204): https://www.telegraph.co.uk/news/2024/03/01/womens-equality-has-gone-too-far-say-half-of-britons

21 'Special Report: State of Gender Inequality in the World 2025: A Full Step Backwards?', Focus 2030 (2025): https://focus2030.org/Gender-inequality-around-the-world-in-2025-special-report

22 'One in four countries report backlash on women's rights in 2024', UN Women (6 March 2025): https://www.unwomen.org/en/

news-stories/press-release/2025/03/one-in-four-countries-report-backlash-on-womens-rights-in-2024

23 G.T. Reyes, 'Nice for Whom? A Dangerous, Not-So-Nice, Critical Race Love Letter', *Education Sciences* (Niceness, Leadership and Educational Equity special issue), 14: 5 (2024), 508. DOI: https://doi.org/10.3390/educsci14050508

24 K. J. Anderson, 'Modern misogyny and backlash', in C. B. Travis et al. (eds), *APA handbook of the psychology of women: History, theory, and battlegrounds* (27–46). American Psychological Association (2018). DOI: https://doi.org/10.1037/0000059-002

25 Sarah Winkler-Reid, 'Friendship, bitching, and the making of ethical selves: what it means to be a good friend among girls in a London school', *Journal of the Royal Anthropological Institute*, 22: 1 (2015), 166–182. DOI: https://doi.org/10.1111/1467-9655.12339

26 Anna Bogutskaya, *Unlikeable Female Characters: The Women Pop Culture Wants You to Hate* (Sourcebooks, 2023), 53.

27 Li Zhou, 'Use of the word "bitch" surged after women's suffrage', Vox (19 August 2020): https://www.vox.com/21365241/19th-amendment-womens-suffrage-backlash

28 Debra Michals (ed.), 'Sojourner Truth', National Women's History Museum (2015): https://www.womenshistory.org/education-resources/biographies/sojourner-truth

29 Marisa Mathias, 'Susan B. Anthony', National Women's History Museum (2024): https://www.womenshistory.org/education-resources/biographies/susan-b-anthony

30 Martha S. Jones, 'For Black women, the 19th Amendment didn't end their fight to vote', National Geographic (7 August 2020): https://www.nationalgeographic.com/history/article/black-women-continued-fighting-for-vote-after-19th-amendment

31 Sumita Mukherjee, 'Black History Month: Diversity and the British Female Suffrage Movement', Fawcett Society (30 October

2017): https://www.fawcettsociety.org.uk/blog/diversity-british-female-suffrage-movement
32. Dr Gillian Murphy, 'Millicent Garrett Fawcett, Lucy Deane and the Boer War', London School of Economics (16 March 2016): https://blogs.lse.ac.uk/lsehistory/2016/03/16/millicent-garrett-fawcett-lucy-deane-and-the-boer-war/
33. 'Emmeline Pankhurst: Suffragette Icon', London Museum: https://www.londonmuseum.org.uk/collections/london-stories/emmeline-pankhurst-suffragette-icon/
34. 'Women's suffrage', Britannica: https://www.britannica.com/topic/woman-suffrage
35. 'Start of the suffragette movement', UK Parliament (2010): https://www.parliament.uk/about/living-heritage/transformingsociety/electionsvoting/womenvote/overview/startsuffragette-/
36. Li Zhou, 'Use of the word "bitch" surged after women's suffrage', Vox (19 August 2020): https://www.vox.com/21365241/19th-amendment-womens-suffrage-backlash
37. Karen Stollznow, *Bitch: The Journey of a Word* (Cambridge University Press, 2024), 30, 38.

Chapter Three: Locker-Room Talk

1. David A. Fahrenthold, 'Trump recorded having extremely lewd conversation about women in 2005', *Washington Post* (8 October 2016): https://www.washingtonpost.com/politics/trump-recorded-having-extremely-lewd-conversation-about-women-in-2005/2016/10/07/3b9ce776-8cb4-11e6-bf8a-3d26847eeed4_story.html
2. Jonathan Lemire, 'Trump caught on video making lewd, crude remarks about women', Associated Press (8 October 2016): https://apnews.com/arts-and-entertainment-events-united-states-presidential-election-television-5906910b70224c62b8013100d8749d3e

3   'US Election: Full transcript of Trump's obscene videotape', BBC News (9 October 2016): https://www.bbc.co.uk/news/election-us-2016-37595321
4   B.P. Cole et al., 'Predicting men's acceptance of sexual violence myths through conformity to masculine norms, sexism, and "locker room talk"', *Psychology of Men & Masculinities,* 21: 4 (2020), 508–17. DOI: https://doi.org/10.1037/men0000248
5   T.P. Patterson and M.S. Ternes, 'Masculine threat and pressures to engage in locker room talk: The moderation effects of self-warmth and self-coldness', *Psychology of Men & Masculinities* (2025). DOI: https://doi.org/10.1037/men0000532
6   B.H.H. Ching, 'The effect of masculinity threat on transprejudice: Influence of different aspects of masculinity contingent self-worth. *Psychology & Sexuality,* 13:3 (2021), 550–64. DOI: https://doi.org/10.1080/19419899.2021.1883724
7   M.C. Parent et al., 'Masculinity contingency and intimate partner violence perpetration among men who have sex with men', *Psychology of Men & Masculinities,* 24: 2 (2023), 167–72. DOI: https://doi.org/10.1037/men0000428
8   R.C. McDermott et al., 'Men's masculinity contingency and social anxiety symptomology in higher education: The moderating role of depressive symptoms', *Psychology of Men & Masculinities,* 23: 2 (2022), 265–70. DOI: https://doi.org/10.1037/men0000390
9   M.J. Vaynman et al., '"Locker room talk": male bonding and sexual degradation in drinking stories', *Culture, Health & Sexuality,* 22: 11 (2019), pp.1235–1252. DOI: https://doi.org/10.1080/13691058.2019.1670864
10 R.M. Leone and D.J. Parrott, 'Misogynistic peers, masculinity, and bystander intervention for sexual aggression: Is it really just "locker-room talk?"' *Aggressive Behavior,* 45: 1 (2019), 42–51. DOI: 10.1002/ab.21795. Erratum in: *Aggressive Behavior,* 45: 5 (2019), 582. DOI: 10.1002/ab.21849

11 Leoma Williams, 'In real life Nemo's dad would become female (and might have even mated with his son) – Discover 10 animals that can amazingly change sex', Discover Wildlife (22 August 2025): https://www.discoverwildlife.com/animal-facts/animals-that-can-change-sex
12 Erin Blakemore, 'How historians are documenting the lives of transgender people', National Geographic (24 June 2022): https://www.nationalgeographic.com/history/article/how-historians-are-documenting-lives-of-transgender-people
13 'Is being trans a new thing?' Trans Hub: https://www.transhub.org.au/101/is-trans-new
14 J. Ristori et al., 'Brain Sex Differences Related to Gender Identity Development: Genes or Hormones?' *International Journal of Molecular Sciences*, 21: 6 (2020), 2123. DOI: 10.3390/ijms21062123
15 Jessica Valenti, Instagram (3 February 2025): https://www.instagram.com/p/DFn-rzUpY8h/?img_index=1
16 'Woman denies self-medicating to induce miscarriage', BBC News (24 April 2025): https://www.bbc.co.uk/news/articles/cwy639j97j2o
17 Phoebe Davis, 'Fourth woman faces illegal abortion charge as UK prosecutions rise', Tortoise (16 August 2023): https://www.tortoisemedia.com/2023/08/16/uk-woman-pleads-not-guilty-to-carrying-out-illegal-at-home-abortion
18 Jennifer Savin, 'Police told how to search a woman's home and her phone for evidence she's had an illegal abortion', *Cosmopolitan* (19 May 2025): https://www.cosmopolitan.com/uk/reports/a64814425/police-guidance-abortion-drugs/
19 'Red Flag Alert on Anti-Trans and Intersex Rights in the UK', Lemkin Institute (30 June 2025): https://www.lemkininstitute.com/red-flag-alerts/red-flag-alert-on-anti-trans-and-intersex-rights-in-the-uk

20 Archie Bland, 'Tuesday briefing: What Reform UK might get from Elon Musk's $100m – and what he might want in return', *Guardian* (24 December 2024): https://www.theguardian.com/world/2024/dec/24/tuesday-briefing-elon-musk-100-million-donation-reform-uk-nigel-farage

21 Alix Cuthbertson, 'Nigel Farage says it is "utterly ludicrous" to allow abortion up to 24 weeks', Sky News (27 May 2025): https://news.sky.com/story/nigel-farage-says-it-is-utterly-ludicrous-to-allow-abortion-up-to-24-weeks-13375431

22 'Opposition', Oxford Learner's Dictionaries: https://www.oxfordlearnersdictionaries.com/definition/american_english/opposition

23 Sarah H. DiMuccio and Eric D. Knowles. 'The political significance of fragile masculinity', *Current Opinion in Behavioral Sciences*, 34 (2020), 25-28. DOI: https://doi.org/10.1016/j.cobeha.2019.11.010

24 Butches refers to a masculine presenting group within the lesbian community.

25 Dr Finn Mackay, 'Who's Afraid of Female Masculinity?', Dr Finn Mackay (21 August 2019): https://www.drfinnmackay.co.uk/blog/whos-afraid-of-female-masculinity

26 Todd W. Reeser, 'Concepts of Masculinity and Masculinity Studies', Brill: https://brill.com/downloadpdf/book/edcoll/9789004299009/BP000003.pdf

27 'Roman Venus', J. Paul Getty Museum: https://www.getty.edu/art/exhibitions/aphrodite/venus.html

28 Vann Orr and Darah Paige, 'A Roman Rape Culture: Sexual Violence in Augustan Era Rome', dissertation, University of Houston (2023): https://uh-ir.tdl.org/items/4b16cfb9-8f7f-4fae-a2b1-7f78edad5c83

29 'Alba Longa', Britannica: https://www.britannica.com/place/Alba-Longa

30 Titus Livius (Livy), Benjamin Oliver Foster (ed.), *The History of Rome, Book 1*, Perseus Digital Library: https://www.perseus.tufts.edu/hopper/text?doc=Perseus%3Atext%3A1999.02.0151%3Abook%3D1%3Achapter%3D3

31 The Legend of Romulus and Remus, Odyssey Online: https://carlos.emory.edu/htdocs/ODYSSEY/ROME/romulus.html

32 Vann Orr and Darah Paige, 'A Roman Rape Culture: Sexual Violence in Augustan Era Rome', dissertation, University of Houston (2023): https://uh-ir.tdl.org/items/4b16cfb9-8f7f-4fae-a2b1-7f78edad5c83

33 'Legal Definitions – stuprum', LSD Law: https://www.lsd.law/define/stuprum

34 'Adulte'rium', William Smith, William Wayte, G. E. Marindin, (eds), *A Dictionary of Greek and Roman Antiquities*, (1890), Perseus Digital Library: https://www.perseus.tufts.edu/hopper/text?doc=Perseus:text:1999.04.0063:id=adulterium-cn

35 'Roman law', Britannica: https://www.britannica.com/topic/Roman-law

36 'Trades of Ancient Rome in the Modern World', National Geographic: https://education.nationalgeographic.org/resource/traces-ancient-rome-modern-world/

37 'History of Sexual Abuse and Harassment', Freedom and Citizenship, Columbia University: https://freedomandcitizenship.columbia.edu/gender-equality-history-2021

38 Rape and sexual assault statistics, Rape Crisis: https://rapecrisis.org.uk/get-informed/statistics-sexual-violence/

39 Alan Travis, 'Rape law change to redefine consent', *Guardian* (28 October 2002): https://www.theguardian.com/uk/2002/oct/28/gender.ukcrime

40 Rape and Sexual Offences – Chapter 7: 'Key Legislation and Offences, Crown Prosecution Service' (21 May 2021): https://

www.cps.gov.uk/legal-guidance/rape-and-sexual-offences-chapter-7-key-legislation-and-offences

41 Jessica Aiston, 'What is the manosphere and why is it of concern?', Internet Matters (4 October 2021): https://www.internetmatters.org/hub/news-blogs/what-is-the-manosphere-and-why-is-it-a-concern/

42 John Burn-Murdoch, 'A new global gender divide is emerging', *Financial Times* (25 January 2025): https://www.ft.com/content/29fd9b5c-2f35-41bf-9d4c-994db4e12998

43 Catherine Kim, 'Young Men Are Swinging Hard Right in Korea. It Could Be a Preview for America', *Politico* (1 July 2024): https://www.politico.com/news/magazine/2024/07/01/south-korea-gender-divide-feminism-00155207

44 Lee Jaeeun, 'Why femicide and dating violence are growing issues in S. Korea', *Korea Herald* (8 May 2024) https://www.koreaherald.com/view.php?ud=20240508050601

45 Filipa Melo Lopes, 'What Do Incels Want? Explaining Incel Violence Using Beauvoirian Otherness', *HYPATIA*, 38: 1 (2023), 134–56. DOI:10.1017/hyp.2023.3

46 Ibid.

47 'Chivalry', Oxford Learner's Dictionaries: https://www.oxfordlearnersdictionaries.com/definition/american_english/chivalry

48 'Knight service', Britannica: https://www.britannica.com/topic/knight-service

49 'What was chivalry and what were its laws?', University of Aberdeen: https://www.abdn.ac.uk/sll/disciplines/english/lion/chivalry.shtml

50 'Chivalry in the Middle Ages', The J. Paul Getty Museum (2014): https://www.getty.edu/art/exhibitions/chivalry/

51 'The results of the Crusades', Britannica: https://www.britannica.com/event/Crusades/The-results-of-the-Crusades

52 Gail Omvedt, Review of *The Origin of Patriarchy*, by Gerda Lerner', *Economic and Political Weekly*, 22: 44 (1987): WS70–72. DOI: http://www.jstor.org/stable/4377665

53 Lindsay Kohler, 'New Research Finds The "Old Boys Club" At Work Is Real – And Contributing To The Gender Pay Gap', Forbes (22 April 2021): https://www.forbes.com/sites/lindsaykohler/2021/04/22/new-research-finds-the-old-boys-club-at-work-is-real---and-contributing-to-the-gender-pay-gap/

54 Zoë Cullen and Ricardo Perez-Truglia, 'The Old Boys' Club: Schmoozing and the Gender Gap', Harvard Business School (2022): https://www.hbs.edu/ris/Publication%20Files/BODY%20--%20Cullen%20and%20Perez-Truglia%20--%20Old%20Boys%20Club_e9d852d9-3277-461c-b7eb-27d46b896318.pdf

55 J.L. Oliffe et al., 'Masculinities and men's emotions in and after intimate partner relationships', *Sociology of Health & Illness*, 45: 2 (2023), 366–85. DOI: https://doi.org/10.1111/1467-9566.13583

56 Chloe Brotheridge, *Brave New Girl: Seven Steps to Confidence* (Michael Joseph, 2019), 19: https://www.penguin.co.uk/books/313922/brave-new-girl-by-brotheridge-chloe/9780241400463

57 T.K. Vescio et al., 'The affective consequences of threats to masculinity', *Journal of Experimental Social Psychology*, 97 (2021), 104195. DOI: https://doi.org/10.1016/j.jesp.2021.104195

58 H.E. Adams et al., 'Is homophobia associated with homosexual arousal?' *Journal of Psychopathology and Clinical Science*, 105: 3 (1996), 440–45. DOI: https://doi.org/10.1037/0021-843X.105.3.440

59 Nathaniel Schermerhorn, 'The Effects of "Gayzing": When the Gaze of Gay Men Poses a Threat to Straight Men's Masculinity', Master Thesis, Penn State University (2019): https://etda.libraries.psu.edu/catalog/16871njs5478

60 Homophobic, Biphobic and Transphobic Hate Crime – Prosecution Guidance, Crown Prosecution Service (3 March 2022): https://www.cps.gov.uk/legal-guidance/homophobic-biphobic-and-transphobic-hate-crime-prosecution-guidance
61 M.L. Borras Guevara et al., 'Fragile Heterosexuality: A Cross-cultural Study Between Germany and Italy', *Sexuality & Culture*, 27 (2023), 1044–63. DOI: https://doi.org/10.1007/s12119-022-10053-z
62 Press release, '12 Sep Andrew Tate's "The Real World" app banned by Google amid claims it's a pyramid scheme', McCue Jury & Partners: https://www.mccue-law.com/andrew-tates-the-real-world-app-banned-by-google-amid-claims-its-a-pyramid-scheme/
63 Matthew Smith, 'One in six boys aged 6–15 have a positive view of Andrew Tate', YouGov (27 September 2023): https://yougov.co.uk/society/articles/47419-one-in-six-boys-aged-6-15-have-a-positive-view-of-andrew-tate

Chapter Four: Social Media

1 Manoel Horta Ribeiro et al., 'The Evolution of the Manosphere Across the Web', UCL Discovery (2021): https://discovery.ucl.ac.uk/id/eprint/10113225/1/no_comments.pdf
2 '*The Matrix* is a "trans metaphor", Lilly Wachowski says', BBC News (7 August 2020): https://www.bbc.co.uk/news/newsbeat-53692435
3 '*The Matrix*'s real-world legacy – from red pill incels to conspiracy and deepfakes', BBC News (21 December 2021): https://www.bbc.co.uk/news/entertainment-arts-57572152
4 Katie Baskerville, 'What Happens When Victims Are Bombarded with Sexual Assault News', *Huff Post* (2 October 2023): https://www.huffingtonpost.co.uk/entry/heres-what-happens-when-victims-have-to-confront-news-about-sexual-assault_uk_651ad915e4b0c39562538035

5   'Roosh V cancels "Return of Kings" events', BBC News (4 February 2016): https://www.bbc.co.uk/news/uk-scotland-35491495
6   Mack Lamoureux, 'Roosh V Shuttering His Godawful Misogynist Website After Successful Boycotts', Vice (2 October 2018): https://www.vice.com/en/article/roosh-v-shuttering-return-of-kings-after-successful-boycotts/
7   Roosh V, *30 Bangs: The Shaping of One Man's Game, from Patient Mouse to Rabid Wolf* (PDF Room, 2012): https://pdfroom.com/books/30-bangs-the-shaping-of-one-mans-game-from-patient-mouse-to-rabid-wolf/315v84D3gYy
8   James McCarthy and Sophie Evans, 'Pro-rape campaigner Roosh V forced to cancel UK "anti-feminist" meetings amid safety fears', *Mirror* (4 February 2016): https://www.mirror.co.uk/news/uk-news/pro-rape-campaigner-roosh-v-7305828
9   The Muslim Skeptic, 'Roosh: Modernity, Christianity, and Islam [Muslim Skeptic Live #37]', YouTube (19 January 2021): https://www.youtube.com/watch?v=W3gMrAGiWHc
10 The 2008 recession 10 years on, Office for National Statistics (30 April 2018): https://www.ons.gov.uk/economy/grossdomesticproductgdp/articles/the2008recession10yearson/2018-04-30
11 Gefjon Orff et al., 'Who perceives women's rights as threatening to men and boys? Explaining modern sexism among young men in Europe', *Frontiers in Political Science*, 4 (2022). DOI: https://doi.org/10.3389/fpos.2022.909811
12 L. García-Favaro and R. Gill, '"Emasculation nation has arrived": sexism rearticulated in online responses to Lose the Lads' Mags campaign', *Feminist Media Studies*, 16: 3 (2015), 379–397. DOI: https://doi.org/10.1080/14680777.2015.1105840

13 Natasha Turner, '"Lose the Lads' Mags" Campaign Causes Stir in U.K.', *Ms.* (6 April 2013): https://msmagazine.com/2013/06/04/lose-the-lads-mags-campaign-causes-stir-in-u-k/

14 Jim Taylor, 'The woman who founded the "incel" movement', BBC News (30 August 2018): https://www.bbc.co.uk/news/world-us-canada-45284455

15 Ashifa Kassam, 'Woman behind "incel" says angry men hijacked her word "as a weapon of war"', *Guardian* (26 April 2018): https://www.theguardian.com/world/2018/apr/25/woman-who-invented-incel-movement-interview-toronto-attack

16 *People* staff, 'Vanessa Hudgens "Embarrassed," Apologizes for Nude Photo', *People* (7 September 2007): https://people.com/celebrity/vanessa-hudgens-embarrassed-apologizes-for-nude-photo/

17 'Cover Exclusive: Jennifer Lawrence Calls Photo Hacking a "Sex Crime"', *Vanity Fair* (7 October 2014): https://www.vanityfair.com/hollywood/2014/10/jennifer-lawrence-cover

18 Caitlin Dewey, 'Absolutely everything you need to know to understand 4chan, the Internet's own bogeyman', *Washington Post* (25 September 2014): https://www.washingtonpost.com/news/the-intersect/wp/2014/09/25/absolutely-everything-you-need-to-know-to-understand-4chan-the-internets-own-bogeyman/

19 Jenna Wortham, 'Founder of a Provocative Web Site Forms a New Outlet', *New York Times* (13 March 2011): https://www.nytimes.com/2011/03/14/technology/internet/14poole.html?_r=2&

20 Brian Holoyda, 'QAnon', Britannica: https://www.britannica.com/topic/QAnon

21 L. Goldstein and M. Linde Murugan, 'Misinformation as woman: anti-feminism, news media, and disinformation's feminized other', *Feminist Media Studies*, 24: 1 (2024), 158–61. DOI: https://doi.org/10.1080/14680777.2023.2284103

22 Erica Hellerstein, 'Silicon Savanna: The workers taking on Africa's digital sweatshops', Coda (11 October 2023): https://www.codastory.com/authoritarian-tech/kenya-content-moderators/

23 Mona Elswah, 'Investigating Content Moderation Systems in the Global South', Center for Democracy & Technology (30 January 2024): https://cdt.org/insights/investigating-content-moderation-systems-in-the-global-south/

24 S. Melbye Larsen, '"Metoo is a terror organization." A Critical Study of How Testimonial Injustice Operates in Danish Facebook Discourses', LUP Student Papers/Lund University Libraries (2022): https://lup.lub.lu.se/student-papers/search/publication/9096579

25 Press release, 'Cyberflashing, epilepsy-trolling and fake news to put online abusers behind bars from today', GOV.UK (31 January 2024): https://www.gov.uk/government/news/cyberflashing-epilepsy-trolling-and-fake-news-to-put-online-abusers-behind-bars-from-today

26 18 U.S. Code § 35 - Imparting or conveying false information, Legal Information Institute, Cornell Law School: https://www.law.cornell.edu/uscode/text/18/35

27 Constance Grady, 'The mounting, undeniable Me Too backlash', Vox (3 February 2023): https://www.vox.com/culture/23581859/me-too-backlash-susan-faludi-weinstein-roe-dobbs-depp-heard

28 'No ifs, many bots? Partisan bot-like accounts continue to amplify divisive content on X, generating over 4 billion views since the UK general election was called', Global Witness (31 July 2024): https://www.globalwitness.org/en/campaigns/digital-threats/no-ifs-many-bots-partisan-bot-accounts-continue-amplify-divisive-content-x-generating-over-4-billion-views-uk-general-election-was-called/

29 'State of the World's Girls 2021: The Truth Gap', Plan International: https://plan-international.org/publications/the-truth-gap/

30 'Decoding Technology-Facilitated Gender-Based Violence: A Reality Check from Seven Countries', Rutgers (2024): https://rutgers.international/wp-content/uploads/2024/06/Decoding-TFGBV-Report-2024.pdf
31 Ibid.
32 'Quick-read guide: gender and countering disinformation', HM Government: https://assets.publishing.service.gov.uk/media/5e4ab31e40f0b677c3e37ff3/Quick_Read-Gender_and_countering_disinformation.pdf
33 'Social media algorithms amplify misogynistic content to teens', University College London (5 February 2024): https://www.ucl.ac.uk/news/2024/feb/social-media-algorithms-amplify-misogynistic-content-teens
34 Alexi Mostrous and Xavier Greenwood, 'Depp v Heard: who trolled Amber?' Tortoise (26 February 2024): https://www.tortoisemedia.com/2024/02/26/depp-v-heard-who-trolled-amber/
35 Jonathan Dean, 'Johnny Depp: "I was a crash test dummy for MeToo"', *The Times* (21 June 2025): https://www.thetimes.com/life-style/celebrity/article/johnny-depp-metoo-amber-heard-interview-73lzdtzt2
36 Mostrous and Greenwood, 'Depp v Heard: who trolled Amber?' Tortoise (26 February 2024): https://www.tortoisemedia.com/2024/02/26/depp-v-heard-who-trolled-amber/
37 Jason Guerrasio, 'Amber Heard has lost up to $50 million due to abuse "hoax" claims, industry expert testifies', Business Insider (24 May 2022): https://www.businessinsider.com/amber-heard-lost-50-million-after-hoax-claims-says-expert-2022-5
38 A. Lüders et al., 'Not our kind of crowd! How partisan bias distorts perceptions of political bots on Twitter (now X)', *British Journal of Social Psychology*, 64: 2 (2025). DOI: 10.1111/bjso.12794

39 Anya Zoledziowski, 'Amber Heard's Vicious Online Trolls Are Coming for Angelina Jolie Now', *VICE* (14 October 2022): https://www.vice.com/en/article/amber-heard-angelina-jolie-abuse-allegations-brad-pitt/

40 Statistics of Sexual Abuse, Hugh James: https://www.hughjames.com/services/sexual-abuse-claims-and-compensation/guide-to-sexual-abuse-claims/statistics-of-sexual-abuse

41 Laura Bates, *The New Age of Sexism: How the AI Revolution Is Reinventing Misogyny* (Simon & Schuster, 2025), 2, 3.

42 Victoria O'Meara et al., 'Just being a bit bitchy: The gendered valences of online anti-social behavior on Tattle Life', Proceedings of the 57th Hawaii International Conference on System Sciences (2024). DOI: 10.24251/HICSS.2024.847

43 Jennifer Savin, 'Revealed: Identity of Tattle Life's publisher is finally unmasked after 7 years, and it's a male influencer', *Cosmopolitan* (13 June 2025): https://www.cosmopolitan.com/uk/reports/a65059691/tattle-life-founder/

44 Ibid.

45 Ethan Alter, 'Louis C.K.'s comeback from cancellation explored in new documentary: "There are no easy answers"', Yahoo! Entertainment (11 September 2023): https://www.yahoo.com/entertainment/louis-ck-comeback-canceled-new-documentary-143133408.html

46 Sam Tobin, 'Kevin Spacey overturns UK ruling in sex assault case over lawyers' mistake', Reuters (7 May 2024): https://www.reuters.com/world/uk/kevin-spacey-overturns-uk-ruling-sex-assault-case-over-lawyers-mistake-2024-05-07

47 Nick Vivarelli, 'Kevin Spacey to Play "The Devil" Character in Italian Thriller "The Contract"', *Variety* (5 March 2024): https://variety.com/2024/film/global/kevin-spacey-devil-italian-thriller-the-contract-1235930332/

48 Chris Willman, 'Can Ryan Adams Be a Rock Star Again? With a New Team and Return to Concerts, Singer Looks to Move Past Sexual Misconduct Allegations', *Variety* (3 June 2022): https://variety.com/2022/music/news/ryan-adams-new-team-concerts-move-past-allegations-1235284292/

49 Todd Martens, 'Chris Brown's "Fortune" sputters to No.1 debut', *Los Angeles Times* (11 July 2012): https://www.latimes.com/entertainment/music/la-xpm-2012-jul-11-la-et-ms-chris-browns-fortune-no-1-debut-20120711-story.html

50 T.R. Graf and L.B. Watson, 'Who Gets Canceled for Sexual Assault?: The Roles of Likeability and Tactic on Perceived Perpetrator Accountability', *Sex Roles*, 90 (2024), 1244–61. DOI: https://doi.org/10.1007/s11199-024-01465-2

51 M. Feinberg et al., 'The virtues of gossip: reputational information sharing as prosocial behavior', *Journal of Personality and Social Psychology*, 102: 5 (2012):1015–30. DOI: 10.1037/a0026650

52 T.D. Dores Cruz et al., 'Gossip and reputation in everyday life', *Philosophical Transactions of the Royal Society B*, 376: 1838 (2021), DOI: https://doi.org/10.1098/rstb.2020.0301

53 Sameer Hinduja, 'The Importance of Your Digital Reputation', Cyberbullying Research Center: https://cyberbullying.org/the-importance-of-your-digital-reputation

54 'What is pile-on harassment', Internet Law Centre, Cohen Davis Solicitors: https://harassmentlawyer.co.uk/information-about-harassment/doxing-legal-help

Chapter Five: Whisper Networks

1 C.L. Johnson, 'The purpose of whisper networks: a new lens for studying informal communication channels in organizations', *Frontiers in Communication*, 8 (2023). DOI: https://doi.org/10.3389/fcomm.2023.1089335

2. Violence against women: Key facts, World Health Organization (25 March 2024): https://www.who.int/news-room/fact-sheets/detail/violence-against-women
3. T.M. Chaplin, 'Gender and Emotion Expression: A Developmental Contextual Perspective', *Emotion Review*, 7: 1 (2015), 14–21. DOI: 10.1177/1754073914544408
4. M. Dittmann, 'Anger across the gender divide', *American Psychological Association*, 34: 3 (2003), 52. https://www.apa.org/monitor/mar03/angeracross
5. Women and mental health, Mental Health Foundation: https://www.mentalhealth.org.uk/explore-mental-health/a-z-topics/women-and-mental-health
6. Daphna Motro et al., 'The "Angry Black Woman" Stereotype at Work', *Harvard Business Review* (31 January 2022): https://hbr.org/2022/01/the-angry-black-woman-stereotype-at-work
7. Mahrukh S.M., 'The stigma around female rage', Assembly (5 January 2022): https://assembly.malala.org/stories/the-stigma-around-female-rage
8. Darlene Clark Hine, '"Ar'n't I a Woman?: Female Slaves in the Plantation South": Twenty Years After', *Journal of African American History*, 92: 1 (2007), 13–21. DOI: http://www.jstor.org/stable/20064151
9. J. Kent, 'Scapegoating and the "angry black woman"', *Group Analysis*, 54: 3 (2021), 354–71. DOI: https://doi.org/10.1177/0533316421992300
10. M. Griffin et al., '#BodyPositive? A critical exploration of the body positive movement within physical cultures taking an intersectionality approach', *Frontiers in Sports and Active Living* (2022), 4: 908580. DOI: 10.3389/fspor.2022.908580
11. Ibid.

12 Viren Swami, 'Why body positivity movement risks turning toxic', Anglia Ruskin University (20 September 2022): https://www.aru.ac.uk/news/why-body-positivity-movement-risks-turning-toxic

13 'More than 12M "MeToo" Facebook posts, comments, reactions in 24 hours', CBS News (17 October 2017): https://www.cbsnews.com/news/metoo-more-than-12-million-facebook-posts-comments-reactions-24-hours/

14 Ted Gregory, 'Tarana Burke discusses her me too movement, Hollywood's hashtag co-opting of it', UChicago News (29 March 2023): https://news.uchicago.edu/story/tarana-burke-discusses-her-me-too-movement-hollywoods-hashtag-co-opting-it

15 R.A.E. Gutierrez et al., 'Confronting *Mean Girls* Niceness: Conceptualizing Whisper Care to Disrupt the Politics of Niceness in Academia', *Education Sciences*, 14: 5 (2024), 473. DOI: https://doi.org/10.3390/educsci14050473

16 J. Tucker and J. Mondino, 'Coming Forward', TIME'S UP Legal Defense Fund and National Women's Law Center (2020): https://nwlc.org/wp-content/uploads/2020/10/NWLC-Intake-Report_FINAL_2020-10-13.pdf

17 Janey Matejka, 'Fetishized and Blamed: Attitudes Toward Asian American Women as Victims/Survivors of Sexual Assault', Scripps Senior Theses, 2377 (2024): https://scholarship.claremont.edu/cgi/viewcontent.cgi?article=3421&context=scripps_theses

18 Jaclyn Diaz, 'Where the #MeToo movement stands, 5 years after Weinstein allegations came to light', NPR (28 October 2022): https://www.npr.org/2022/10/28/1131500833/me-too-harvey-weinstein-anniversary

19 'Weinstein & Hollywood's "open secret"', Ethics Unwrapped, McCombs School of Business, University of Texas at Austin: https://ethicsunwrapped.utexas.edu/video/weinstein-hollywoods-open-secret

20 A. Rysman, 'How the "Gossip" Became a Woman', *Journal of Communication*, 27: 1 (1977), 176–80. DOI: https://doi.org/10.1111/j.1460-2466.1977.tb01814.x

21 Ed Pilkington, 'Donna Rotunno: the legal Rottweiler leading Harvey Weinstein's Defense', *Guardian* (9 February 2020): https://www.theguardian.com/film/2020/feb/09/donna-rotunno-lawyer-leading-harvey-weinsteins-defense

22 Donna Rotunno, 'Jurors in My Client Harvey Weinstein's Case Must Look Beyond the Headlines', *Newsweek* (16 February 2020): https://www.newsweek.com/jurors-my-client-harvey-weinsteins-case-must-look-past-headlines-opinion-1487564

23 Shannon H.P. Ward, 'Combatting the Harvey Weinstein Defense', *Advocate* (May 2020): https://www.advocatemagazine.com/article/2020-may/combatting-the-harvey-weinstein-defense

24 Deconstructing the Myths About Victims, Stronghearts Native Helpline: https://strongheartshelpline.org/abuse/deconstructing-the-myths-about-victims

25 Anti Victim Blaming Guidance, Health Surrey: https://www.healthysurrey.org.uk/domestic-abuse/professionals/anti-victim-blaming-guidance

26 Rape and Sexual Assault Statistics, Rape Crisis England & Wales: https://rapecrisis.org.uk/get-informed/statistics-sexual-violence/

27 Graeme Baker, 'Harvey Weinstein's 2020 rape conviction overturned in New York', BBC News (25 April 2024): https://www.bbc.co.uk/news/world-us-canada-68899382

28 Terry Gross, 'Reporters Dig into Justice Kavanaugh's Past, Allegations of Misconduct Against Him', NPR (16 September 2019): https://www.npr.org/2019/09/16/761191576/reporters-dig-into-justice-kavanaughs-past-allegations-of-misconduct-against-him

29　Bess Levin, 'The FBI Confirms Its Brett Kavanaugh Investigation Was a Total Sham', *Vanity Fair* (5 August 2022): https://www.vanityfair.com/news/2022/08/brett-kavanaugh-fbi-investigation

30　Aisha Doherty, 'Woman wins payout after "sexsomnia" rape case dropped', BBC News (14 August 2024): https://www.bbc.co.uk/news/articles/cwyxdpezyllo

31　Vikram Dodd, 'Met police found to be institutionally racist, misogynistic and homophobic', *Guardian* (21 March 2023): https://www.theguardian.com/uk-news/2023/mar/21/metropolitan-police-institutionally-racist-misogynistic-homophobic-louise-casey-report

32　Gordon B. Dahl and Matthew M. Knepper, 'Why is Workplace Sexual Harassment Underreported? The Value of Outside Options Amid the Threat of Retaliation', National Bureau of Economic Research (2021), 29248. DOI: 10.3386/w29248

33　Lauren Brown, 'Half of employees do not report workplace sexual harassment, survey finds – how can businesses encourage speaking up?' People Management (26 March 2024): https://www.peoplemanagement.co.uk/article/1866611/half-employees-not-report-workplace-sexual-harassment-survey-finds

34　'Women @ Work 2024: A Global Outlook, Deloitte (2024): https://www.deloitte.com/content/dam/assets-shared/docs/collections/2024/deloitte-women-at-work-2024-a-global-outlook.pdf?dl=1

35　Lucy Webster, 'The everyday assault of disabled women: "It's inappropriate sexual touching at least once a month"', *Guardian* (25 November 2021): https://www.theguardian.com/world/2021/nov/25/the-everyday-assault-of-disabled-women-its-inappropriate-sexual-touching-at-least-once-a-month

36　Sexual Harassment in Our Nation's Workplaces, U.S. Equal Employment Opportunity Commission: https://www.eeoc.gov/data/sexual-harassment-our-nations-workplaces

37 D. Cheng et al., 'How Organizational Responses to Sexual Harassment Claims Shape Public Perception', *Basic and Applied Social Psychology*, 46: 3 (2024), 169–86. https://doi.org/10.1080/01973533.2024.2313536

38 'New TUC poll: 2 in 3 young women have experienced sexual harassment, bullying or verbal abuse at work', Trades Union Congress (12 May 2023): https://www.tuc.org.uk/news/new-tuc-poll-2-3-young-women-have-experienced-sexual-harassment-bullying-or-verbal-abuse-work

39 Carrie Ann Johnson, 'The purpose of whisper networks: a new lens for studying informal communication channels in organizations', *Frontiers in Communication*, 8 (2023). DOI: https://doi.org/10.3389/fcomm.2023.1089335

40 R. Bowen et al., 'Why Report? Sex Workers who Use NUM Opt out of Sharing Victimisation with Police', *Sexuality Research and Social Policy*, 18, 885–96 (2021). DOI: https://doi.org/10.1007/s13178-021-00627-1

41 P. Struyf, 'To Report or Not to Report? A Systematic Review of Sex Workers' Willingness to Report Violence and Victimization to Police', *Trauma, Violence, & Abuse*, 24: 5 (2022), 3065–77. DOI: https://doi.org/10.1177/15248380221122819

42 Baroness Casey, 'An Independent Review into the Standards of Behaviour and Internal Culture of the Metropolitan Police Service', Metropolitan Police (2023): https://www.met.police.uk/SysSiteAssets/media/downloads/met/about-us/baroness-casey-review/update-march-2023/baroness-casey-review-march-2023a.pdf

43 '"Institutional racism applies to South Wales Police", says chief constable', Police Professional (11 October 2023): https://policeprofessional.com/news/institutional-racism-applies-to-south-wales-police-says-chief-constable/

44 'South Wales Police has worst record for allegations of violence against women and girls of all Welsh forces', Nation Cymru (15 March 2023): https://nation.cymru/news/south-wales-police-has-worst-record-for-allegations-of-violence-against-women-and-girls-of-all-welsh-forces/

45 Dame Vera Baird KC, 'The Baird Inquiry' (2024): https://www.greatermanchester-ca.gov.uk/media/9861/the-baird-inquiry.pdf

46 'Inquiry finds Greater Manchester Police unlawfully arrested and stripsearched victims of abuse', End Violence Against Women (18 July 2024): https://www.endviolenceagainstwomen.org.uk/inquiry-finds-greater-manchester-police-unlawfully-arrested-and-stripsearched-abuse-victims/

47 N. Westera et al., 'Police Investigators' Perceptions of the Challenges Associated with Interviewing Adult Sexual Assault Complainants', Violence Against Women, 29: 2 (2022), 276–99. DOI: https://doi.org/10.1177/10778012221120447

48 Wallace et al., 'Framed as (Un)Victims of Sexual Violence', 19: 3 (2024), 243–68. DOI: https://doi.org/10.1177/15570851241227937

49 Request information under Clare's Law: Make a Domestic Violence Disclosure Scheme (DVDS) application, Metropolitan Police: https://www.met.police.uk/rqo/request/ri/request-information/cl/triage/v2/request-information-under-clares-law/

50 'Research finds that 97% of women in the UK have been sexually harassed', Open Access Government (7 October 2022): https://www.openaccessgovernment.org/97-of-women-in-the-uk/105940/

51 'Five essential facts to know about femicide', UN Women (25 November 2024): https://www.unwomen.org/en/news-stories/feature-story/2022/11/five-essential-facts-to-know-about-femicide

52 'Why do we say domestic abuse is gendered?' Women's Aid: https://www.womensaid.org.uk/information-support/what-is-domestic-abuse/domestic-abuse-is-a-gendered-crime/

53 Domestic abuse victim characteristics, England and Wales: year ending March 2023, Office for National Statistics: https://www.ons.gov.uk/peoplepopulationandcommunity/crimeandjustice/articles/domesticabusevictimcharacteristicsenglandandwales/yearendingmarch2023#sex

54 K.R. Hanson et al., '"It's Getting Difficult to Be a Straight White Man": Bundled Masculinity Grievances on Reddit', *Sex Roles*, 88 (2023), 169–86. DOI: https://doi.org/10.1007/s11199-022-01344-8

55 r/AWDTSGisToxic, 'Dr Murrey's response to questions from the manosphere – video 2', Reddit: https://www.reddit.com/r/AWDTSGisToxic/comments/1f174ym/dr_murreys_response_to_questions_from_manosphere/

56 r/AWDTSGisToxic, 'Does anyone have recent success with getting your post in are we dating the same guy removed?', Reddit: https://www.reddit.com/r/AWDTSGisToxic/comments/1f26fln/does_anyone_have_recent_success_with_getting_your/

57 E. Harmer and S. Lewis, 'Disbelief and counter-voices: a thematic analysis of online reader comments about sexual harassment and sexual violence against women', *Information, Communication & Society*, 25: 2 (2020), 199–216. DOI: https://doi.org/10.1080/1369118X.2020.1770832

58 Zoe Williams, 'The nasty noughties: Russell Brand and the era of sadistic tabloid misogyny', *Guardian* (18 September 2023): https://www.theguardian.com/culture/2023/sep/18/the-nasty-noughties-russell-brand-and-the-era-of-sadistic-tabloid-misogyny

59 H. Eslen-Ziya, 'Establishing networked misogyny as a counter movement: The analysis of the online anti-Istanbul convention presence', *Convergence*, 28: 6 (2022), 1737–53. DOI: https://doi.org/10.1177/13548565221089218

60 R. Weidmann et al., 'Age and gender differences in narcissism: A comprehensive study across eight measures and over 250,000

participants', *Journal of Personality and Social Psychology*, 124: 6 (2023), 1277–98. DOI: 10.1037/pspp0000463

61 Arwa Mahdawi, 'There are no secrets on the internet. Just ask the women who entrusted their data to Tea', *Guardian* (30 July 2025): https://www.theguardian.com/commentisfree/2025/jul/30/there-are-no-secrets-on-the-internet-just-ask-the-women-who-entrusted-their-data-to-tea

62 Faith Hill, 'First Came Tea. Then Came the Male Rage', *Atlantic* (30 July 2025): https://www.theatlantic.com/family/archive/2025/07/tea-app-dating-data-breach-misogyny/683712/

63 'Defamation', Cambridge Dictionary: https://dictionary.cambridge.org/dictionary/english/defamation

64 Dr Lucas Murrey, X (25 August 2024): https://x.com/MurreyLucas/status/1827594147940995505

65 Manosphere Highlights Daily, YouTube: https://www.youtube.com/@manospherehighlightsdaily

66 Lucas Murrey, *Nietzsche: The Meaning of Earth* (Lehigh University Press, 2015): https://www.amazon.co.uk/Nietzsche-Meaning-Earth-Lucas-Murrey/dp/1611461545

67 Sean Illing, 'The alt-right is drunk on bad readings of Nietzsche. The Nazis were too', Vox (30 December 2018): https://www.vox.com/2017/8/17/16140846/alt-right-nietzsche-richard-spencer-nazism

68 Peter Sheridan, 'The world's most vilified man speaks for the first time: An online female hate-mob has accused him of stalking, extortion and MURDER. But, we reveal, there are also dark episodes in his past...', *Daily Mail* (14 April 2024): https://www.dailymail.co.uk/news/article-13305141/stewart-lucas-murrey-sue-women-social-media.html

69 Lucas Murrey, 'Are We Being Murdered by the Same "Intelligence" Mafia? From Epstein's Pedophile Network to Facebook, United States and Israeli Cyber-Criminals', Sickoscoop

(2023): https://sickoscoop-media.sfo2.digitaloceanspaces.com/pdf/68663684f9279ee89580cb1f/1752628225062-y4bsb-3.6_DrMurreyAreWeBeingMurderedByTheSame-Intelligence-Mafia--compressed_4.pdf

70 Lucas Murrey, 'Who I am, and what I suspect happened to me', Sickoscoop (19 February 2025): https://sickoscoop-media.sfo2.digitaloceanspaces.com/pdf/68663684f9279ee89580cb1f/1752627686091-7xlu2k-WhoAmI_DrMurrey.pdf

71 Taryn Kaur Pedler (2024), 'Judge dismisses a $2.6 million claim by a bachelor, 32, against dozens of women who mocked him for being a "bad date" in a viral Facebook group: "They did nothing wrong"', *Daily Mail* (9 April 2024): https://www.dailymail.co.uk/news/article-13287847/Judge-dismisses-defamation-lawsuit-brought-LA-bachelor-against-50-women-discovered-discussing-Facebook-group-called-dating-guy.html

72 Niamh Lynch, 'Man suing women who claimed he was a bad date has first of his 50 cases thrown out', Sky News (9 April 2024): https://news.sky.com/story/man-sues-50-women-who-said-he-was-a-bad-date-13111414

Chapter Six: Defamation

1 'Moral Truth', Science Direct: https://www.sciencedirect.com/topics/psychology/moral-truth

2 Edmund Jacobson, 'The Relational Account of Truth', *Journal of Philosophy, Psychology and Scientific Methods*, 7: 10 (1910): 253–61. DOI: https://doi.org/10.2307/2011964

3 Janne van Doorn and Nathalie N. Koster, 'Emotional victims and the impact on credibility: A systematic review', *Aggression and Violent Behavior*, 47 (2019), 74–89. DOI: https://doi.org/10.1016/j.avb.2019.03.007

4 Alexandra Repke, 'The Power of Presentation: How Attire, Cosmetics, and Posture Impact the Source Credibility of the

Female Expert Witness', PhD thesis (2021), Aquila, University of Southern Mississippi: https://aquila.usm.edu/dissertations/1796/

5   Katherine M. Cole, 'She's Crazy (to Think We'll Believe Her): Credibility Discounting of Women with Mental Illness in the Era of #MeToo', *Georgetown Journal of Gender and the Law*, 22: 173 (2021–2022): https://heinonline.org/HOL/LandingPage?handle=hein.journals/grggenl22&div=8&id=&page=

6   L. Khoury et al., 'Substance use, childhood traumatic experience, and Posttraumatic Stress Disorder in an urban civilian population', *Depression and Anxiety*, 27: 12 (2010):1077–86. DOI: 10.1002/da.20751

7   Post-traumatic stress disorder, OASH: Office on Women's Health, US Department of Health & Human Services: https://www.womenshealth.gov/mental-health/mental-health-conditions/post-traumatic-stress-disorder

8   Jessica Lake, 'Whores Aboard and Laws Abroad: English Women and Sexual Slander in Early Colonial New South Wales', *Gender & History*, 35: 3 (2022), 916–34. DOI: https://doi.org/10.1111/1468-0424.12632

9   Christopher Hutchings and Mollie Jackson, 'A decade of the Defamation Act 2013', Hamlins (4 April 2024): https://hamlins.com/insight/a-decade-of-the-defamation-act-2013

10 'Defamation and whistleblowing: What does it mean?', Protect: https://protect-advice.org.uk/defamation-whistleblowing/

11 Joel Simon et al., 'Weaponizing the Law: Attacks on Media Freedom', Thomas Reuters Foundation and Tow Center for Digital Journalism (2023): https://www.trust.org/documents/weaponizing-law-attacks-media-freedom-report-2023.pdf

12 'Weaponizing defamation lawsuits against survivors violates international human rights', Equality Now: https://equalitynow.org/news_and_insights/

weaponizing-defamation-lawsuits-against-survivors-violates-international-human-rights

13 Leonie Cooper, 'What did Amber Heard's Washington Post op-ed actually say?' *Independent* (1 June 2022): https://www.independent.co.uk/arts-entertainment/films/news/amber-heard-op-ed-washington-post-article-b2091446.html

14 'CL-2019-2911 John C. Depp, II v. Amber Laura Heard Defendant's Motion for Briefing Schedule and Evidentiary Hearing', Fairfax County Court (2019): https://www.fairfaxcounty.gov/circuit/sites/circuit/files/assets/documents/pdf/high-profile/depp%20v%20heard/cl-2019-0002911_motion_8871451_04_11_2019.pdf

15 Amber Heard, 'Amber Heard: I spoke up against sexual violence – and faced our culture's wrath. That has to change', *Washington Post* (18 December 2018): https://www.washingtonpost.com/opinions/ive-seen-how-institutions-protect-men-accused-of-abuse-heres-what-we-can-do/2018/12/18/71fd876a-02ed-11e9-b5df-5d3874f1ac36_story.html

16 Strategic Lawsuits against Public Participation (SLAPPs), Solicitors Regulation Authority (28 November 2022): https://www.sra.org.uk/solicitors/guidance/slapps-warning-notice/

17 Tejal Jesrani, 'Weaponizing the Law: The Rise of Abusive Private Criminal SLAPPs and Their Chilling Effect on Justice', Columbia Law School, Human Rights Institute (11 April 2024): https://hri.law.columbia.edu/weaponizing-law-rise-abusive-private-criminal-slapps-and-their-chilling-effect-justice

18 Sara Sanabria and Christopher Dietzel, '"I Can Be Sued for That?" When University Community Members Are Sued for Defamation in Response to Allegations of Sexual Violence', *Education & Law Journal*, 32: 2 (2023), 151–84: https://www.proquest.com/openview/bac98d09de0876d23c4854cc06178bd3/1?pq-origsite=gscholar&cbl=44752

19 Nicole Pelletiere, 'Has #MeToo changed men? Guys respond to the movement and how they feel about masculinity', ABC News (20 June 2018): https://abcnews.go.com/GMA/Family/metoo-changed-men-guys-respond-movement-feel-masculinity/story?id=55971752
20 M. Harradine, 'Defamation Law and Epistemic Harm in the #MeToo Era', *Australian Feminist Law Journal*, 48: 1 (2022), 31–55. DOI: https://doi.org/10.1080/13200968.2022.2146303
21 A/76/258, 'Promotion and protection of the right to freedom of opinion and expression', United Nations General Assembly (30 July 2021): https://documents.un.org/doc/undoc/gen/n21/212/16/pdf/n2121216.pdf?OpenElement
22 S.J. Harsey and J.J. Freyd, 'Defamation and DARVO', *Journal of Trauma & Dissociation*, 23: 5 (2022), 481–89. DOI: https://doi.org/10.1080/15299732.2022.2111510
23 '26 April 2023 – Hays v Cresswell – Summary of Judgment', Bindmans: https://www.bindmans.com/wp-content/uploads/2023/04/26-April-2023-Hays-v-Cresswell-Summary-of-Judgment.pdf
24 Amy Novotney, 'Women who experience trauma are twice as likely as men to develop PTSD. Here's why', American Psychological Association (13 April 2023): https://www.apa.org/topics/women-girls/women-trauma
25 J.P. Hayes et al., 'Emotion and cognition interactions in PTSD: a review of neurocognitive and neuroimaging studies', *Frontiers in Integrative Neuroscience*, 6: 89 (2012). DOI: 10.3389/fnint.2012.00089
26 Catriona Innes and Jennifer Savin, '"I was sued by my rapist": The rise in abusers silencing women who dare to speak out', *Cosmopolitan* (13 June 2023): https://www.cosmopolitan.com/uk/reports/a44171616/sued-by-abuser-darvo/
27 Professor Betsy Stanko, 'Operation Soteria Bluestone Year 1 Report 2021–2022', Secretary of State for the Home Department

(December 2022): https://assets.publishing.service.gov.uk/media/63c02994d3bf7f6c287b9ff7/E02836356_Operation_Soteria_Y1_report_Accessible.pdf

28 'Op Soteria rolled out across England and Wales', National Police Chiefs' Council (10 July 2023): https://news.npcc.police.uk/releases/victims-rights-and-needs-at-centre-of-transformative-new-approach-to-rape-investigations-and-prosecutions

29 'Operation Soteria is a "game-changer for policing"', National Police Chiefs' Council (22 August 2024): https://news.npcc.police.uk/releases/operation-soteria-is-a-game-changer-for-policing

30 Rape and sexual assault statistics, Rape Crisis England & Wales: https://rapecrisis.org.uk/get-informed/statistics-sexual-violence/

31 R. Harding et al., 'Competing concepts of public value and legitimacy in the police: Organisational challenges in the investigation of rape and serious sexual offences', *International Journal of Law, Crime and Justice*, 76 (2024), 100646, ISSN 1756-0616 DOI: https://doi.org/10.1016/j.ijlcj.2023.100646

32 Baroness Newlove, 'Statement – rape review progress "risks being undermined by systemic issues eroding victim confidence"' (2 February 2024): https://victimscommissioner.org.uk/news/feb-2024-cjs-dashboard

33 'P Diddy: What are the allegations against Sean Combs and when is his trial?' Sky News (23 January 2025): https://news.sky.com/story/p-diddy-what-is-sean-combs-accused-of-and-what-has-he-said-13103248

34 Myriam Page, 'Diddy's lawyer offers bizarre explanation for the 1,000 bottles of baby oil found in home raid', *Independent* (26 September 2024): https://www.independent.co.uk/news/world/americas/crime/sean-diddy-combs-baby-oil-lawyer-b2619493.html

35 Ian Youngs and Helena Wilkinson, 'Russell Brand pleads not guilty to rape and assault', BBC News (30 May 2025): https://www.bbc.co.uk/news/articles/cvgvknwxjdqo

36 Peter Birks, 'Iniuria (Contempt)', in Eric Descheemaeker (ed.), *The Roman Law of Obligations* (Oxford, 2014; online edn, Oxford Academic, 18 Sept. 2014). DOI: https://doi.org/10.1093/acprof:oso/9780198719274.003.0010

37 Sir John Baker, 'Defamation', *The Oxford History of the Laws of England: Volume VI 1483–1558* (Oxford, 2003; online edn, Oxford Academic, 22 Mar. 2012). DOI: https://doi.org/10.1093/acprof:oso/9780198258179.003.0044

38 The Italian Renaissance (1330–1550), Sparks Notes: https://www.sparknotes.com/history/european/renaissance1/section9/

39 'The legal sector in the Commonwealth', Commonwealth of Nations (2013): https://www.commonwealthofnations.org/?sectors=business/legal/

40 Steven Veerapen, 'Slander and Sedition in Elizabethan Law, Speech and Writing', PhD thesis, University of Strathclyde (2019): https://stax.strath.ac.uk/downloads/9p290955k?locale=zh

41 Slander of Women Act 1891 (repealed), Legislation.gov.uk: https://www.legislation.gov.uk/ukpga/Vict/54-55/51

42 J. Lake, 'Protecting "injured female innocence" or furthering "the rights of women?" The sexual Slander of Women in New York and Victoria (1808–1887)', *Women's History Review*, 31: 3 (2021), 451–75. DOI: https://doi.org/10.1080/09612025.2021.1949822

43 K. Fischer, '"False, Feigned, and Scandalous Words" Sexual Slander and Racial Ideology Among Whites in Colonial North Carolina', in Catherine Clinton and Michele Gillespie (eds), *The Devil's Lane: Sex and Race in the Early South* (1997; online edn, Oxford Academic, 3 October 2011), 139–149. DOI: https://doi.org/10.1093/acprof:oso/9780195112436.003.0010

44 D. Pilgrim, 'The Jezebel Stereotype', Jim Crow Museum (2012): https://jimcrowmuseum.ferris.edu/jezebel/index.htm

45 K. Markey, 'Unlawful Intimacy: The Criminalization of Interracial Relationships in Progressive-Era Chicago', *Law and Social Inquiry*, 49: 2 (2024), 1169–91. DOI: https://doi.org/10.1017/lsi.2023.29

46 Lake, 'Protecting "injured female innocence"', (2021), 451–75. DOI: https://doi.org/10.1080/09612025.2021.1949822

47 Valerie Fridland, 'Why Do We Think Women Talk Too Much?' *Psychology Today* (12 July 2020): https://www.psychologytoday.com/gb/blog/language-in-the-wild/202007/why-do-we-think-women-talk-too-much

48 Afghanistan-related sanctions: 928. Do U.S. sanctions on the Taliban and the Haqqani Network prohibit the provision of humanitarian assistance to Afghanistan? Office of Foreign Assets Control, US Department of the Treasury: https://ofac.treasury.gov/faqs/928

49 Select Committee on International Relations and Defence: The UK and Afghanistan, '2nd Report of Session 2019–21', Chapter 5: 'The Taliban and other security issues', Section 296, UK Parliament (13 January 2021): https://publications.parliament.uk/pa/ld5801/ldselect/ldintrel/208/20808.htm

50 Arpan Rai, 'Afghan women "banned from hearing each other" in bizarre new Taliban rule', *Independent* (30 October 2024): https://www.independent.co.uk/asia/south-asia/afghanistan-taliban-women-hearing-speak-b2637984.html

51 Annie Kelly and Zahra Joya, '"Frightening" Taliban law bans women from speaking in public', *Guardian* (26 August 2024): https://www.theguardian.com/global-development/article/2024/aug/26/taliban-bar-on-afghan-women-speaking-in-public-un-afghanistan

52 Mary Kalantzis and Bill Cope, 'Aristotle on Inequality', Works & Days: https://newlearningonline.com/new-learning/chapter-5/supproting-materials/aristotle-on-inequality

53 'Philomela', Britannica: https://www.britannica.com/topic/Philomela
54 Farah Karim-Cooper, 'Dismemberment and mutilation in *Titus Andronicus*', Shakespeare's Globe (21 April 2016): https://www.shakespearesglobe.com/discover/blogs-and-features/2016/04/21/dismemberment-and-mutilation-in-titus-andronicus
55 'Sirach (Ecclesiasticus) 26 GNB', Bible Society (2020): https://www.biblesociety.org.uk/explore-the-bible/read/eng/gnb/sir/26/
56 Nishat Choudhury, 'Research finds that 97% of women in the UK have been sexually harassed', Open Access Government (7 October 2022): https://www.openaccessgovernment.org/97-of-women-in-the-uk/105940/
57 Lorna Adams et al., '2020 Sexual Harassment Survey', Government Equalities Office: https://assets.publishing.service.gov.uk/media/60f03e068fa8f50c77458285/2021-07-12_Sexual_Harassment_Report_FINAL.pdf
58 Tim Kiely, 'Criminal barrister says UK normalises "violent male behaviour towards women"', Open Access Government (12 March 2021): https://www.openaccessgovernment.org/violent-male-behaviour/106138/
59 Jonathon Keats, '*Edge of Memory*: Distrusting oral tradition may makes us more ignorant', *New Scientist* (29 August 2018): https://www.newscientist.com/article/mg23931932-900-edge-of-memory-distrusting-oral-tradition-may-make-us-more-ignorant/
60 Seema Yasmin, 'Witch Hunts Today: Abuse of Women Superstition and Murder Collide in India', *Scientific American* (11 January 2018): https://www.scientificamerican.com/article/witch-hunts-today-abuse-of-women-superstition-and-murder-collide-in-india/
61 'Witch Trials in the 21st Century', National Geographic: https://education.nationalgeographic.org/resource/witch-trials-21st-century/

62　B.L. Meel, 'Witchcraft in Transkei Region of South Africa: case report', *African Health Sciences*, 9:1 (2009), 61–4. https://www.ncbi.nlm.nih.gov/pmc/articles/PMC2932523/

Chapter Seven: Rags to Reality TV

1　Sally Engle Merry, '10 – Rethinking Gossip and Scandal', *Toward a General Theory of Social Control* (1984), 271–302. DOI: https://doi.org/10.1016/B978-0-12-102801-5.50016-9
2　Felicia Appell, 'Victorian Ideals: The Influences of Society's Ideals on Victorian Relationships', McKendree University (2012): https://www.mckendree.edu/academics/scholars/issue18/appell.htm
3　Elena Escobar Gil, 'Beyond the gossip: Why reality is so popular', Aceprensa (2 November 2023): https://www.aceprensa.com/english/beyond-the-gossip-why-reality-tv-is-so-popular/
4　'Walter Winchell', Britannica: https://www.britannica.com/biography/Walter-Winchell
5　C. Lee Harrington and Denise D. Bielby, 'Where did you hear that? Technology and the Social Organization of Gossip', *Sociological Quarterly*, 36: 3 (1995), 607–28. DOI: https://doi.org/10.1111/j.1533-8525.1995.tb00456.x
6　Perez Hilton: https://perezhilton.com/
7　John Plunkett, 'Perez Hilton interview: "I'm sassy, without being nasty"', *Guardian* (4 December 2011): https://www.theguardian.com/media/2011/dec/04/perez-hilton-interview-itv2-show
8　William Turvill, 'Perez Hilton interview: How Hollywood's "most hated" sacrificed clicks (and ad revenue) for his conscience', *Press Gazette* (14 October 2021): https://pressgazette.co.uk/news/perez-hilton-interview/
9　Anne Petersen, 'Celebrity juice, not from concentrate: Perez Hilton, gossip blogs, and the new star production', *Jump Cut: A Review of Contemporary Media*, 49, (2007): https://www.ejumpcut.org/archive/jc49.2007/PerezHilton/text.html

10 Steven McIntosh, 'Perez Hilton: I never needed to be so cruel', BBC News (6 October 2020): https://www.bbc.co.uk/news/entertainment-arts-53662800
11 Hope Schreiber, 'Mila Kunis blames Perez Hilton for creating internet "trolling" and "ugly news"', Yahoo! Life (23 July 2018): https://www.yahoo.com/lifestyle/mila-kunis-blames-perez-hilton-creating-internet-trolling-ugly-news-213050104.html
12 R. Tiger, 'Perez Hilton and the Celebrity Body', *Humanity & Society*, 37: 2 (2013), 189–91. DOI: https://doi.org/10.1177/0160597613481736
13 'Why is "Big Brother" called "Big Brother"? Name meaning explained', IMDB: https://www.imdb.com/news/ni63380411/
14 Closer Staff, '35 completely outrageous Celebrity Big Brother moments', Closer (7 April 2025): https://closeronline.co.uk/entertainment/tv-movies/cbb-fights-controversial-moments/
15 Constance Grady, 'The bubblegum misogyny of 2000s pop culture', Vox (25 May 2021): https://www.vox.com/culture/22350286/2000s-pop-culture-misogyny-britney-spears-janet-jackson-whitney-houston-monica-lewinsky
16 Josh Milton, 'Vile paparazzo took upskirt pictures of Britney Spears to prove she wasn't pregnant', Pink News (19 February 2021): https://www.thepinknews.com/2021/02/19/britney-spears-photographer-paparazzi-mental-health-nick-stern/
17 Emily Maddick, 'Photographer who trailed Britney Spears, but quit over her terrible treatment, reveals what he witnessed – and it's shocking', *Glamour* (19 February 2021): https://www.glamourmagazine.co.uk/article/britney-spears-paparazzi-interview
18 Ramon Antonio Vargas, 'Britney Spears settles legal dispute with estranged father over conservatorship', *Guardian* (27 April 2024): https://www.theguardian.com/music/2024/apr/27/britney-spears-father-legal-dispute-settlement

19 'Worldwide study shows reality TV gender disparity', Televisual (17 July 2024): https://www.televisual.com/news/worldwide-study-shows-reality-tv-gender-disparity/
20 '*Love Island*: Adam sparks warning from charity Women's Aid', BBC News (9 July 2018): https://www.bbc.co.uk/news/newsbeat-44558478
21 'Mike Thalassitis: Love Island star left notebook at scene of death', BBC News (5 June 2019): https://www.bbc.co.uk/news/uk-england-essex-48507026
22 LeAnn Cain, 'Lights, Camera, Contracts: The Legal Side of Reality TV', Campbell Law Observer (6 December 2024): https://campbelllawobserver.com/lights-camera-contracts-the-legal-side-of-reality-tv/
23 Loren A. Seeger, 'The Rest Is Still Unwritten: Female Adolescents' Cultivation of Gender from MTV's Reality Television Series *The Hills* Through Celebrity Gossip Blog Commentary', master's thesis, University of Texas (2007): https://krex.k-state.edu/server/api/core/bitstreams/f8120d50-6456-40b4-8257-775d9a27afe8/content
24 Kasper H. Ulmanen and Stella Fogelberg, 'Reality (TV) constructing women: A discourse analysis of how "The Real Housewives of Beverly Hills" portray women stereotypes', thesis, Uppsala University (2024): https://www.diva-portal.org/smash/get/diva2:1875656/FULLTEXT01.pdf
25 S. Reiss and J. Wiltz, 'Why People Watch Reality TV', *Media Psychology*, 6: 4 (2004), 363–78. DOI: https://doi.org/10.1207/s1532785xmep0604_3
26 Eric Jaffe, 'Reality Check', Association for Psychological Science (22 March 2005): https://www.psychologicalscience.org/observer/reality-check
27 Ibid.

28 Reiss and Wiltz, 'Why People Watch Reality TV' (2004), 363–78. DOI: https://doi.org/10.1207/s1532785xmep0604_3
29 Raghu Malhotra, 'Explained: Who is a gold digger – the derogatory expression used to describe a certain kind of greedy woman?' *Indian Express* (20 July 2022): https://indianexpress.com/article/explained/explained-who-gold-digger-derogatory-expression-describe-a-certain-kind-of-greedy-woman-8042032/
30 Lindsey Spencer, 'Being a feminist and a reality TV fan is possible', *Michigan Daily* (28 November 2022): https://www.michigandaily.com/opinion/being-a-feminist-and-reality-tv-fan-is-possible/
31 'Reasons for watching reality TV in the United States as of March 2017, by gender', Statista: https://www.statista.com/statistics/692691/reasons-watching-reality-tv-gender/
32 Darshita Goyal, 'Can a Reality TV Addiction Warp Your Entire Personality?', *Vogue* (9 August 2024): https://www.vogue.co.uk/article/reality-tv-addiction
33 Danielle J. Lindemann, *True Story: What Reality TV Says About Us* (Farrar, Straus & Giroux Inc, 2022), 212.
34 Robin Dunbar, *Grooming, Gossip and the Evolution of Language* (Faber and Faber, 2004), 58.

Chapter Eight: Biddies, Codswallop and Witches

1 Carter Sherman, 'Sundresses and rugged self-sufficiency: "tradwives" tout a conservative American past ... that didn't exist', *Guardian* (24 July 2024): https://www.theguardian.com/lifeandstyle/ng-interactive/2024/jul/24/tradwives-tiktok-women-gender-roles
2 Fortesa Latifi, 'How the Trad Wife Trend on TikTok Sells Biblical Gender Roles', *Teen Vogue* (29 April 2024): https://www.teenvogue.com/story/how-the-trad-wife-trend-on-tiktok-sells-biblical-gender-roles

3   S.A. Crabtree, 'The Mother, the Warrior, the Midwife and the Holy Whore: An Ethnographic Study of Women's Faith, Sacralisation and Embodiment', *Feminist Theology*, 32: 1 (2023), 40–59. DOI: https://doi.org/10.1177/09667350231183073
4   Judith Butler, *Gender Trouble: Feminism and the Subversion of Identity* (Routledge, 1990), 5.
5   J.M. Mansilla-Domínguez et al., 'The role of duty, gender and intergenerational care in grandmothers' parenting of grandchildren: a phenomenological qualitative study', *BMC Nursing*, 23: 477 (2024). DOI: https://doi.org/10.1186/s12912-024-02151-0
6   Jillian Jimenez, 'The History of Grandmothers in the African-American Community', *Social Service Review*, 76: 4 (2002). DOI: https://doi.org/10.1086/342994
7   'Codswallop', Oxford English Dictionary: https://www.oed.com/dictionary/codswallop_n?tl=true
8   'Biddy', Google Oxford Languages: https://www.google.com/search?sca_esv=adc7fa8b48536f88&rlz=1C5GCCM_en&q=biddy
9   'How men and women experience ageism differently revealed in new survey', Centre for Ageing Better (27 November 2024): https://ageing-better.org.uk/news/how-men-and-women-experience-ageism-differently-revealed-new-survey
10   '*Daily Mail* urges "legs-it" critics to "get a life"', BBC News (28 March 2017): https://www.bbc.co.uk/news/uk-39421279
11   Barbara H. Chasin and Laura Kramer, 'Chapter 7: Ageism and Sexism: Invisibility and Erasure', in Marcia Texler Segal, Vasilikie Demos (eds), *Gender Visibility and Erasure* (Emerald Publishing Ltd, 2022). DOI: https://doi.org/10.1108/S1529-212620220000033015
12   Kirsten Weir, 'Ageism is one of the last socially acceptable prejudices. Psychologists are working to change that', *Monitor*

on Psychology, 54: 2 (1 March 2023): https://www.apa.org/monitor/2023/03/cover-new-concept-of-aging
13 Mariarosa Dalla Costa and Selma James, Chapter 7: 'The Power of Women and the Subversion of the Community', Stanley Aronowitz and Michael J. Roberts (eds), *Class: The Anthology* (Wiley, 2017). DOI: https://doi.org/10.1002/9781119395485.ch7
14 Clegg, *Woman's Lore* (2023), 69.
15 Ronald Hutton, *The Witch: A History of Fear, from Ancient Times to the Present* (Yale University Press, 2017), 64.
16 Chapter 8: 'The Middle Ages in Europe: The Catholic Church in Western Civilization', Lumen: https://courses.lumenlearning.com/atd-herkimer-westerncivilization/chapter/the-catholic-church/
17 'Heresy', Britannica: https://www.britannica.com/topic/heresy
18 R.W. Thurston, 'Violence towards Heretics and Witches in Europe, 1022–1800', R. Antony, S. Carroll and C.D. Pennock (eds), *The Cambridge World History of Violence* (Cambridge University Press, 2020), 513–30: https://www.cambridge.org/core/books/abs/cambridge-world-history-of-violence/violence-towards-heretics-and-witches-in-europe-10221800/010E6D80D5BAE3F236DD2EF51471203E
19 Nicola A. Ring et al., 'Healers and midwives accused of witchcraft (1563–1736) – What secondary analysis of the Scottish survey of witchcraft can contribute to the teaching of nursing and midwifery history', *Nurse Education Today*, 133 (2024), 106026. DOI: https://doi.org/10.1016/j.nedt.2023.106026
20 'Toil and Trouble: Witchcraft in Scotland', University Collections, University of Aberdeen: https://exhibitions.abdn.ac.uk/university-collections/exhibits/show/toil_and_trouble/witch-hunts
21 Johannes Dillinger, 'Germany: "The mother of the witches"', Radar, Oxford Brookes University: https://radar.brookes.ac.uk/radar/file/c3645b3f-5537-403e-a629-6829cad914d1/1/

Germany%20mother%20of%20the%20witches%20-%20 9781138782204%20-%202019%20-%20Dillinger.pdf
22 James I and Anne of Denmark, Historic Royal Palaces: https://www.hrp.org.uk/banqueting-house/history-and-stories/james-i-and-anne-of-denmark/#gs.hlwk29
23 'Salem witch trials', Britannica: https://www.britannica.com/event/Salem-witch-trials
24 Lauren Nitschke, 'European Witch-Hunting (A Brief History)', The Collector (13 February 2022): https://www.thecollector.com/european-witch-hunting/
25 'Why did the witch hunts end in Scotland?', BBC Bitesize: https://www.bbc.co.uk/bitesize/articles/zj2r4xs
26 Jasmine Niblett, 'The Tool of the Senseless and Bitchy? Reclaiming Gossip as an Act of Female Agency', *Glasgow University Magazine* (8 March 2024): https://glasgowuniversitymagazine.co.uk/articles/culture-2/the-tool-of-the-senseless-and-the-bitchy-reclaiming-gossip-as-an-act-of-female-agency/
27 Brendan C. Walsh, '"Witches" are still killed all over the world. Pardoning past victims could end the practice', The Conversation (29 April 2024): https://theconversation.com/witches-are-still-killed-all-over-the-world-pardoning-past-victims-could-end-the-practice-228613
28 Mukesh Ranjan, 'Elderly woman beaten to death allegedly for practising witchcraft in Jharkhand', *New Indian Express* (26 June 2023): https://www.newindianexpress.com/nation/2023/Jun/26/elderly-woman-beaten-to-death-allegedly-for-practising-witchcraft-in-jharkhand-2588670.html
29 Sally Howard, 'Why the witch-hunt victims of early modern Britain have come back to haunt us', *Guardian* (24 October 2021): https://www.theguardian.com/uk-news/2021/oct/24/why-the-witch-hunt-victims-of-early-modern-britain-have-come-back-to-haunt-us

30 Human Rights Council, Forty-seventh session, 21 June–14 July 2021, Agenda item 3, Promotion and protection of all human rights, civil, political, economic, social and cultural rights, including the right to development, United Nations General Assembly: https://documents.un.org/doc/undoc/gen/g21/191/99/pdf/g2119199.pdf

31 Jonny Humphries, 'Liverpool parade crash accused appears in court', BBC News (15 July 2025): https://www.bbc.co.uk/news/articles/cq53p67n76zo

32 Martin Brunt, 'Officers who confronted "coward" Southport killer Axel Rudakubana win police bravery award', Sky News (11 July 2025): https://news.sky.com/story/officers-who-confronted-coward-southport-killer-axel-rudakubana-win-police-bravery-award-13394408

33 Jonny Humphries and Kara O'Neill, '"Evil" Southport killer jailed for minimum 52 years', BBC News (23 January 2025): https://www.bbc.co.uk/news/articles/c4gweeq1344o

34 Holly Evans, 'Who is Paul Doyle, the father and ex-Royal Marine commando accused of Liverpool parade crash', *Independent*/Yahoo! News (29 May 2025): https://uk.news.yahoo.com/paul-doyle-father-ex-royal-201811809.html

35 Shereen H. Shaw, 'Gendered Islamophobia: Evidence of Disproportionate Abuse Against Muslim Women and Girls', Committees – UK Parliament: https://committees.parliament.uk/writtenevidence/138836/pdf

Chapter Nine: Tea

1 Edward Siddons, 'A Common Ear', *Tank*, The Gossip Issue, 70 (spring 2017): https://magazine.tank.tv/issue-70/features/edward-siddons

2 Ciara O'Rourke, 'Being against same-sex marriage isn't homophobic', *Trinity News* (13 March 2014): https://trinitynews.ie/2014/03/being-against-same-sex-marriage-isnt-homophobic/

3   William Antonelli, 'Mark Zuckerberg's end to factchecking is a desperate play for engagement', *Guardian* (10 January 2025): https://www.theguardian.com/technology/2025/jan/10/mark-zuckerberg-meta-factchecking
4   Julia Cohen, 'A Platform Problem: Hate Speech and Bots Still Thriving', University of Southern California Viterbi School of Engineering (12 February 2025): https://viterbischool.usc.edu/news/2025/02/a-platform-problem-hate-speech-and-bots-still-thriving-on-x/
5   Amelia Hansford, 'Meta "removes LGBTQ+ and Pride themes from Facebook Messenger app', Pink News (13 January 2025): https://www.thepinknews.com/2025/01/13/meta-facebook-messenger-pride-themes/
6   Salvador Rodriguez, 'Facebook's Mark Zuckerberg joins San Francisco gay pride parade', *Los Angeles Times* (1 July 2013): https://www.latimes.com/business/technology/la-fi-tn-zuckerberg-facebook-pride-san-francisco-20130701-story.html
7   Serena Smith, 'Meet the young trans activists taking on Wes Streeting', *Dazed* (12 December 2024): https://www.dazeddigital.com/life-culture/article/65702/1/young-trans-activists-trans-kids-deserve-better-wes-streeting-office
8   Paul Baker, *Fabulosa!: The Story Polari, Britain's Secret Gay Language* (Reaktion Books, 2019), 21.
9   Baker, *Fabulosa!* (2019), 18–19.
10 Siddons, 'A Common Ear', *Tank* (2017): https://magazine.tank.tv/issue-70/features/edward-siddons
11 Andrew Johnson, 'Carry on laughing: Kenneth Williams was glad to be gay', *Independent* (13 April 2008): https://www.independent.co.uk/news/uk/this-britain/carry-on-laughing-kenneth-williams-was-glad-to-be-gay-808482.html
12 Baker, *Fabulosa!* (2019), 27.
13 Ibid., 127–8.

14 Nuno Marques, 'Cants and Anti-Languages: The Hidden World of Secret Languages', Babbel (22 March 2022): https://www.babbel.com/en/magazine/cants-and-anti-languages-the-secret-history-of-cryptolects

15 'Cockney', Britannica: https://www.britannica.com/topic/Cockney

16 Rebecca Stewart, '*Verlan* (France)', Global Informality Project: https://www.in-formality.com/wiki/index.php?title=Verlan_(France)

17 Martha Vicinus, *Intimate Friends: Women Who Loved Women, 1778–1928* (University of Chicago Press, 2006), 20.

18 Caroline Derry, 'Lesbianism and the criminal law of England and Wales', Open University (10 February 2021): https://www.open.edu/openlearn/society-politics-law/law/lesbianism-and-the-criminal-law-england-and-wales

19 '14 romantic quotes from the love letters of Virginia Woolf and Vita Sackville-West', Penguin (1 February 2021): https://www.penguin.co.uk/discover/articles/valentines-day-14-romantic-quotes-from-the-love-letters-of-virginia-woolf-and-vita-sackville-west

20 r/SapphoAndHerFriend, Reddit: https://www.reddit.com/r/SapphoAndHerFriend/

21 Siobhan, 'Swords, Satan and Sexuality: Queer Nuns of the Past', Autostraddle (17 November 2016): https://www.autostraddle.com/swords-satan-and-sexuality-queer-nuns-of-the-past-358331/

22 Tim Brinkhof, 'The strange case of Benedetta Carlini: how the Catholic Church investigated fraudulent saints', Big Think (21 April 2022): https://bigthink.com/the-past/benedetta-carlini-catholic-saint-trial/

23 Hannah Steinkopf-Frank, 'Lesbianism (!) at the Convent', JSTOR Daily (16 May 2018): https://daily.jstor.org/lesbianism-at-the-convent/

24 Esther Newton and students, 'Lesbians in the twentieth century', Out History (2008): https://outhistory.org/exhibits/show/lesbians-20th-century/beginnings
25 Victoria A. Brownworth, 'Erasing lesbians erases women's history', *Philadelphia Gay News* (29 March 2023): https://epgn.com/2023/03/29/erasing-lesbians-erases-womens-history/
26 Ciara E. Pruett, 'Institutionalizing Femininity: A History of Medical Malpractice and Oppression of Women Through 19th century American Mental Asylums', Young Historians Conference (2023): https://pdxscholar.library.pdx.edu/cgi/viewcontent.cgi?params=/context/younghistorians/article/1272/&path_info=Institutionalizing_Femininity_A_History_of_Medical_Malpractice_and_Oppression_of_Women_Through_19th_century_American_Mental_Asylums_by_Ciara_Pruett.pdf
27 Dr Jasna Magić and Peter Kelley, 'Barriers to accessing services for LGBT+ victims and survivors', Safe Lives (9 April 2018): https://safelives.org.uk/news-views/barriers-to-accessing-services-for-lgbt-victims-and-survivors/
28 Lara Stroudinksy, 'Queer Erasure in History', Heriot-Watt University Student Union (7 June 2021): https://www.hwunion.com/news/article/6013/queer-erasure-in-history/
29 Lily Lindon, 'Virginia Woolf's (not so) secret lesbian relationship – in her own words', Penguin (4 February 2021): https://www.penguin.co.uk/discover/articles/virginia-woolf-vita-sackville-west-letters-love-affair
30 P. VanHaitsma, 'Gossip as Rhetorical Methodology for Queer and Feminist Historiography', *Rhetoric Review*, 35: 2 (2016), 135–47. DOI: https://doi.org/10.1080/07350198.2016.1142845
31 Ziyun Fan and Patrick Dawson, 'Gossip as evaluative sensemaking and the concealment of confidential gossip in the everyday life of organizations', *Management Learning*, 53: 2 (2021), 146-166. DOI: https://doi.org/10.1177/1350507620979366

32 Kwame Holmes, 'What's the Tea: Gossip and the Production of Black Gay Social History', *Radical History Review*: 122 (2015), 55–69. DOI: https://doi.org/10.1215/01636545-2849531

33 '10 ways to be an ally to Black LGBTQ people', Stonewall (1 October 2020): https://www.stonewall.org.uk/news/10-ways-be-ally-black-lgbt-people

34 Elle Hunt, '"It's not whether you do it – it's how you do it:" the expert guide to healthy gossiping', *Guardian* (7 February 2025): https://www.theguardian.com/lifeandstyle/ng-interactive/2025/feb/07/expert-guide-to-healthy-gossiping

Chapter Ten: Unbelievable

1 Julianne Schultz, 'None of us saw digital colonialism coming, now we must live with its consequences', *Guardian* (11 May 2024): https://www.theguardian.com/commentisfree/article/2024/may/11/none-of-us-saw-digital-colonialism-coming-now-we-must-live-with-its-consequences

2 Shaleen Khanal et al., 'Why and how is the power of Big Tech increasing in the policy process? The case of generative AI', *Policy and Society*, 44: 1 (2025), 52–69. DOI: https://doi.org/10.1093/polsoc/puae012

3 Pat de Brún, 'Talk on Big Tech's catastrophic impact on human rights', SOAS University of London (22 February 2024): https://www.soas.ac.uk/about/news/talk-big-techs-catastrophic-impact-human-rights

4 Eric Levitz, 'Why Big Tech turned right', Vox (31 January 2025): https://www.vox.com/politics/397525/trump-big-tech-musk-bezos-zuckerberg-democrats-biden

5 Andrea Dworkin, *Right-Wing Women* (Tarcherperigree, 1983), 3.

6 Moira Donegan, 'Why the US is burning $10m worth of birth control', *Guardian* (1 August 2025): https://www.theguardian.com/commentisfree/2025/aug/01/why-the-us-is-burning-10m-worth-of-birth-control

7 'Sarah Everard: Met Police missed Wayne Couzens indecent exposure link', BBC News (30 September 2021): https://www.bbc.co.uk/news/uk-england-london-58755391

8 Operation Argens – Final Report, Independent Office for Police Conduct: https://www.policeconduct.gov.uk/publications/operation-argens-final-report

9 Carter Sherman, 'Texas woman died after being denied miscarriage care due to abortion ban, report finds', *Guardian* (30 October 2024): https://www.theguardian.com/us-news/2024/oct/30/texas-woman-death-abortion-ban-miscarriage

10 John Yang and Ryan Connelly Holmes, 'Investigation links Georgia's abortion ban to preventable deaths of 2 women', PBS News (18 September 2024): https://www.pbs.org/newshour/show/investigation-links-georgias-abortion-ban-to-preventable-deaths-of-2-women

11 Max Colbert, 'Nigel Farage Teams Up With Extreme Anti-Abortion Group and Calls for Debate on Restricting Abortion Rights in the UK', *Byline Times* (29 November 2024): https://bylinetimes.com/2024/11/29/nigel-farage-teams-up-with-extreme-anti-abortion-group-and-calls-for-debate-on-restricting-abortion-rights-in-uk/

12 Amelia Abraham, 'Is Feminism in Its Flop Era?' *ArtReview* (3 May 2024): https://artreview.com/is-feminism-in-its-flop-era-alice-cappelle-collapse-feminism-review/

13 Alice Giddings, 'Half of women have been dumped for this reason – toxic masculinity is alive and well', *Metro* (20 March 2025): https://metro.co.uk/2025/03/20/half-women-dumped-this-reason-toxic-masculinity-alive-well-22740543/

14 Dworkin, *Right-Wing Women* (1983), 185.

15 Dworkin, *Right-Wing Women* (1983), 7.

16 Gefjon Off, 'Complexities and Nuances in Radical Right Voters' (Anti)Feminism', *Social Politics: International Studies in Gender,*

State & Society, 30: 2 (Summer 2023), 607–29. DOI: https://doi.org/10.1093/sp/jxad010

17 Dworkin, *Right-Wing Women* (1983), 33.
18 Ash Sarkar, *Minority Rule: Adventures in the Culture War* (Bloomsbury, 2025), 14.
19 'Distribution of Meta Platforms employees worldwide as of June 2022, by gender and department', Statista: https://www.statista.com/statistics/311836/facebook-employee-gender-department-global/
20 PowerfulJRE, 'Joe Rogan Experience #2255 – Mark Zuckerberg', YouTube (10 January 2025): https://www.youtube.com/watch?v=7k1ehaE0bdU
21 A. Bedrov and S.L. Gable, 'Thriving together: the benefits of women's social ties for physical, psychological and relationship health', *Philosophical Transactions of the Royal Society of London, Series B, Biological Sciences*, 378 (2023), 1868. DOI: 10.1098/rstb.2021.0441